CINEMA AND DEVELOPMENT IN WEST AFRICA

CINEMA AND DEVELOPMENT IN WEST AFRICA

James E. Genova

INDIANA UNIVERSITY PRESS
Bloomington and Indianapolis

This book is a publication of

Indiana University Press
Office of Scholarly Publishing
Herman B Wells Library 350
1320 East 10th Street
Bloomington, Indiana 47405 USA

iupress.indiana.edu

Telephone orders   800-842-6796
Fax orders   812-855-7931

© 2013 by James E. Genova

All rights reserved

No part of this book may be reproduced or utilized in any form or by any means, electronic or mechanical, including photocopying and recording, or by any information storage and retrieval system, without permission in writing from the publisher. The Association of American University Presses' Resolution on Permissions constitutes the only exception to this prohibition.

♾ The paper used in this publication meets the minimum requirements of the American National Standard for Information Sciences—Permanence of Paper for Printed Library Materials, ANSI Z39.48-1992.

Manufactured in the United States of America

Library of Congress Cataloging-in-Publication Data

Genova, James Eskridge.
    Cinema and development in West Africa / James E. Genova.
      pages cm
    Includes bibliographical references and index.
    ISBN 978-0-253-01002-5 (cl : alk. paper) — ISBN 978-0-253-01008-7 (pb : alk. paper) — ISBN 978-0-253-01011-7 (eb)   1. Motion picture industry—Africa, French-speaking West—History—20th century 2. France—Colonies—Africa—History—20th century. I. Title.
    PN1993.5.A35G46   2013
    791.43′0966—dc23

                                        2013011314

1 2 3 4 5   18 17 16 15 14 13

To my wife Stephanie and daughter Eva

Contents

	Acknowledgments	*ix*
	Abbreviations	*xi*
	Introduction: Cinema as Art and Industry	*1*
1	The Cinema Industrial Complex in French West Africa to the 1950s	*20*
2	The Colonialist Regime of Representation, 1945–60	*45*
3	West African Anticolonial Film Politics, 1950s–60s	*70*
4	The Postcolonial African Regime of Representation	*97*
5	The West African Cinema Industrial Complex, 1960s–70s	*128*
	Postscript: Francophone West African Cinema to the Present	*158*
	Notes	*165*
	Bibliography	*183*
	Index	*193*

Acknowledgments

THIS BOOK IS the culmination of several years of research and has benefited from the support, encouragement, and critical insights of many colleagues, friends, family, and institutions. I wish to thank Herman Lebovics for providing the inspiration for undertaking a study of the intersection of culture, economics, and the state. He has been a wonderful mentor and very dear friend. His unwavering support, unvarnished critiques, and guidance have been invaluable to me. Olufemi Vaughan has been a constant source of energy, intellectual engagement, and profound friendship. Our long conversations together through the years have generated vital questions and led to the significant rethinking of fundamental issues around the role of the state, civil society, and globalization in shaping postcolonial Africa. I thank Nwachukwu Frank Ukadike, who read the entire manuscript and provided important suggestions for improving the narrative. His work on African cinema has strongly influenced on my own engagement with the subject. Toyin Falola also read parts of the manuscript and offered support and encouragement for the project. I thank Mamadou Diouf, whose humor, intellectual adroitness, and deep commitment to the general welfare of Senegal's people is an inspiring model of committed academic work.

I wish also to express my profound thanks to Ahmad Sikainga, Alamin Mazrui, and the late John Conteh-Morgan for welcoming me to the African American and African Studies Department at the Ohio State University and providing an immediate community of Africanist colleagues that made me feel at home. I will always miss John's humanity and cheerful smile. I thank my colleagues in the History Department at OSU as well as those on OSU's Marion campus who contributed to making this book possible.

I owe gratitude for the support of the following institutions that provided the structural means to bring this study to fruition. The College of the Arts and Sciences at OSU awarded a Research Enhancement Grant to fund work in Senegal's national archives. The History Department furnished an RTAP Fellowship to finance three years of overseas research in West Africa and France. The Marion campus of OSU provided a Professional Development Grant that enabled me to present some of the project's preliminary findings at conferences in the United States and overseas. I wish to thank the staff at several archives, whose generous assistance was vital to compiling the substantive material that made this study a reality. They include the remarkable and knowledgeable personnel at the Centre des archives d'outre-mer in Aix-en-Provence, France, the Archives de la République du Sénégal in Dakar, Senegal, the Centre des archives contemporaines in Fontainebleau, France, and the

Centre Georges Pompidou in Paris, France. The Pompidou hosted a retrospective exhibit on African cinema in 2005, featuring the work of Manthia Diawara, that strongly influenced the direction of this investigation.

I also thank Dee Mortensen at Indiana University Press for so strongly embracing this project, helping to improve the manuscript, and being a wonderful editor. Sarah Jacobi also provided crucial assistance in ushering the study through the publication process.

Most importantly, I offer my deepest thanks and owe the greatest debt to my wife, partner, companion, and colleague Stephanie Smith. Her insights into the vital role of artists and culture in shaping identities as well as state practices in Latin America have contributed immensely to improving this study's argument and opening new vistas for inquiry. She is the love of my life, the source of all of my happiness, a person without whom I cannot imagine experiencing life's journey.

Abbreviations

Agence de coopération culturelle et technique	ACCT
Afro-American Films Inc.	AFRAM
American Motion Picture Export Company-Africa	AMPECA
Consortium audio-visuel international	CAI
Commission fédérale de contrôle cinématographique	CFCC
Centre national du cinéma et de l'image animée	CNC
Compagnie africaine cinématographique industrielle et commercial	COMACICO
Fonds d'aide et de coopération	FAC
Fédération panafricaine des cinéastes	FEPACI
Fonds d'équipement rural et de développement économique et social	FERDES
Festival panafricain du cinéma et de la télévision de Ouagadougou	FESPACO
Fonds pour l'investissement en développement économique et social	FIDES
Front de libération nationale	FLN
Groupe africain du cinéma	GAC
Gosudarstvenyi institut kinematografii	GIK
Institut des hautes études cinématographiques	IDHEC
Journées cinématographiques de Carthage	JCC
Motion Picture Export Association of America	MPEAA
Parti communiste français	PCF
Rassemblement démocratique africaine	RDA
Société d'éxploitation cinématographique africaine	SECMA
Société national voltaïque de cinéma	SONAVOCI
Union pour la démocratie française	UDF

CINEMA AND DEVELOPMENT IN WEST AFRICA

Introduction:
Cinema as Art and Industry

I RETURNED TO DAKAR, Senegal, in the summer of 2011 to complete research for this project and took my usual path walking along Avenue Hassan II (ex-Albert Sarraut) through the Place de l'indépendance toward the administrative building in the basement of which is housed the National Archives of Senegal. For years a movie theater stood at the southwest corner of the central plaza, although it was clearly run down and did not offer many showings. Now, though, the building was gone, replaced with a pile of rubble. Barely concealing the rubble was a fence that seemed to offer more perils than protection from the debris. No evidence remained that this location once offered audiences celluloid entertainment. Instead, the ruins blended into the generally decaying architecture that characterizes this once majestic space. In fact, much of downtown Dakar resembles the plaza—a mixture of crumbled buildings, others in better repair, frozen in 1970s architectural style, and some in a perpetual process of construction. Downtown Dakar was at that moment bustling with new construction projects promoted by then-president Abdoulaye Wade and financed by international lending agencies, China, and Morocco, among other outside sources. Much of the money appeared destined to develop a tourist infrastructure—hotels and a cultural park, financed entirely by China, which would contain "the Seven Wonders of Dakar," one of which was to be a new site for the archives near the location of the historic train station, scene of the 1947–48 railway strike. This strike was one of the heroic moments in the saga of the anticolonial struggle, immortalized in Ousmane Sembène's 1960 novel *God's Bits of Wood*.

Weaving unceasingly through this urban landscape were multitudes of people headed to work, shopping, or school or going out in search of a job; still others wandered, hustled, or sat on the sidewalks in no apparent hurry to be anywhere else. In fact, there were far too many of the last groups, although they had been made less visible in the city center with President Wade's construction boom. It's been more than fifty years since Senegal and the other countries of French West Africa achieved independence (celebrated in the plaza that bears its namesake), but the scenes of contemporary Dakar, marked by coterminous signs of renewal and decline, belie the heritage of that half century. It is a composite of hope for a self-directed future leading to economic development and cultural regeneration and of frustration as those aspirations have been blunted by a neocolonial system that has trapped Senegal and

1

much of sub-Saharan Africa in a dependent relationship with their former colonial overlords and fostered a vicious cycle of impoverishment and nondevelopment. It is ironic that one of the Seven Wonders of Dakar, the realization of Senegal's first President Léopold Sédar Senghor's longtime dream of a museum dedicated to black civilizations (Musée des civilisations noires), has only been made possible with a grant from the government of the People's Republic of China.

The image of the building that used to show films reduced to rocks and dust on the Place de l'indépendance, replete with its central water fountain from whence water does not flow, evokes the central theme of this book—the struggle by early African filmmakers to found a truly independent African cinema that would simultaneously contribute to the cultural renaissance of Africa's peoples and play a central role in postcolonial economic development. This aspiration is still very much alive, but it has been severely mitigated by the vicissitudes of a global imperialist capitalist system that relinquished formal colonial rule in Africa but did not give up its ultimate domination of Africa's peoples and societies. African filmmakers struggle today to ply their craft under conditions that their predecessors would easily recognize from the 1960s. This is both encouraging and disheartening. It is encouraging because despite the seemingly insuperable odds that confront them, African cineastes have continued to strive for aesthetic innovation and to find a means to use film as a vehicle to foster the material improvement of the lives of their compatriots. It is disheartening because the evidence for progress, at least in the arena of structural development, is minimal at best. This book seeks to tell the story of the early years in that battle, as cultural activists from Francophone West Africa sought to invent an African cinema that would be a vital part of constructing a liberated and developed postcolonial Africa.

That role was sketched emphatically in 1975 when representatives from thirty-nine national film organizations from across Africa met in Algiers, Algeria, at the second congress of the Fédération panafricaine des cinéastes (FEPACI). In the wake of the organization's founding in 1970 the African filmmakers gathered in Algiers to issue a clear statement of purpose and direction for postcolonial African cinema. In the Algiers charter, endorsed at the conclusion of the congress, the assembled delegates proclaimed that in order "to assume a genuinely active role in the process of development, African culture must be popular, democratic and progressive in character, inspired by its own realities and responding to its own needs." At the heart of that project was the development of "a responsible, free, and committed cinema."[1] From the inception of African cinema, the continent's filmmakers viewed the motion picture industry as a vital component of the social, political, economic, and cultural development of their societies as they emerged from the yoke of colonial rule. Film became central to the thinking of cultural activists when they were seeking a vehicle that could help overcome decades of negative cultural representations of Africa and Africans and thereby instill a new, positive identity among their people in a multilingual environment where most of the population was illiterate. Beyond being attracted to the aesthetic imprimatur of film, the earliest African filmmakers viewed the establishment of an African cinema as an essential means by which to assist in the material regeneration of their societies. Paulin Soumanou Vieyra, one of the progenitors of African filmmaking, enunciated that bond between the imperative to forge an African film aesthetic and economic development. Speaking at the Second World Congress of Black Writers and Artists held in Rome, Italy, in 1959, Vieyra said, "There must be economic development. At the [very] least in the vital sectors, and the cinema is one of them."[2]

African filmmakers of the pioneer generation did not inaugurate the idea of a politics of film or even of political film. They adapted the concepts of a film politics and political film to the contexts of societies newly free from nearly a century of foreign rule, a century during which cinematography was invented and certain structural aspects of the cinema as an industry and an art form emerged. In that sense, African cineastes in the 1960s made a profound contribution to the history of film by charting the path for the development of a distinctively "African cinema" while also intervening in crucial theoretical debates about the nature and purpose of moving pictures in the modern world. Contrary to the assertions of some film theorists, most notably those associated with the Frankfurt school, the first generation of African filmmakers viewed the mechanics of the cinema, specifically its associated technology and the capacity for a film's reproduction and widespread dissemination, as virtues that could be harnessed to the project of liberation from all forms of oppression.[3] Early filmmakers such as Sembène (Senegal) and Med Hondo (Mauritania) consciously appropriated the technology and practices of Western filmmaking in order to challenge prevailing colonialist representations of Africa and Africans as well as the former imperialist powers' monopoly over the cinema industrial complex. Operating generally from a Marxist perspective, the first filmmakers in postcolonial West Africa did not attach inherent moral attributes to the tools associated with film but instead viewed them as the patrimony of humankind. The instruments of the cinema industrial complex were not the source of oppression; rather, by gaining access to and using them, one was able to locate the structural impediments to development and liberation. Consequently, I argue that the caution offered by Roy Armes is misplaced when he writes, "We must never forget that the technology of filmmaking introduced after independence was a borrowed technology and that the prestige of existing Western applications of this technology could not fail to impress emergent African filmmakers."[4] To appropriate the technology monopolized by the West and (re)deploy it to serve the interests of Africans in their own societies was precisely the point of the work carried out by West African filmmakers in the early years of political sovereignty. One of the greatest impediments to the emergence of a fully autonomous and self-sustaining

African cinema has been the continued need to borrow the technology of filmmaking from those who monopolized it at the time of decolonization.

In this study I am specifically concerned with the emergence of filmmaking in Francophone West Africa. Therefore, I do not offer a comprehensive history of film in Africa or of African filmmaking. There are many excellent works that have tackled those daunting tasks.[5] I have chosen a more limited study in order to explicate some specific dynamics at work in the emergence of African cinema and to tackle the subject from an angle that it has not been systematically addressed from before. My focus on this region results from two overriding factors. The first is the prominent place that France gave to cinema as both an art and an industry. Following the devastation and disruption of the Second World War, successive governments in France viewed film as a central element in the country's regeneration culturally and economically.[6] In the colonies this translated into the articulation of a "film politics" structured by a series of decrees that bounded the aesthetic and material practice of cinema in the overseas territories. West Africa was a primary geographic site for the enactment of France's approach to cinematic practices, as it was for most French imperial policies. West Africa was a market that had to be secured for French films and a space that would be permanently marked by French culture. The result was a flurry of regulations that tightly controlled what could be viewed on African movie screens, what kinds of films could be made in and about West Africa, and even what languages were acceptable for film dialogue. It is a perfect illustration of what Gary Wilder identifies as the "French imperial nation-state," "an internally contradictory artifact of colonial modernity that was simultaneously imaginary and real, abstract and concrete, universalizing and particularizing, effective and defective, modern and illiberal, republican and racist, welfarist and mercantilist, Franco-African and Afro-French, national and transnational."[7] Consequently, centering the analysis on Francophone West Africa enables the interrogation of the idea of a film politics in the site that was its target as well as the context in which it achieved its most elaborate expression.

Edward Said remarks that "scarcely any attention has been paid to what I believe is the privileged role of culture in the modern imperial experience, and little notice taken of the fact that the extraordinary global reach of classical nineteenth- and early twentieth-century European imperialism still casts a considerable shadow over our own times." However, if there has been a dearth of scholarly research, only recently being redressed, on the interconnectedness of imperialism and culture, the links were not at all missed by colonialists constructing France's imperial apparatus in West Africa nor among those who resisted those structures of alien domination. In fact, "the cultural question" was a central feature, perhaps even a distinguishing one, of the history of France's colonial adventure and its continuing postcolonial relationship with the ex-colonies. Moreover, it was a terrain on which some of the most important battles in the imperial context were fought, as colonized peoples struggled to protect their own cultural practices from expurgation by the French or sought to (re)construct a post- (even anti-) colonial culture to repair the inevitable damage wrought and transcend the corruption induced by the colonial experience. As Said notes, those skirmishes, especially on the cultural terrain, have endured into the present, growing more desperate as the patent failures or incompleteness of decolonization become too painful to ignore.[8]

One of the foremost theorists on the importance of the cultural question in the struggle to overcome the negative colonial legacies wreaking havoc across Africa is Ngũgĩ wa Thiong'o. A leader by example as well as through intellectual expression, Ngũgĩ argues that "the biggest weapon wielded and actually daily unleashed by imperialism against that collective defiance [of the colonized] is the cultural bomb. The effect of a cultural bomb is to annihilate a people's belief in their names, in their languages, in their environment, in their heritage of struggle, in their unity, in their capacities and ultimately in themselves."[9] From the moment French imperialists launched their part of the European scramble for Africa in the late nineteenth century they deployed a cultural bomb intended to eradicate, through denial if necessary, African cultures and replace them with French civilization. As General Joseph Gallièni, the conqueror of Madagascar, notes in his memoirs, France's explicit goal through colonization was to "Frenchify" the indigenous populations through promotion of the French language, a physical reordering of social space, and the introduction of a battery of legal changes meant to alter patterns of behavior and worldviews.[10] That ambition was shared by many officials of all ranks who ruled over the vast federation of French West Africa after it was formed in 1895 until the final independence of its eight territories in 1960.[11] It was a vision also embraced to some degree by elements of the colonized society—those trained by French colonial or missionary schools to be the day-to-day administrators of empire, sections of the emergent working class who modeled their future on the French workers' present, the small, but powerful planters' class, and even some chiefs grafted onto the lower echelons of France's colonial power structure.[12]

However, there were signs from the start that this would not be an uncontested mission. Early resisters to the French conquest invoked existing elements of local culture, in particular religious brotherhoods and secret societies, as a means of countering the invader and preserving their independence. Even after the military engagements ended, resistance continued unabated in the field of culture. It took the form of newly emergent Muslim brotherhoods, syncretic religious movements, and even the appropriation of the rhetoric of France's own *mission civilisatrice* as a means by which to highlight the failings and outright hypocrisy of the colonial project and thereby articulate an independent and distinctive African modernity.[13] Consequently, the cultural realm was never entirely left to the colonizers. What changed over time were the forms that struggle took and the issues over which the fight was waged. But it is important to be cognizant that there was a continuous fight over mentalities, systems of representation, and claims to identity during the period of French rule in West Africa. By the 1950s the terrain on which the fight against cultural imperialism was fought had begun to shift to the cinema.

"What is claimed," writes John Tomlinson, by the notion of cultural imperialism "is that a form of domination exists in the modern world, not just in the political and economic spheres but also over those practices by which collectivities make sense of their lives."[14] However, it is not just a question of an additional form of domination supplementing or even reinforcing the economic and political aspects of control exerted by one force in an attempt to subsume another. Such a rendering allows for the analysis of cultural aspects of imperialism without explicit reference to the material dimensions of the relationship between the imperial center and its dominated periphery. A central theme of this book is that the cultural and material dimensions of power relations are part of a complex whole that is greater than the sum of its parts. Consequently, African filmmakers of the pioneer generation viewed cultural production as intricately bound up with the question of material development, technology transfer, and skill acquisition. Their approach often approximated what Frantz Fanon called for in his explication of the elements necessary for a thorough and meaningful decolonization.[15] Moreover, this study requires a look at processes of cultural diffusion that are not necessarily imperialistic in the sense of having as their overarching objective the replacement of one set of cultural values with another but that rather seek to cut through misrepresentations and offer new images from previously silenced perspectives.

Pierre Bourdieu's analysis of the field of cultural production as a contested space wherein power relations (evidenced in access to and control over the material means of production and distribution in a society), as well as the parameters that define the zone of engagement, are at stake is particularly useful for this study. In addition to possessing structural aspects, the field is also a location wherein the capacity to impose meanings is worked out by competing elements.[16] In the course of that struggle, new values and their forms of representation take shape and are articulated by those who emerge as what Antonio Gramsci called the "organic intellectuals" of subaltern groups, or as West African filmmakers called themselves, "modern griots."[17] Cineastes from West Africa sought to formulate a distinctive African film aesthetic in order to forge a space within the global field of cinematic cultural production that would both add to it (in terms of contributing heretofore unseen images) and reconfigure it by forcing others in the field to engage with the emergent African aesthetic. The particular framework in which they had to operate had already been structured through the actions of French colonial officials, their colleagues in Paris, and African film audiences. Thus, the film politics generated in the context of late-French colonial rule makes West Africa a particularly important site for investigating the major themes of this book.

The second element that makes Francophone West Africa a fruitful site for investigating this study's central themes is the overwhelming dominance of filmmakers from the region in terms of production and theoretical contributions in the early history of African moviemaking, especially in sub-Saharan Africa. This is a factor that scholars and critics of African cinema have commented on extensively.[18] The number of "firsts" that accrued to the work of French-speaking West African cineastes is too long to list here. However, a few of those inaugural highlights include the first full-length feature made by an African director (Sembène's *La noire de...*, produced in Senegal in 1966), the first full-length feature made in an African language (Sembène's *Mandabi*, produced in Senegal in 1968), and the first historical epic made by an African filmmaker (Hondo's *Soleil Ô*, produced in Mauritania in 1967). Throughout this period Vieyra, who was born in Benin and raised from the age of ten on in Senegal, offered critical theoretical and aesthetic commentary on the fundamental question that exercised the thinking of the pioneers of African film: what is African cinema? He also was one of the first to challenge the barrier to African access to filmmaking, even before the end of colonial rule. Finally, Francophone West Africa was the site for the first Pan-African film festival, the Festival panafricain du cinéma et de la télévision de Ouagadougou (FESPACO), held in 1969, in Ouagadougou, Upper Volta (now Burkina Faso), as well as the home region for most of the founding members of FEPACI. Not unrelated to the study of film in West Africa, in 1970 the inaugural meeting of what would become the Francophonie (today formally known as the Organisation international de la Francophonie) took place in Niamey, Niger, at which the Agence de coopération culturelle et technique (ACCT) was launched, with France's minister of culture, André Malraux, attending as an observer. The Francophonie's founding included a public commitment to technology transfer, again linked to cultural production, as attested to in the original name of the organization. That event was itself the culmination of efforts begun by Senghor through an article he published in the French journal *Esprit* in 1962. Francophone West Africa, then, was uniquely positioned to become the site where the struggle to found an African cinema would unfold. As such, the works of those progenitors of sub-Saharan African filmmaking served at the very least as reference points, providing cineastes in other parts of Africa with a starting point for their own careers as well as supplying the elements that would structure the pattern of African filmmaking for subsequent generations.

Significantly, what bound the French tradition of film politics to the politically engaged film of the first West African filmmakers was precisely their mutual comprehension of cinema as both an art and an industry that together comprised a "cinema industrial complex." It was an understanding that filmmakers from other parts of Africa would come to much later, after years of difficulty trying to get their productions shown on screens in their own countries. As the Ethiopian cineaste and film theorist Haile Gerima explains in a 2002 interview, "I believe that the struggle in the world is determined decisively on the basis of who controls the story narrative.... So to me, the right to express one's own story is the battleground.... Now I have become more realistic that films are nothing without the power of distribution, and I have become more realistic about the economic aspects of cinema."[19] This point is reinforced by the Sudanese filmmaker Gadalla Gubara in a 1995 interview with Nwachuckwu Frank Ukadike: "As you know, the film industry is called film industry and art, not art and industry. Industry is first because to make a film you must have money.... [F]or the cameraman, actors, raw film stock, a laboratory, the soundman, etc. The foreigners who support African cinema have the cash, but they use it to stifle the growth of Africa's film industry in order to ensure lack of competition from African filmmakers."[20] The notion of Francophone West African motion picture production as transpiring within a "cinema industrial complex" provides the conceptual framework for this study. It allows for the interrogation of emergent Francophone West African cinema as part of the overarching struggle for development in the early postcolonial years. In order to carry out this interrogation, I deploy a broader understanding of the idea of development that reflects the significance of the cultural aspect as well as an expanded notion of the nature of the cinema that encompasses its essential material aspects.

This book offers a new approach to understanding the emergence of West African filmmaking from the 1950s to the 1970s. Typically, scholars have analyzed African films in terms of their aesthetic dimensions or have presented general narratives of the history of African cinema, such as a chronological explication of film production. Missing from both approaches is an interrogation of the essential social and economic aspects of the cinematic process. This study reveals the link between the struggle to articulate an African film aesthetic and the urgent task of postcolonial economic development. I argue that the difficulties African filmmakers confronted as they developed their craft during the 1960s were indicative of the broader crisis of underdevelopment that today continues to challenge African societies. In fact, the barriers that inhibited the establishment of a self-sustaining and independent cinema industry in West Africa during the 1960s reveal the neocolonial structures that allowed former colonial powers like France to maintain significant influence in their ex-colonies, as well as the complicity of postcolonial governments in that relationship.

This investigation places the culture industry at the center of discussions about economic development in postcolonial African societies. Rather than focus on problems connected with international aid, loans, and trade, I stress how an analysis of the fight to establish an independent African cinema responsive to the aspirations and needs of the people exposes the structural inequalities in the global economy that constrained the prospects for economic growth in postcolonial Africa. Moreover, this book makes a significant contribution to contemporary discussions about technology transfer and socially responsible development. One of the problems that vexed the pioneers of African cinema was the lack of access to basic filmmaking equipment and especially postproduction facilities. Since cinema was and continues to be a capital-intensive industry, my research on early West African filmmaking provides unique insights into the ways in which a lack of access to financial resources and the inability to control domestic markets not only preserves global inequalities but also constrains cultural development in poorer countries. Throughout the period of this study, colonial-era monopolies tied to non-African film conglomerates dominated the film distribution network in West Africa, and instead of promoting domestic films, those theater companies featured movies produced in Hollywood, India, Europe, and Hong Kong. Thus, not only were African audiences regularly bombarded with foreign images but African filmmakers could not even show their films in their own countries.

The book draws on a multidisciplinary methodology that combines aspects of film analysis, archival work, and development studies. Consequently, I examine individual films in order to uncover what they tell us about the formation of an African film aesthetic, the issues that filmmakers regarded as most urgent, and shifts in theme over time. In addition, I analyze film treatments and records of the creative process in order to trace the path leading to the finished product. Unlike most scholars working on film in general and African cinema specifically, I make extensive use of archival materials because they provide a means by which to understand how film production and distribution was organized, as well as how filmmakers and governments interacted in the early postcolonial period. Specifically, I examine the reports of censorship boards and police and surveillance agencies and financial statements detailing revenues from movie theaters. By bringing together analyses of the creative process, the finished films, and the material context of the movies' production and distribution, this study offers a comprehensive and nuanced picture of the successes and failures of postcolonial African development in the first decade after independence.

The book's narrative structure maps the emergence of West African cinema from the years after 1945 to the early 1970s. As French power waned in West Africa following the Second World War, cultural activists throughout the region came to play a vital role in the mobilization of the people to end colonial rule. In that struggle, two themes recurred as essential to the restoration of real independence to Africa: regaining control over the construction of African identities through the kinds of images presented to and articulated on behalf of the people and economic development. Cinema, as an industry and a form of cultural expression, was uniquely able to meet those two objectives. In 1959, on the eve of West African independence, Vieyra wrote that cinema "will assume particular responsibilities in an underdeveloped independent country" because of its basic attributes as a modern industrial art. He viewed filmmaking as a collective process that relied on a variety of specialists in front of and behind the camera. Moreover, a successful cinema industry encompasses the use of chemistry, technical training, optics, movie theater construction, marketing, and distribution, in addition to other fundamental material components.[21] It is, in a word, about much more than the film itself, however important the images on the screen may be. Vieyra and the first generation of African filmmakers, therefore, argued that cultivating a national cinema would contribute to general economic development and foster social change. The pioneers of West African cinema insisted that the material aspects of film production were inseparable from the aesthetic attributes of motion pictures that made movies powerful tools in constructing images and conveying messages to broad audiences, especially in areas where literacy was minimal and visual cues were prominent as a form of communication. My research takes those claims seriously and resituates the advent of African cinema within the general process of postcolonial nation building.

During the 1960s West African filmmaking blossomed. By the end of the 1960s there were a sufficient number of directors and films to convene the first FESPACO as well as to found FEPACI. At its inception, FEPACI explicitly cited the "liberating economic capacity" of film as well as its importance as a vehicle for controlling "Africa's image and imagination."[22] With the emergence of an institutional framework that could facilitate the further development of an African cinema industry, Upper Volta took the lead in 1970 and broke the stranglehold of the European distribution monopolies that owned almost all the movie theaters in the region. In their place, a nationalized film industry took root with a mandate to foster African visual arts and generate revenue for additional economic development. I conclude my study with a discussion of FEPACI's second congress in 1975 and the definitive declaration issued by the filmmakers gathered for that meeting in Algiers, Algeria. This promising moment in the history of Francophone West African cinema starkly illustrates the contrast between the possibilities for meaningful social change that inhered within the efforts of the pioneer African filmmakers and the structural forces in the global economy that circumscribed Africa's potential for postcolonial economic and cultural development.

In this study I make critical use of certain strains of film theory and criticism in order to explicate the linkages between the position of the filmmaker as auteur, the instruments (tools) of cinema, and the social contexts in which the film narratives were produced and meant to be received. In doing so I argue that it is necessary to complicate conventional theoretical approaches to the cinema by insisting on the integral importance of the material aspects of film production and distribution in any conversation about the affective attributes of a given movie. This is particularly relevant in an investigation of African cinema. The question posed by Jean-Louis Baudry of whether "the work [is] made evident" in the final film, the "consumption of the product bring[ing] about a 'knowledge effect,'" or whether "the work [is] concealed," was not, I argue, a preoccupation of the pioneers of West African cinema.²³ Baudry's question elides the fundamental differences in cinematic styles that inform the struggle over film production, especially in the developing world. For Baudry the central issue in film analysis is its alienating potential, which was also a concern of African cineastes. Film has the seductive power to present a reality that is not real and can, therefore, lead the consumer of the product into the realm of fantasy. Theodor Adorno also identifies that danger when he writes that "the consumers are made to remain what they are: consumers. That is why the culture industry is not the art of the consumer but rather the projection of the will of those in control onto their victims."²⁴ However, for the progenitors of African film the site of alienation was located in the final images produced on the screen as well as in the ownership/control of the means of the film's production and distribution. Sembène and others explicitly constructed an alternative reality to counter the "realities" about Africa and Africans that had been produced and circulated around the world for decades during colonial rule. The founders of African cinema viewed "objective reality" as a site of struggle, always in the process of construction. Thus, the question of whether or not the labor that went into the finished commodity was elided by the images conveyed to the public or is reducible to some ideological control of the auteur over the viewer displaces the materialist analysis of film onto the aesthetics of the cinema.

The materialism that concerns Baudry and Adorno, among others, is in the effects of the film on the audience and, consequently, is limited to the psychological/ideological realm. It is an immaterial materialism. Again, according to Baudry, "We must first establish the place of the instrumental base in the set of operations which combine in the production of a film (we omit consideration of economic implications).... [O]ne may ask, do the instruments (the technical base) produce specific ideological effects, and are these effects themselves determined by the dominant ideology?"²⁵ In a subtle maneuver, Baudry transforms the camera into the agent and leaves the filmmaker and even the audience in the roles of secondary participants in the construction/dissemination process or at least reduces them to passive recipients of the products emanating from the tools. Baudry reproduces one of the salient aspects of capitalism that Karl Marx critiqued in the nineteenth century: the reification of the tool by which the tool is made into the agent controlling the labor of the worker. For African cineastes in the 1960s the camera was not a limiting device that obfuscated their labor; it was rather a desired technology that had the capacity to carry new, liberating images to mass audiences, and it had to be appropriated because of its potential to aid in the material development of the former colonies.

In this regard the early African filmmakers embraced a conceptualization of cinema close to that being articulated by their contemporaries in Latin America. Beginning with *cinema novo* in Brazil in the early 1960s and continuing with the Third Cinema movement later in the decade, cultural and political activists sought to reinvent cinematic practice and put moviemaking squarely in the service of the liberation of the people from capitalist and imperialist oppression. It was precisely against the kind of auteurist cinema of the New Wave in France and the commercially driven movies of Hollywood, both of which informed Baudry's concerns, that Fernando Solanas and Octavio Getino articulated a vision of revolutionary filmmaking as a vital weapon in the struggle for social change in the Third World. In the manifesto that formed the theoretical basis of the Third Cinema movement, Solanas and Getino state that their goal was the formation of "a cinema of subversion" that "prepares the terrain for the revolution to become reality": "Every image that documents, bears witness to, refutes or deepens the truth of a situation is something more than a film image or purely artistic fact; it becomes something which the System finds indigestible."[26] Yet even among Third Cinema theorists, film remained within the conceptual orbit of an aesthetic meant to affect the material reality of the audience in the act of viewing and the filmmakers in the act of production. The materiality of film as a commodity situated at the nexus of complex productive processes continued to be elided. For Solanas and Getino the film becomes a weapon in the fight for liberation, as it would be for African cineastes, but filmmaking is not understood as a mechanism for the material development of those societies that are to be so transformed. African filmmakers offered a more comprehensive approach to cinema that recognized the imperative to engage in the contest to forge an African cinema in the service of the people on the material/technological terrain as much as at the level of the images and narratives conveyed to the audiences.

Scholars of African cinema have also tended to underplay or ignore the industrial nature of filmmaking in their studies. Yet the linkages are there. As Ukadike notes, "Since political independence in black Africa has not been followed by economic and cultural independence, film production, even when under the control of Africans in independent countries, has mimicked the general uneven pattern of Africa's overall development. . . . Instead of being utilized as an integral arm of the sociopolitical and economic infrastructure, serving useful development purposes, [electronic media's] function has been to perpetuate the leadership of powerful oligarchs." I would add that the work of cineastes such as Sembène or Hondo has also not been promoted by their own governments and in some cases has been banned or severely censored. Despite Ukadike's acknowledgment of the fundamental connection between film as art and industry, he concentrates the discussion on the emergent aesthetic of African cinema. His analysis follows "African filmmaking as emerging out of the excitement of nation-building and a quest for the revivification of Africa's lost cultural heritage and identity, a quest that has inspired innovative and creative diversification in the cinema and the arts."[27] This is certainly a crucial component of the project to found an African cinema, but it was one that the pioneers of the 1960s viewed as unattainable absent the economic development that would accompany the establishment of a cinema industry in Africa.

Ukadike partly addresses this aspect in his subsequent compendium of interviews with African cineastes, *Questioning African Cinema,* although it is the filmmakers, in their responses to questions that Ukadike poses, who insist on those linkages.[28]

This leads to a discussion of the two main theoretical concepts that inform the current study. One is the idea of representation and the other is the notion of materialism. Both were central to early West African filmmakers' understanding of their project of establishing an African cinema. Roland Barthes writes, "Representation is not defined directly by imitation: even if one gets rid of notions of the 'real,' of the 'vraisemblable,' of the 'copy,' there will still be representation for so long as a subject (author, reader, spectator, or voyeur) casts his *gaze* toward a horizon on which he cuts out the base of a triangle, his eye (or his mind) forming the apex." He continues, "The 'Organon of Representation' ([of] which today it is becoming possible to write because there are intimations of *something else*) will have as its dual foundation the sovereignty of the act of cutting out [*découpage*] and the unity of the subject of that action."[29] Representation in film, as Barthes explains, involves a deliberate and conscious process of selection. The image is entirely intentional and is the product of a continuous editing that seeks to circumscribe the range of meanings available to the consumer of the film. The sequence of shots is designed to lead the viewer through the journey of denotative discovery, but to do so the images must be encoded with culturally relevant symbols. In other words, the film must speak a cinematic language that resonates with the epistemology of the viewing public. As Christian Metz observes, "*The fact that must be understood is that films are understood,*" and, I would add, films must be comprehensible within the culturally encoded language of images that the spectator brings to the viewing of the movie.[30] Meaning does not exist outside of context and one is made cognizant of the context through the construction of meaning.

From its origination to the sketching of its narrative structure to its filming and editing, a movie revolves around choices of inclusion and exclusion. The camera must accurately capture the director's desired and (deliberately) constrained image. The audience should see the shot that the filmmaker wants viewed. As Barthes puts it, "Such demiurgic discrimination implies high quality of thought: the tableau is intellectual, it has something to say (something moral, social), but it also says that it knows how this must be done; it is simultaneously significant and propaedeutic, impressive and reflexive, moving and conscious of the channels of emotion."[31] Metz further sums up this process: "It is well known that the nature of the cinema is to transform the world into discourse." To do this the director must be the master of "two main types of signifying organization: *cultural* codes and *specialized* codes."[32] Thus, the project of making a film is structured around intent, conveyance of meaning, and contextual relevance. All must be present and technically well executed for the end product to be consumed by the audience in a way that approaches the objectives of the filmmaker as adumbrated in the inaugurating idea.

For the early West African filmmakers the problem of representation was fundamental to articulating what would constitute an African cinema. The struggle, as Thiong'o put it, to "decolonize the mind" was an urgent task following the achievement of political sovereignty.[33] For decades, African film audiences had been bombarded with images about them constructed by others with the intent of fostering a colonized mentality that would naturalize the imperialist system. Western filmmakers forged representations of Africa and Africans that legitimated the colonialist project and reinforced racist ideologies that confirmed the privilege of the West over the rest. As Kenneth Cameron and others have noted, "'Africa' came into filmmaking almost with cinema's beginnings."[34] Africa and Africans were subjects and Africa was backdrop and location for many films from the earliest days of the Lumière Brothers' productions through the advent of ethnographic filmmaking in the 1930s. David Henry Slavin remarks that "colonial film reflected and reinforced the machinery of cultural hegemony, noncoercive social control, and the underlying politics of privilege."[35] Motion pictures from the first part of the twentieth century deployed the trope of Africa as a site of savagery, violence, and mystery. Africa was a setting for the actualization of masculine virtues said to be in decline in Europe as well as the primeval zone where civilization could be transplanted in its pure form on a benighted population. Africans were either to be combatted as threats to human society or coached into the light from their eternal darkness. However, this early cinematic experience, as Ukadike describes it, was targeted largely at extra-African audiences; Africans in these films figured merely as props in a political morality play directed back at its source.[36]

West African directors sought to counter those representations on both levels; however, the main focus in the initial years had to be the images Africans consumed of themselves. As Joseph Ki-Zerbo sums up the task confronting African filmmakers, "The cinema must address sick, battered consciousnesses to make them upright and militant."[37] This required that cineastes explore what it meant to label a film as "African" in contradistinction to "Western." For filmmakers like Sembène and Hondo in the 1960s, African identity had to be constructed through a simultaneous process of recovery and invention that responded to the immediate material context of postcolonial African society. The final product had to be judged according to whether it advanced the cause of liberating the mind from negative colonial cognitive patterns and, by extension, by its capacity to empower viewers to transform their material conditions to better serve their own needs as opposed to those of the former imperial ruler. Thus, the selection and sequencing of shots, the construction of images, was determined by an understanding of the state of social relations and development of newly independent Africa. The film's "Africanness" was located in its cultural coding (the images were said to be rooted in a recognizable system of social meaning) as well as in its contribution to the material transformation of the society in which the viewer lived in the direction of greater development and social equality. The African film had to connect with and move its consumers in Africa. As David Murphy and Patrick Williams note, "African cinema exists in a Western-dominated global system and its politics of representation must be understood within the full complexity of this situation."[38] Thus African cinema was oppositional from its very beginnings. It constituted an antithesis to the thesis of hegemonic images that pervaded the cinematic field at the time of West Africa's independence.

This leads to a discussion of materialism as a key component in the practices of early West African filmmaking. The representations of and directed at Africa/Africans during the colonial period were connected to a specific set of material relations that structured a system of Western dominance exploiting Africa (and other colonized parts of the world) for the further enrichment and development of the ruling capitalist class in Europe and North America. The production of those visual markers was not accidental or incidental to imperialism as a socioeconomic system. This point is well documented by Slavin in his study of colonial cinema and has been confirmed in the work of many other scholars of film in the colonial/third world.[39] For the purposes of this study I take "materialism" to refer to that intellectual tradition that arose to counter a prevailing "idealist" philosophy and that roots cultural artifacts in the specific historical conditions from which they emanate and that, in turn, legitimate the extant social relations of production. Systems of representation correspond to their material conditions of production and are, as such, grounded in the historical moment of their manufacture. In the dialectics of history those "ideological apparatuses," as Louis Althusser describes them, either sustain the existing relation of social forces or they seek to subvert them, presaging a new order of power that reflects the interests of subaltern groups.[40]

Thus, the images generated by early West African filmmakers directly related to prevailing, already existing visual tropes of Africa and Africans and were meant to undermine the ideological legitimacy of the hegemonic material system. From the start, African cinema had to be engaged and politically subversive because of Africa's objective position in the world system.[41] African directors had to participate in the "complete calling into question of the colonial condition," as Frantz Fanon describes it, in order to forge a cinema that was distinctive and responsive to the African situation after years of colonial rule. In the absence of a cinematic tradition other than that of the West during the period of foreign rule, African film had to emerge as an existential challenge to that monopoly over both representation and production.[42] As such, early West African filmmakers sought out examples of subversive and revolutionary cinema from other contexts that approximated their own in the 1960s. This would lead some like Sembène and Malian Souleymane Cissé to explore Soviet cinematographic traditions or to seek inspiration from other disruptive cinematic styles like Italian neorealism, Latin American *cinema novo*, and Third Cinema.

The concept of materialism is also important for this study because a film is, after all, a commodity. It results from the collective work of the entire production staff and performers as well as the intellectual labor of the filmmaker. It makes use of sophisticated technology and scientific principles relating to lighting, angles, chemistry, optics, and aurality, among others. It also deploys the artistic notions of framing, narrative structure, and sensory evocation. The end result is a product forged from raw materials (mental and physical) through the infusion of a significant amount of labor and capital (which itself represents labor) invested in it that is distributed in order to be consumed by audiences who are, generally, expected to pay for access to the screening and also perform the work of interpretation, bringing their own meanings to the viewing. The original is such that it is designed for mass reproduction; the copies are exact replicas, indistinguishable from the master. This process gave Walter Benjamin pause; he warned about the loss of "sacrality" in the modern world and the potential fascist implications of art in the age of mechanical reproduction. However, he also saw the potential for this new system of manufacture in the realm of "art" to be appropriated in a way that would restore deep meaning in the world, precisely through disruptive techniques that were often at the heart of African film practices in the 1960s in conscious fealty to Berthold Brecht's experimentations in theater.[43] Benjamin was careful to highlight the potential for motion pictures to contribute to the project of social liberation, as exemplified in the production of many early Soviet cinematographers, wherein "work itself is given a voice" and the tendency evident in the capitalist West to appropriate film technology to promote illusion and fantasy is combatted.[44] In such conditions, the filmmaker could be cast in the role of organic intellectual for the subaltern classes or groups.[45]

This is exactly how early African moviemakers viewed their task in the years following independence. Consistent with the idea of drawing on existing cultural codes as a marker of connection and relevance as well as using their specialized codes to advance the cause of social liberation, Sembène and his contemporaries frequently described their position as that of the "modern griot," a label likewise claimed by earlier cultural activists in the literary terrain.[46] The griot in West Africa is the traditional storyteller who has the specific social role of preserving the history and knowledge of a particular community while also acting as a moral guide in the manner of the retelling of important cultural narratives. They are not merely praise singers, although that is one of their functions. They are both a "living library" and interpreters of the wisdom contained therein, adapting it to contemporary circumstances. The filmmakers sought to harness modern technology to those traditional functions and thereby participate in the representational and material regeneration of their societies. Early West African cineastes, according to Mbye Cham, regarded "film as a crucial site of the battle to decolonise minds, to develop radical consciousness, to reflect and engage critically with African cultures and traditions, and to make desirable the meaningful transformation of society for the benefit of the majority."[47]

But it involved so much more than that. The film is a commodity produced and circulated within a cinema industrial complex that Aminata Barry describes in detail as involving electricity, cameras, sound recording, marketing, financing, distribution, reproduction, and skill training, among other essential activities.[48] Without engaging with the materialism of filmmaking, the representation projected on the screen lacks meaning, and without the struggle over representation, the prevailing material conditions that preserve the power of the former imperialist powers and their ruling capitalist class cannot be changed to improve the lives of those subjugated by the world system. This was the dual front on which the progenitors of West African cinema battled in the early postcolonial years.

To tell that story, the narrative begins with the articulation of a film politics during the last phase of French colonial rule in West Africa. The first chapter follows the administrative process through which the film industry was regulated and structured beginning with the Laval decree of 1934 and subsequently with the flurry of decrees issued in the wake of the Second World War. France's leaders in Paris and West Africa viewed the cinema as a special industry to be protected and developed not only because it could be used to project French cultural influence around the world but also because it was an economic sector vital to reconstruction after years of occupation and war. In the colonies, the film politics of the 1940s and 1950s aimed to shore up a tottering imperial apparatus by more tightly controlling and directing the minds of the colonized populations, who, as it turned out, had a growing appetite for consuming films. Thus the struggle to control the images (representation) available to and about Africans as well as the functioning of the market (materialism) in French West Africa were joined in the film politics of the postwar era.

Chapter 2 offers a survey of colonialist representation by looking at some of the prevailing images of Africa/Africans projected to the outside world as well as those directed at the local audiences themselves. Here I examine shifting French sensitivities about what kinds of visual cues were being offered about Africans to non-African viewers. French colonial officials expressed growing alarm at the "negative" perceptions of Africans generated by certain movies popular in the West. Their concern was not so much that the imagery was morally abhorrent and racist but that the films suggested that Europe's presence in Africa had not brought any appreciable change to the lives of Africans from before colonial rule. French officials were thus anxious that the "progress" the colonizers had brought to benighted Africans be taken into account. At the same time that they worried about the messages conveyed to the extra-African world about conditions in the colonies, administrators in West Africa also sought to constrict the kinds of images shown to African audiences lest they produce undesirable (i.e., destabilizing) results that would call into question the colonial project from an entirely different direction.

The first two chapters serve to frame the remainder of the book. Establishing the film politics and the battle over representation that already existed when the transition to political sovereignty began enables a better appreciation of the context in which West African cultural activists operated. Chapter 3 looks at the emergence of an African anticolonial film politics. This chapter pays special attention to the role played by the journal *Présence africaine* and the critical interventions of Vieyra as he sought to persuade his fellow cultural activists of cinema's important place in the decolonization struggle. That process entailed making claims as to the specificity of the film industry's contribution to Africa's cultural and material liberation, which in turn necessitated a discussion of the unique language of films and its effects on the spectator. In a statement that many early West African filmmakers would second, Metz writes, "The creative filmmaker exerts more influence on the diachronic evolution of cinematographic language than the imaginative writer on the evolution of his idiom, for idiom may exist in the absence of art, whereas the cinema must be an art to become a language with a partial denotative code." He goes on to observe that "the reverse of this coin, however, is that a given narrative receives a very different semiological treatment in the cinema than it would in a novel, in classical ballet, in a cartoon, and so on."[49] Stretching Metz's point a bit, one might say that African cineastes were also literally concerned with the question of language, as the prose writing of the 1950s was entirely in French and therefore did not reach the professed targets of the writers. Film was a medium that could redress that fundamental problem.

Chapter 4 moves to an examination of the products of early Francophone West African filmmaking. In this section I argue that postcolonial West African cinema was strongly influenced by and built on the work of anticolonial documentaries made during the 1950s. The chapter shows the important continuities between films like *Afrique 50* and *Les statues meurent aussi* and Sembène's early work. However, the Senegalese cinematographer did more than simply replicate French anticolonial cinema. He built on those precursors while incorporating elements of the region's motion picture tradition, including the hegemonic and counterhegemonic film politics that framed West Africans' experiences of the cinema industrial complex. Sembène's first movies, in turn, became structuring devices for subsequent cinematic production in the region and throughout sub-Saharan Africa. They were foundational works not only because they established a pattern that could be replicated by those who followed in his footsteps but also because they became markers from which other African cineastes could distinguish their own work. This chapter also isolates key points of representation that sought to articulate a postcolonial African modernity while marking the region's films as specific to the context of the material circumstances of their production.

Chapter 5 turns to the question of the cinema industrial complex in the postcolonial period. Moving from the terrain of representation back to the materialism of the 1960s and early 1970s, this last chapter looks at the emergent structures of independent African cinematic production. It approaches the founding of the

African film festival system as well as the organization of African filmmakers as signs of an emergent autonomous African cinema industry. The narrative brings to light the difficult battle over production and distribution that posed the greatest threat to the possibilities for developing a truly independent filmmaking tradition in Africa. The analysis includes a discussion of the efforts by national governments to break the distribution monopolies that persisted in West Africa from the colonial period as well as of the controversial issue of French government funding for African moviemaking. Specifically, it examines the role played by France's Ministère des affaires culturelles and its Ministère de la coopération, especially the latter's Bureau de cinéma, as part of the materialist context within which African filmmakers had to function in order to practice their craft. The establishment of the Francophonie (in the form of the ACCT) in 1970 offered yet other challenges and opportunities for the emergence of African cinema. Finally, the founding and growth of FEPACI as well as its important links with Latin American Third Cinema reveals the growing prospects for the realization of Vieyra's idea of a cinema in the service of the people that would drive Africa's postcolonial economic and cultural regeneration.

In conclusion, this book assesses the successes and limitations of the early Francophone West African cineastes. Like the twenty-first-century architecture of downtown Dakar, the record of the pioneer generation of African directors is a mixture of heroic struggle and deep frustration. Sembène, Cissé, Hondo, and others managed to significantly impact the terrain of representation with regard to the images of Africa projected to the outside world. It is less clear how successful they have been in altering the images Africans see of themselves. Moreover, in the materialist realm the victories are harder to locate, although they are there as well. After all, as Cham reminds us, "One is . . . talking here about a very young, if not the youngest, creative practice in Africa," and cinema as a global industrial complex and an art form had a more than sixty-year head start by the time Francophone West Africans grabbed the camera and framed their first celluloid images for projection on the screen.[50] When assessing the role and impact of cineastes in Francophone West Africa during the early postcolonial period, it is worth recalling that independent Africa was a very young place that had to overcome the legacies of five centuries of the slave trade and colonialism that had simultaneously scarred and fortified the continent and its peoples. The material conditions in which the filmmakers labored and the representational material from which they worked were forged in those circumstances. Their successes, then, mark the steady, but sometimes painfully slow, progress of humanity toward liberation from those oppressive structures and into a better world. Like Dakar's architecture, construction is a continual process of renewal in shifting environments. It is that story of hope, frustration, and perseverance to which the narrative now turns.

1 The Cinema Industrial Complex in French West Africa to the 1950s

In 1949, André Lemaire submitted a report to Commission du cinéma d'outre-mer, a division of the Ministère de la France d'outre-mer (formerly the Ministère des colonies) that addressed matters pertaining to cinema in the French colonies, that signaled the emergence of a new dimension to the cultural politics of empire in French-ruled West Africa. In this report, Lemaire discussed the problem of "raising the level of the Africans," which he argued had been solved for the elite but not the masses. To further France's objectives, Lemaire said officials should recognize that "in most cases" they were operating in social contexts in which societies "are organized on traditional bases of oral culture and [are] more open to the concrete thing than the abstract thing." Consequently, he continued, "it seems that the image is particularly designed to resolve in part the problem here posed." Lemaire then came to the point of his recommendations. He argued that "in effect, there is by now no doubt that the procedures of visual education, and in particular the cinema, are extremely powerful means of expression and susceptible of rapidly diffusing among the nonevolved population the most diverse [forms of] knowledge. The subtlety of that means of expression enables addressing practically all the problems in adapting the level of the exposé to that of the spectator." Lemaire concluded that "the use of audiovisual procedures" to generate "reciprocal information" and "to culturally orient the populations in all areas, technical, economic, and social, is liable to ameliorate the human climate and favor a harmonious entente" between Africans and Europeans. He urged the French administrators to study how the Belgians, English, and Americans used film to advance their interests.[1]

Lemaire's notes addressed a growing interest among colonial officials and French politicians in the efficacy of cinema as a tool of empire, especially as an integral part of French cultural politics projected in its overseas territories and more broadly around the world. As Sue Harris and Elizabeth Ezra note, "The French recognized earlier than most the importance of cultivating a national image," as well as "the central role of cinema in constructing and disseminating this image." The importance of filmmaking in France confirms, they conclude, "cinema's role as possibly the single most important medium for the transmission of French cultural values and identity in the twentieth and twenty-first centuries."[2] While officials tacitly recognized to an extent the power of film in the colonies as early as the 1930s, it was not until the post–World War II era that the cinema industrial complex took a more concrete form in Africa. With it came an expanding concern over the impact moving pictures might be having in France's empire. There followed a series of regulations concerning what constituted acceptable films for African audiences, quotas to promote the French film industry as part of postwar economic and cultural recovery, and questions as to how to integrate Africans into the cinema industrial complex without handing control over the making of films to Africans. However, by the mid-1950s, cultural activists from French West Africa had also begun to appropriate film as part of their arsenal in the struggle to resist imperialism and assert their independence. Cinema, then, was becoming one of the terrains on which the fight for control over representation and for the minds of Africans was engaged while political authority in the colonies slipped from France's hands into those of the Westernized elite.[3] In addition, the struggle over moving pictures played out directly on the materialist terrain, as colonial officials explicitly connected the fundamental question of economic development in France and West Africa to making motion pictures. This chapter examines the articulation of a colonial film politics in the federation from the 1930s to the 1950s, focusing on the structural aspects of the cinema industrial complex as it took shape in the late imperial era.

In the particular case of French colonialism in West Africa, cinema has recently attracted scholars' attention. The result has been the development of two distinct lines of analysis. One approach, evident in the work of Kenneth Cameron, Rachel Moore, David Henry Slavin, and Dina Sherzer, has focused on an examination of the ways in which, through film, empire has served as a constitutive element in metropolitan identities and imaginings of places such as Africa.[4] Chapter 2 deals more extensively with the issues raised by researchers drawn to that dimension of film and empire. The other, represented by Frank Ukadike, Imruh Bakari and Mbye Cham, June Givanni, Manthia Diawara, Joseph Gugler, and Femi Shaka, has centered around a reconstruction of narratives on the origins of African cinema and the uses of film in the postcolonial African context and is the focus of this chapter.[5] Neither approach to the treatment of cinema in the colonial context provides an analysis of how the French imperial government set out to purposely articulate a film politics as an essential pillar of colonial rule, and neither examines the processes whereby that project was made integral to French postwar reconstruction.

Diawara poses the basic question that frames the current discussion, namely determining " the role played by the French government and individuals in furthering film production in their former colonies in a manner that has not interested other ex-colonial powers such as England and Belgium." I extend that query backward to the last decades of imperial rule as well, since what came after decolonization was presaged in the colonial era. Diawara takes the position that "the French had no policy of producing films that were especially intended for their subjects in Africa" and concludes with the sweeping claim that "the French colonial system ... had no economic, political, or cultural policy encompassing the majority of its subjects."[6] However, while it is true that France did not create anything approximating the British anthropological film programs of the Bantu Educational Kinema Experiment or the Colonial Film Unit that attempted to incorporate Africans into the making of educational documentaries aimed at their colonial subjects, the French imperial nation-state did concern itself with "film politics" as it related to all of their colonial subjects in West Africa and helped to produce docu-fiction films aimed at autochthonous audiences.[7] Officials at every level of the imperial administration stretching back to the corridors of power in Paris filed reports, issued circulars, promulgated decrees, and solicited regular surveys on the subject of the place and impact of film in West Africa. Moreover, the absence of a formal and fully functioning government institution solely directed to produce films for an African audience should not be taken to indicate a willful indifference to the kinds of images African moviegoers consumed or a lack of engagement in manufacturing those representations. The litany of regulations and careful parsing of film treatments and movies to vet their appropriateness for West Africans suggests the depth of French interest in cinema aimed at the African colonial subject.

In a similar vein, Murphy and Williams categorically state that France's policy with respect to cinema in West Africa "was simply to show French films to Africans." In contradistinction to other colonizing powers, they argue that "the French approach at least allowed Africans to be considered as a proper audience for proper films." Like Diawara, Murphy and Williams cite the 1934 Laval decree as "a rare example of government intervention" in the realm of cinema, and on top of that, they suggest it was "rarely invoked." This approach leads them to conclude that "unlike a range of other cultural forms—poetry, song, music, stories—film had, for very obvious reasons, almost no part to play in the anticolonial process."[8] It is true that Francophone West African cinema is "a child of African political independence," as Cham notes, but that does not mean the cinema industrial complex wasn't a crucial site of the decolonization struggle.[9] The objective material conditions in West Africa may have precluded the actual making of films by Africans in Africa (I discuss the special place of Vieyra's Groupe africain du cinéma and its 1955 production *Afrique-sur-Seine* in chapter 3 of this study), but cultural activists did discuss the important role film had to play in (re)constructing a truly independent Africa in both representational and materialist terms. Moreover, the French colonial state was very cognizant of the power of movies and the connection between what Africans saw on the screen and France's capacity to maintain power in the region. This is attested to by the *frequent* invocation of the Laval decree (especially after 1945) and its further systematic elaboration during the 1950s.

For his part, Ukadike describes French colonial film policy as merely seeking to maintain the monopolies of the distribution cartels Compagnie africaine cinématographique industrielle et commercial (COMACICO) and Société d'éxploitation cinématographique africaine (SECMA) in the region. Ukadike reduces film politics, such as it existed, to the collusion between capitalist enterprises and the state. Their interests were confined to preventing the conditions for the emergence of an "African cinema [that] would bring competition and a change in audience taste that might challenge their exclusive hold on the African market."[10] However, although Ukadike makes this gesture toward a consideration of the materialist dimension of film politics in late colonial Francophone West Africa, in his analysis of the economics of filmmaking he does not venture beyond the calculations of market share. Subsequently, he traces the aesthetic aspects of the emergence of West African cinema, making occasional mention of the problems confronted by directors in terms of financing and distribution. While the French imperial nation-state certainly did not take any active role in undermining the dominance of the two distribution monopolies, it did express an interest in developing an African cinema under *its* direction that would sustain France's influence, if not political power, in the region. As part of the expanding legislation through which officials formulated a "film politics" in the postwar years, the government in Paris envisaged the formation of a full cinema industry in West Africa, replete with all its attendant technologies and processes, under French management, of course. Moreover, France's economic concerns as they related to film redounded on metropolitan economic reconstruction, a point entirely missed in Ukadike's discussion.[11] For the French government, the market dimensions of cinema in West Africa were not limited to simply assuring a profit for COMACICO and SECMA. In fact, the distributors often clashed with colonial officials because of Paris's insistence that they show French films in sufficient quantities or face stiff fines and potentially the loss of their license to screen movies. Consequently, the relationship between the distribution monopolies and the imperial nation-state was not as cozy as it would appear at first blush.

My aim in this chapter is to explore France's conscious articulation of a "film politics" for West Africa as challenges mounted to its political mastery in the region. Cinema was an important field within which colonial officials and anticolonial cultural producers worked out the process of decolonization. In the formulation of this late colonial film politics, the salient features that structured the emergence of Francophone West African cinema in the 1960s became evident. Some of the issues that constituted the nexus around which West African cineastes had to work to develop their art are strikingly apparent in the debates over France's film politics in the 1950s. In this regard, representation and materialism were overriding concepts that informed the discourse of imperial officials and metropolitan governments alike as they wrestled with defining (and controlling) the place of moving pictures in West Africa. How they framed the field, then, determined the access points available to the postcolonial filmmakers who came in their wake.

France and Cinema in Colonial West Africa before 1945

The notes submitted by Lemaire to the Ministère de la France d'outre-mer in 1949 were part of an effort among French imperial officials after 1945 to create a coherent film policy in the colonies. Just two months later, the Academie des sciences d'outre-mer forwarded its own notes to the Ministère de la France d'outre-mer in which it stated that "cinema constitutes, with radio, one of the most powerful weapons of which a nation could make use, in the present period, for its propaganda." "Documentary film, in particular," the academy continued, "possesses, from this point of view, a capacity and an action infinitely more expansive and more effective than the book or the newspaper, which touches a much more limited public." The documentary film "does not present any point [of reference] except for the image," and owing to "its magic" that is "even at times [constitutive of] its undeniable reality," documentary film "presents an undeniable value."[12] I examine the theoretical debates over the particular efficacy of documentary filmmaking in chapter 4. But at this point it is interesting to note, as discussed in the introduction, that the radical cineastes of the Third Cinema movement in Latin America also embraced documentary filmmaking as the most appropriate cinematic form for galvanizing the masses to revolutionary action. The current focus, though, is on the broader articulation of a film politics within the context of the French imperial nation-state.

The desire among colonial officials for a clear and consistent "politics of film" was not new in the post-1945 period. In fact, it dated to the early 1930s. However, the arguments for such a policy were expressed in more urgent terms following the war as a result of the explosive growth of the film industry, reflected in the rapidly increasing number of movie houses in French West Africa and the vastly expanded demand among African audiences for film.[13] First, though, it is important to sketch the early presence of moving pictures in West Africa and the colonial state's approach to the cinema. As Ukadike observes, "Cinema came to Africa as a potent organ of colonialism." In addition to the Christian missionaries who came armed with "film and slide projectors," there were European filmmakers and fledgling distributors who began to set up "mobile cinemas" by at least 1905 in Dakar, Senegal.[14] However, motion pictures in the region at this time were not integrated into a coherent strategy of imperial rule. Private filmmakers and distributors made and showed movies in Africa to largely European expatriate communities, while missionaries operated mostly independently of (and sometimes in conflict with) the colonial state.[15] The infrastructure for the cinema industrial complex was nowhere evident in French West Africa until the 1920s. Moreover, those who made films about Africa and Africans did so within a conceptual universe that already carried centuries-old tropes of the "primitive native." The images of Africans produced by non-African filmmakers and projected almost entirely to audiences outside the continent participated in an extant hegemonic representational environment in which they added their own inflections but did not offer any ruptures with the past.

Like governments in Europe and North America, the colonial state did not at first recognize how important film could be as an integral part of colonial rule. It was part of an imperialist process, an organ, but not yet a tool. Moreover, for Africans the period before the 1920s was one of very selective encounters with moving pictures. Those conscripted to serve in the slaughterhouse of the western front during the First World War probably had more sustained contact with the cinema than any other community from the colonies.[16] But even then, their exposure would have been in Europe, not in their own land; this was an entirely different contextual space within which the conscripts became "spectators" in the sense that Nick Browne discusses it in his analysis of *Stagecoach*.[17] At some level, where the viewer is physically seated shapes the reading of the filmic text.

Little information is available about the early presence of cinema in French West Africa. However, scholars have arrived at a consensus that the first permanent movie theaters were established by the 1920s in the federation. Not surprisingly, those spaces existed only in a select few major cities; Dakar, as the capital of French West Africa, was the epicenter. Many of those first theaters appear to have been owned by Lebanese migrants, France having acquired Lebanon as a League of Nations mandate from the Ottoman Empire following the First World War. Thus, as happened in other imperial contexts (the Indian diaspora throughout the British Empire is another example) intracolonial migratory patterns emerged that reflected the reach of a particular metropole's territorial power. In the case of the Lebanese in West Africa, though, there was a longer history that predated French rule in the region. A Lebanese commercial diaspora had spread to West Africa at least as early as the period of the Mali Empire (thirteenth to fifteenth centuries), although many of the later arrivals were Christian Lebanese rather than Muslim Lebanese, as were the members of the first commercial networks.[18] These film theater owners, then, came from a marginal outside community that stood between the French colonial rulers and the subjugated African population. They were not only foreign in terms of ethnicity but religion as well. Moreover, while the Lebanese did not have citizenship rights like the French, they nonetheless were not reduced to the abject position of colonial subject, at least in West Africa.

The early cinematic venues catered to resident French citizens and not to the Africans, very few of whom would have had the income, leisure time, or freedom of movement that would have permitted access to the cinema. The films they screened came almost entirely from France and the United States and generally were consistent with those that the audience would have had access to had they been in Europe instead of West Africa. This was a purely "entertainment cinema" meant to provide diversion to those serving the colonial state. Significantly, though, the very act of viewing a movie in West Africa at this time was a mark of distinction that further delineated the boundaries between colonizers and colonized.[19] This made access to the world of film viewing an object of desire on the part of those seeking to break down the barriers of colonial society.[20] Cinema, even if prohibited to African audiences through the material realities of colonial rule, was already becoming a contested field in West Africa.

In fact, Africans soon found ways around the restrictions on their ability to become an audience for "entertainment" films. Not only that, but some were also exploring how to break the Lebanese monopoly on showing movies. By the 1930s colonial officials were complaining that since the movie houses catered mostly to the French expatriate community, enterprising Africans were purchasing films and showing them in their own homes to meet the emergent demand among the subject population for cinema.[21] Robert de Guise, commissioner of French Togoland, a League of Nations mandate territory often governed as part of French West Africa, was practically beside himself with concern about Africans showing films privately to African audiences. In several letters to the governor general of the federation as well as to the minister of colonies in France in 1932 he complained that since the 1920s Africans had purchased films and were turning their homes and businesses into illicit cinemas. He used the example of Albert John Mensah of Lomé, who had regularly turned his café, Tonyeviadji, into a theater for up to thirty people since at least 1929.[22] This was problematic for administrators, as a legal framework for cinematic practices did not yet exist in the colonies. Even the home government had not grasped film's potential in the colonies both as a support for the imperial project and a potential site for the subversion of French rule.

Nothing in the hated *indigénat*, the native law code under which most West Africans suffered, proscribed the indigenous population from viewing films, even if they contained content that could be construed as undermining official notions of the French colonial mission. While the *indigénat* prohibited certain forms of speech, did not permit colonial subjects to wear the insignia of the colonial military without justification, and even required that they show deference to imperial officials, it did not specifically ban viewing images that could carry out the work of defaming French civilization or destabilizing the framework of white privilege that undergirded the imperial system. There also was nothing in the existing legal framework that said Africans could not own movies or show them as entrepreneurs. Finally, while this was not specifically at issue in the 1920s and 1930s, nothing prevented an African from actually making a movie, if he or she could ever get access to the requisite technology. In a word, France did not have a film politics in the early 1930s and only began to develop one in response to the interventions of colonized African subjects into the cinematic field.

As more theaters were built in the 1930s and increasing numbers of Africans turned out to view the latest releases from France and Hollywood, even becoming the distributors themselves, the imperial apparatus made its first halting intervention into the politics of film in the colonies with the issuance of the Laval decree of 1934. That act set a pattern of "film politics" that carried over into the post–World War II period. Named after Pierre Laval, the minister of colonies at the time and a future Nazi collaborator, the decree was fundamentally reactionary in nature, seeking through censorship to control the distribution, content, and audiences of films. Consistent with a paradigmatic shift in the nature of France's civilizing mission that occurred following the First World War, the objective of this regulation was "the conservation of local and national mores and traditions."[23] The decree provided for the establishment in each colony of a commission "to examine the treatments and scenarios, the advertisements, programs, and, if there are any, the films themselves with a view to accord or refuse the control visa" licensing the showing of the film in that territory.[24] The Laval decree engaged in the cinematic field from at least three reactionary directions encompassing dimensions of both representation and materialism. First, the new act sought to constrict the images available to African audiences, implicitly acknowledging, as Murphy and Williams observe, that Africans could be a legitimate audience for films.[25] Thus, ironically, the Laval decree can be read as granting "permission" for the colonized to enter the cinema field, but on France's terms. Second, the guidelines mapped out the parameters for the kinds of pictures the imperial nation-state wanted to be projected about Africa to extra-African audiences.[26] To that end, France was already thinking in terms of countering tropes of African primitivism in the hope that the "positive" work of French colonialism could be shown to Western audiences. Even though the British at that time were constructing a documentary filmmaking program aimed at African audiences, hoping to convince their own colonial subjects of the beneficence of British rule, the French did not take that extra step, perhaps out of a supreme imperial arrogance that such accomplishments should be self-evident to those living under France's control. Third, the Laval decree established a system of licensing for showing films in West Africa.[27] This brought the French colonial state directly into the purview of distribution and marketing.

The Laval decree was the culmination of several years of debate within the colonial government. Once Africans intervened in the cinematic field, colonial officials on site took notice and sought to regulate their entry into that area of engagement. De Guise's complaints to the Ministère des colonies in 1932 highlighted the problem. As he put it, "There does not exist in Togo any act regulating the presentation and the control of films. The operators of cinematographic enterprises are not under any regulations."[28] That spring Louis de Chappedelaine, minister of colonies, launched a full discussion within the imperial hierarchy with the aim of formulating a universal "politics of film." In a general directive sent to all governors general, governors, and commissioners of mandated territories, Chappedelaine assessed the situation with regard to cinema in the colonies and offered guidance on the parameters that would define the place of moving pictures within the imperial project. He wrote, "Over the course of the last few years, cinematographic production, because of increased technical perfection and following the invention of talkies, has reached everywhere a [level of] development that merits holding our attention. A source of recreation, [as well as] artistic and documentary information, the cinematograph has, apart from that, become increasingly an instrument of propaganda." Chappedelaine added that the camera " can reveal itself to be useful or harmful, according to the objectives pursued by the film's editor; the impression produced varies, on the other hand, with the degree of receptivity of the public. In this regard, the dispositions of the spirit are, among the spectators, different according to their personal convictions, their intellectual development, the concepts appropriate to their race, [and] the ideas received in the social group to which they belong." Finally, he acknowledged that cinema was becoming an important element in the psychological development of the colonial subjects and concluded that "it is indispensible, in the end, to understand the genres of the spectacles that *garner* the favor of the public, the subjects that are likely to respond to their preferences. . . . My department will be able to determine the principles to put in place as the foundation of this 'politics of film.'"[29]

Chappedelaine's directive set in motion the articulation of France's colonial film politics and was crucial in the elaboration of the cinematic field of engagement in the empire. While not explicitly putting it in these terms, his letter to the colonial officials marked an important intervention in film theory by positing that the filmic text was constituted by both the intentions of the filmmaker, starting from his or her goals or vision, and the mentality or position of the spectator. Thus, the final product was the result of the interaction of cineaste and audience, the film itself serving as a mediating device. The job of the colonial state, as articulated by Chappedelaine, was to control that in-between space in order to manage the relationship constituted by filmmaker and spectator in the cinematic field in a way that redounded to the advantage of the colonial mission.

Nick Browne's insights on "the specular text" are useful in this context. In his study of *Stagecoach* he discusses how both the narrator (the filmmaker) and the spectator are constitutive of the film's discourse. The cineaste constructs a narrative seeking to lead the spectator to a common goal, but the viewer brings his or her own perspectives that shape the outcome. In addition, Browne argues, "the filmic spectator is a plural subject: in his reading he is and is not himself."[30] Browne's view of the movie-watching process is remarkably close to Chappedelaine's understanding of the film viewer. Both see the plurality of the audience and the important role that plays in determining how the narrator constructs the film. In short, the filmmaker has to know his or her audience in order to make a product that has meaning. The product is also meant to shape the context in which it is viewed. Thus, cinema is a dynamic element in the cultural field, as it is formed from multiple interventions. The task of the colonial government was to figure out the most effective means for controlling that process and for harnessing film to the imperial project.

Over the next two years the process Chappedelaine inaugurated generated a lively discussion among government officials; letters, reports, and intergovernmental meetings produced a wealth of new information about the place of cinema in the colonies, West Africa being a particularly rich site of activity. Government officials discovered that a network of film clubs already existed in their territories and that there was a growing interest among filmmakers in generating documentary, educational, and scientific films that could aid in France's colonial mission. As one production company, Les films mercure, put it in a request to the general government of French West Africa in 1929, "Our project consists of furnishing you 1,000 to 1,200 meters of film illustrating the benefits of French domination from the point of view of agriculture, forest exploitation, sanitation, etc."[31] The government also received reports from schools inspectors urging the incorporation of film into the colonial education curriculum. They went so far as to discuss the composition of the performers on the screen, with one official noting that the success of using film to reach the indigenous masses depended on putting "a certain number of actors of color" in the films.[32] However, by 1938 the idea had been effectively tabled as a result of several structural obstacles. Among them were that the format of 35 mm was incompatible with the 16 mm equipment available in the colonies, that the film stock was flammable, that the overall cost of integrating film into the colonial education infrastructure was high, and, perhaps most importantly, that the colonies lacked equipment necessary to sustain such a program.[33]

Although film did not end up being used systematically in the colonial classroom, the cinema continued to expand in West Africa. By 1930 government officials noted that there existed in the federation a Société des films exotiques et coloniaux. A 1935 report mentions the Société d'études pour la propagande colonial par la film. And the Haute comité Méditerranéan artinisat-cinéma was well established in West Africa by 1938. Through it all, the colonial government wrestled with how to manage the powerful attraction of film among audiences in the region. One report claimed that "the projection of theatrical films does not touch the indigenous soul," but police shoot-up films and others that "wound their beliefs or their traditions" were to be avoided at all costs.[34] Consequently, at the very least the colonial state had to regulate the "theatrical cinema" that was growing up in West Africa during the 1930s. The Laval decree, then, was not a marginal intervention in the cinematic field or an isolated act in an area the colonial state was otherwise indifferent toward. It was part of a comprehensive examination of the means by which film might be integrated into the overall colonial project. The fact that the colonial government lacked the means to fully take advantage of film in the 1930s was not the result of disinterest. The Laval decree set the baseline for what colonial officials expected would be a further elaborated film politics in the coming years. It signaled the beginning of a process, not its culmination.

By the time France promulgated the Laval decree, the two film distribution companies that eventually came to monopolize West Africa's theater system had already been established in the region. By 1926 the corporation that would be known by the acronym COMACICO had branched out from other colonies, notably Morocco, adopting its specific West African form. It took its final name, Compagnie africaine cinématographique industrielle et commerciale in 1959. By 1934 SECMA had also developed a presence in West Africa. It took the definitive appellation of the Société d'éxploitation cinématographique africaine in 1948. Together these two conglomerates over time managed to muscle the competition out of the business of showing movies in West Africa, effectively removing the Lebanese from the equation. Already by 1948 COMACICO owned ten of the seventeen movie theaters in Dakar, the center of film viewing in the federation, and SECMA owned another four. The independent Lebanese operator Abdou Karim Bourgi possessed the remaining three.[35] The most popular place to watch films was the Vox Theater, established at least by the early 1930s, and it would remain the most important movie house well into the postcolonial era.[36] When the eight territories of the West African federation achieved independence by 1960 the two conglomerates owned upward of 80 percent of all movie theaters in the region. Beyond the actual ownership of venues, their sheer dominance was enough to effectively control what was available for viewing at the independent theaters. In addition, COMACICO and SECMA both had subsidiary importing wings that served as agents through which almost every film screened in West Africa was purchased by the 1960s.[37] I return to the specific roles played by these conglomerates in shaping the emergence of Francophone West African cinema in chapter 5.

Despite those fleeting efforts to control the cinema in West Africa, locals continued to find ways of getting around the law, and complaints mounted against filmmakers, movie house owners, and residents of the colonies who violated the decree. As a youth, even the legendary Senegalese filmmaker Ousmane Sembène participated in subversion of the Laval decree. He and his friends routinely caused disturbances at the entrances to cinemas in the late 1930s so that others could sneak in without paying or being stopped by security enforcing restrictions on the films that Africans could see and the cinemas that they could attend.[38] Commenting on incidents in Madagascar, Eric Jennings writes that during the Second World War movie theaters became surprising locales for "outbursts of Free French and anti-Vichy sentiments," since their "dark confines facilitated precisely such anonymous political expression" and their "very socialness transformed them into popular political tribunes."[39] For those youths in urban colonial contexts, film was rapidly becoming a site for engaging in fantasy, confronting the colonial state, and forging a sense of community. The physical site of the movie theater was where young people could gather, plot, and share experiences. The images to which they surreptitiously gained access became references in the construction of their representational universe. The cinema industrial complex as well as the cinematic field of engagement was coming into its own. What remained was for the colonial state to catch up to these developments through a further elaboration of its colonial film politics.

Film Politics à l'urgence after 1945

The intervention of the Second World War and its attendant disruptions precluded the colonial state from paying much closer attention to film at the time. In the case of West Africa most of the activity on the film front centered on efforts by COMACICO to expand its market share. From 1939 to 1942 the company sought to open several new theaters in the federation in an effort to undermine its major competitors. Despite its pleas that more screens "would permit a greater and more effective diffusion of propaganda and news films," some of their requests were denied on the grounds that the new theaters would be "too close" to existing ones. For example, in 1941, the Commission des théâtres et spectacles refused to grant a permit for a new movie house in Dakar, explaining that "in the general interest and for [the sake of] public tranquility, it is important not to add a new source of troubles to that which already exists due to the presence of the 'Palace' cinema." The commission added that "public hygiene requires that [we] not multiply the [number of] movie theaters in the same quarter.... In Dakar there exists a deplorable practice of public urination along the walls, despite the presence of sanitary installations in the interior of the establishments."[40] Interestingly, despite the lack of development in film politics during the war, the drive by COMACICO to rapidly expand the number of theaters in the federation speaks to the growing audience for films in the colonies.

Nevertheless, as Jennings argues, "the Vichy regime quite unwittingly set in motion several forms of opposition in its 'loyal colonies.' It did so on two levels; first by hardening an already ruthless colonialism; second, and more ironically, by introducing to the empire Pétain's cherished themes of authenticity, tradition, and folklore."[41] The liberation of France, then, brought with it the urgent task of reconstructing French imperial power overseas in the context of heightened anticolonial mobilization and nationalist consciousness. As part of that project, after 1945 the Ministère des colonies embarked on a thorough rethinking of its "film politics" that included both the introduction of further reactionary policies in the tradition of the 1934 Laval decree and a new proactive dimension designed to use the power of film to promote certain outcomes in the colonies that would benefit the interests of French power in the world, France's influence in Africa, and the French film industry, struggling (as was the entire metropolitan economy) to recover from the ravages of the recently concluded war. In part, the result was a string of new regulations building on the 1934 decree that culminated in the 1954 issuance of an order establishing strict guidelines for the entire range of activities connected with the cinema industrial complex in the colonies, including the screening of French films in West Africa.[42] However, that rethinking went beyond legislation to a deeper conceptualization of the nature of film as a medium of communication and of the ways in which cultures constructed their universes of meaning.

While not explicitly framing their project in the terminology of film theorists, French administrators had begun to grasp the links between narrator and spectator in the cinema and they were determined to control that relationship. As Browne describes it, "If a discourse carries a certain impression of reality, it is an effect not exactly of the image but of the way the image is placed by the narrative or argument. . . . As a production of the spectator's reading, the sense of reality that the film enacts, the 'impression of the real,' protects the account the text seems to give of the absent narrator." This, he concludes, is "an illustration of the process of constructing a spectator's attitudes in the film as a whole through the control of point of view."[43] By the late 1940s colonial officials had come to appreciate the cinema as a constitutive element of modern culture and a vehicle for the circumscription of the future trajectory of social development. The imperial nation-state sought to position itself as the mediator between narrator and spectator by controlling the construction and dissemination of images to and about Africans. Henceforth, the French colonial state would assume the role of positioning narrator and spectator in relation to each other, bringing them together in a specific way to promote the übernarrative of imperialism. Film was already being thought of as part of the politics of development before such thinking became central to global conversations. Consequently, the cinema would be understood as an industry with economic and technological implications as well as a means for crafting attitudes, behaviors, and social relations within and between societies. It was to be a vehicle through which France could continue to influence its colonies even as they assumed greater political sovereignty.

The creation of the Commission du cinéma d'outre-mer within the Ministère de la France d'outre-mer in 1949 gave institutional expression to the articulation of a film politics for the colonies. The edict that created the commission included an exposition of the motives for its establishment. It was formed, according to the edict, "principally to study the problem of educational cinema. Now, in the course of its work, it became apparent that the overall problem of the development of cinema in Overseas France and that [dealing with] information on the Overseas Territories [conveyed] by cinema in the metropole required, with no less urgency, the attention of the public authorities." It mandated the commission to find the "conditions for the use of cinema as an instrument of information, education and knowledge in the Overseas Territories and as an instrument of information on those Territories in the metropole."[44] Interestingly, the commission's origins lay in the desire to create a filmmaking tradition targeted explicitly at African audiences, and in seeking to realize this goal, it closely followed the path charted by the British prior to the Second World War.[45] The French state was seeking a means to become a player in the cinematic field as an independent agent, a way of filling a gap in the construction of knowledge deemed necessary for the further augmentation of France's colonial mission. That in itself was an admission of the limitations of French "accomplishments" in the colonies fully half a century after the conquest of West Africa.

Once treading down that road, however, the officials charged with exploring the prospects for such an intervention in the field of filmmaking came to the realization that their task had to immediately and massively expand to take into consideration the entirety of the cinema industrial complex. Thus, the final charter for the commission included the added dimensions of promoting the development of cinema *in the colonies* and constructing educational films targeting *metropolitan* audiences. Apparently, French audiences were in dire need of edification on the work of imperialism in the overseas territories, perhaps suggesting that after the horrors of the Second World War, public opinion was less in favor of France's remaining a colonial power.[46] By seeking to create such films for French moviegoers the commission also staked a claim to control the representation of Africans to extra-African audiences. Consistent with the Laval decree that inaugurated France's film politics, cinema was conceived as simultaneously a commodity encompassing both representational and materialist aspects. The commission could not carry out even the work of making educational films for West African audiences without the requisite material infrastructure for producing a sufficient number of products for consumption. This was particularly important if the commission meant to expand its purview to making films for French viewing as well. Kristin Thompson notes that "a film depends on materiality for its existence; out of image and sound it creates its structures, but it can never make all the physical elements of the film part of its set of smooth perceptual cues."[47] The commission recognized that its mission would succeed or fail based on the ability to develop all those "physical elements of the film" on site in the colonies.

In the following months, the Conseil économique de l'Afrique occidentale française, through its publication *Bulletin du Conseil économique,* published a series of resolutions, notes, and articles weighing in on the importance of cinema for France and West Africa and for sustaining French interests in the federation. In full concord with the charge of the Commission du cinéma d'outre-mer, the Conseil économique de l'Afrique occidentale française asserted that cinema should be conceptualized as a total industry designed to convey information to and from West Africa and France. That, of necessity, involved developing physical infrastructure in the region (movie houses, film equipment, and training facilities, etc.) as well as paying specific attention to the content of films shown in West Africa, which were mainly to be understood as "agents of propaganda and for the dissemination of

French ideas" to the region's people.[48] Diawara, then, is mistaken when he asserts that France did not have a "cultural policy encompassing the majority of its subjects."[49] France's film politics went further to include the French themselves, not just the colonial subjects. French officials envisioned a representational/materialist apparatus that was coterminous with the empire and all its residents.

Moreover, in the field of cinema there was a stunning reversal of interwar French colonial policy that explicitly banned industrial development in West Africa, a policy that gained momentum following the defeat of Albert Sarraut's *mise en valeur* scheme in 1923. This went even further than the "development-oriented" programs—Fonds pour l'investissement en développement économique et social (FIDES) and Fonds d'équipement rural et de développement économique et social (FERDES)—that France set up in 1946 and 1949 respectively to upgrade West Africa's economic infrastructure. Those programs were limited, in the first instance, to funding the construction of roads, railroads, port facilities, and communications and, in the second, to promoting further agricultural production through financing irrigation, land clearance, and other locally managed projects.[50] It should be noted, however, that in the absence of a fully functioning film agency for the colonies, funds from FIDES were being tapped to make educational or technical films, the latter of which focused on the subjects of "exploitation of palm oil, the peanut industry, the port of Dakar, and forestry."[51] However, the Commission du cinéma d'outre-mer actually carried a charge to go further and encourage the transfer of technology to the colonies, not just to forge the shell of a developed economy.

Building on the commission's recommendations, the Ministère de la France d'outre-mer produced decrees and guidelines for the regulation of the cinema industrial complex, in the process exposing the deep anxieties of an imperial system that felt itself to be under threat from a variety of external forces. The new strictures sought to circumscribe the range of possible images available to Africans as well as the source of those images while simultaneously promoting the projection of French films as a means to assist France's cinema industry's recovery from the privations of occupation and war. Films from Egypt were banned entirely, regardless of content, because of French trepidations over the influence of Gamal Abdel Nasser's regime among Muslim populations in West Africa as well as the role Egypt's government was playing in support of the Algerian resistance after 1954.[52] In fact, by 1957 colonial officials in West Africa were expressing deep concern about the "attraction" Egyptian films held for the youth in particular. According to a report from August of that year, "One could not find a more striking example of anti-French nor even anti-European propaganda than the [Egyptian films] that are no more than hymns to the glory of Greater Egypt, 'Leader of the Arab World.'"[53] In the wake of Nasser's triumph over France and its allies, the United Kingdom and Israel, in the Suez crisis of 1956 as well as the controversy that erupted among the

French public over its government's brutal tactics during the "battle of Algiers" in 1957, colonial administrators in West Africa were especially sensitive to anything that might generate enthusiasm for Nasser's regime or the anti-imperialist politics he promoted.

Along related lines, films in Arabic were also banned because of the feared cultural influence that promotion of the Arabic language would have in the region as well as the potentially subliminal subversive messages that might be lodged in the recesses of meaning within Arabic words and phrases. Even subtitling Arab language films in French was insufficient protection against the damage that such products could potentially cause. As an official put it in the late 1940s, "The commentaries in the Arab language often go beyond the inscribed texts and contain allusions [that are] hostile or otherwise unfavorable to the cause of a country, such as France, which administers Arab populations." The letter's author also cited the link between Arabic and "Egyptian nationalism" in a marginal comment.[54] French officials explicitly addressed the role Arabic could have in the promotion of Islamic solidarity and exciting religious passions against the colonial overlords.[55] In fact, as the hour of political independence neared for West Africa, concerns escalated about the potential unforeseen links between Egyptian films and Islamic religious revivalism. In its explanation for banning *Aube de l'Islam,* a film that had been approved for viewing as recently as 1953, the censorship commission in 1959 remarked, "With the unfolding of the action [in the film], essentially religious [in nature], one can see within a glorification of holy war."[56] It is not clear what prompted official concern about the appeal of jihad to West African audiences, since Islamic movements as such were marginal to the general decolonization process in the region, and the aspirations of those more likely to be in the audience viewing films tended toward the modern and secular.[57]

Films from the United States were also tightly regulated in terms of quantity, running time, and content. Colonial officials expressed alarm at the "pro–U.S. propaganda" carried by Hollywood productions and urged the censorship and outright prohibition of some films that "presented [the United States] in a magnificent light," since this could set "a harmful example for the autochthonous population."[58] Additionally, the French government was deeply troubled by the westerns and gangster films emanating from Hollywood because they showed violence, which might upset the morals of the viewing public as well as give viewers dangerous ideas about the effectiveness of guns against white people.[59] Bernard Cornut-Gentille, high commissioner for French West Africa from 1951 to 1956, noted in a 1955 letter to M. Josse, senator from Côte d'Ivoire, that "a great number of foreign (i.e., American) productions were comprised of Westerns" and that "their influence on the development of criminality among the African youth" had been the object of a recent debate within the Conseil de la République.[60] In fact, the discussions among colonial officials about the nefarious influence of western and gangster films on

West African youth is reminiscent of the contemporary debates about the behavioral impact of video games on young people in the United States. According to memoranda detailing debates in the Assembly of the French Union, the territorial assemblies in West Africa, and other deliberative bodies of the empire, American western and gangster films exercised an "undo" influence on African youth, causing them to develop antisocial mannerisms that threatened public order. Therefore, the colonial state had to take a more proactive role in restricting the African population's access to such films.[61]

Pornography from the United States was also singled out as disturbing to African audiences and was to be banned entirely. The grounds for prohibiting Africans (as opposed to Europeans) from viewing pornographic films were twofold. On the one hand, sexually explicit movies were said to exert a "subversive influence" on African youth, destroying their morality and opening them up to other negative behaviors, including alcoholism. Throughout the 1950s government officials in West Africa sounded the alarm over the growth of alcoholism, crime in general, and declining morals among young West Africans. For many administrators, film was the obvious source of such antisocial behaviors, since what was portrayed on the screen ran contrary to "all local customs." Once again, the colonial state arrived at the conclusion that it had to act as the guardian of African traditions that were deemed to be under threat from deleterious foreign influences. On the other hand, French officials expressed concern about the "debasement of the white women" portrayed in such films. This had the effect, much like gangster movies or westerns, of undermining the image of European civilization carefully crafted to sustain the "moral imperative" of colonialism and the legitimacy of France's civilizing mission.[62] Concern over the potential damage that could be done to France's position in the colonies by way of a questioning of the virtues of its women was not new to the 1950s nor was it confined to concerns about film. Such issues were commonly debated during the First World War, when some African conscripts struck up relations with French women while serving on the western front as well as with German women during the occupation of the Rhineland that followed the conflict.[63]

A final category of films that were categorically prohibited were those from the USSR. Colonial officials were acutely aware of the potential impact that Soviet "propaganda" might have on impressionable and otherwise naïve African minds. For example, the governor of the territory of Niger fired off a strong appeal in late 1949 to ban all Soviet films after a showing of *Tête brûlée* spawned raucous political celebrations. The colonial official noted with approbation that the Rassemblement démocratique africaine (RDA) applauded the film because it "pronounced the USSR and its army [to be] invincible." In response to this appeal, and in light of escalating Cold War tensions, all films that "glorified the USSR, its army, and the regime" were banned in West Africa.[64] The following year *Les partisans,* another film from the USSR, was banned and classified as "a dangerous film" for its portrayal of the heroic resistance of the Soviet Red partisans behind German lines in the occupied parts of the USSR during the Second World War.⁶⁵

Unlike the regressive Laval decree, though, France's postwar film politics presented a more comprehensive approach to the cinema that recognized its usefulness as a tool of empire and the potential benefits that would redound to the metropolitan economy. In addition to the censorship provisions, another level of regulations promoted the showing of French films as a means to assist an industry hard hit by the experiences of war and occupation. In late 1954 the colonial government had established a quota system whereby movie houses in the federation were required to screen thirty-five French films each trimester. Furthermore, the new rules specified that the total length of each film screened must be thirteen hundred meters, which in the standard 16 mm format preferred by the colonial government at the time meant about two hours. To guarantee that they were compliant with the mandate, each theater had to file a report at the end of the trimester that detailed the films shown, their nationality (presumably of the film's origin), the length of the movie, and the number of days it was shown.⁶⁶ A typical report from March 1957 submitted by a SECMA-owned movie house in Dakar indicated that it screened movies every three or four days and usually had two shows a day, which during this period included *East of Eden, The Sons of Sinbad,* and *The Phantom of the Rue Morgue.* A COMACICO-run theater in Dakar listed *Ecrit sur du Vent, Le dos au Mur,* and *Le bandit* among its offerings in November 1958 and has a similar schedule to the SECMA-owned theater, screening films every three to four days.⁶⁷ Interestingly, SECMA included a note that it had produced and showed a film titled *Pelerinage Touba* (1958), a documentary on the annual Mouride pilgrimage to Touba in Senegal, perhaps as a means to curry favor with the colonial administration.⁶⁸ The new government strictures that all movie theaters file such reports certainly promised to generate a significant amount of detailed information on the cinematic experience in West Africa. But it also represented a massive and systematic intervention in the field of film. In practical terms, the major distribution firms were being drawn into the process of French economic reconstruction as well as being made participants in circumscribing the range of representations available to African audiences. One government report hinted at some of the pitfalls inherent in the structures of the new regulations when it noted that French studios averaged producing one film every five weeks, an insufficient quantity to meet the guidelines specified in the original *arrêté*.⁶⁹

In the very first year of the quota system's implementation (1954–55), a survey found that the major movie house chains (COMACICO and SECMA) were far from reaching their goals and routinely were being fined. According to the high commissioner's office, in the first six months of the new guidelines, 178 foreign and 64 French films had been screened in the federation (9 October 1954 to 13 April 1955), well short of the 105 French films required annually when one considers that many of the 64 French movies did not meet the thirteen-hundred-meter length requirements to qualify.[70] Despite frequent protests from COMACICO and SECMA that the French studios simply did not churn out enough product to meet the quotas, the general government of French West Africa regularly doled out fines to force compliance. In turn, the distribution companies fired off angry protests to the high commissioner saying that the fines and the new regulations were undermining their businesses.[71] The colonial administration did respond by setting up an inquiry commission to look into revising this aspect of the decree. However, nothing came of it, and the original guidelines remained in force until the end of colonial rule.[72]

The remainder of the decade witnessed a back-and-forth struggle between the movie chains and government officials over the quota system. By the time West Africa won its independence in 1960, the two sides were still far from agreement, and it was left to the new sovereign governments to establish their own guidelines in tripartite negotiations among themselves, the distribution chains, and France.[73] Chapter 5 explores that phase of the story. Thus, the relationship between the colonial state and capitalist distribution conglomerates was at best contentious. Each needed the other; there is no question that their existence was both mutually dependent and reinforcing. However, the manner of their liaisons was not one of automatic agreement or even cooperation in the achievement of their disparate specific objectives. The colonial state acted to protect the monopoly position of COMACICO and SECMA in West Africa just once, when Adolphe Touffait, the minister for overseas France, expressed his "wish that the choice and the distribution of films should remain, in French West Africa, under French direction."[74] That note was prompted by efforts of the Motion Picture Export Association of America (MPEAA) to open movie theaters in West Africa. It did not explicitly endorse the position of COMACICO or SECMA, nor did the colonial government take any action to prohibit "foreign" companies from opening theaters in the region. They refrained from such action despite some administrators' fear of "an offensive by the large American, English, and Indian companies" aimed at dumping their products on screens in West Africa.[75] The main concern seemed to be not so much market share but how to manage the kinds of images available to West African audiences, and government officials thought French companies would be easier to control than those based in the United States.

The Cinema Industrial Complex

Another difficulty with complying with the quotas mandated by the colonial government was that even the limited number of French films that theater owners were required to screen had to be scrutinized for content—some films were even banned outright. The regulations designed to aid French economic reconstruction were part of a package that simultaneously sought to control the flow of images into and about Africa. In other words, by 1954 a fully articulated cinema industrial complex had taken shape in the federation that integrated the fundamental aspects of representation and materialism into a single field of engagement. The cinema industrial complex involved censorship of films (both those that could be shown and those that could be made in West Africa) and led to the establishment of a program for making films useful to the imperial enterprise, regulating theaters in terms of categories based on size and permits to construct new ones, controlling the type of film stock that should be used (16 mm vs. 35 mm), and managing the revenue generated in the cinemas.[76]

In the realm of censorship, in 1954 the general government of West Africa formed the Commission de contrôle des films cinématographiques (CFCC) to review all films proposed for release in the federation. Its nine members were appointed by the high commissioner in Dakar and included an agent of the colonial government, a member of the grand council of the federation, delegates from the director general of education and the director of the security services, a magistrate specializing in questions of juvenile delinquency, and representatives of the medical association, cultural centers, family associations, and importers-distributors.[77] In 1956, one additional member was added after a consolidated association of parents of students of public schools petitioned the colonial government to be represented in its deliberations.[78] The purpose of the commission was outlined in instructions forwarded to the territorial governors. The commission was "to protect, according to the national plan, the French cinematography industry, which must permit, according to the local plan, the sensible limitation of the projection of foreign films, and particularly Egyptian films." The commission also served to guarantee that "the African populations" were not exposed to images that did not correspond to the "French spirit" or did not buoy up "local customs and traditions." After acknowledging "the ever increasing attraction that the cinema exercises on the masses," the instructions observed that the government was concerned about the potentially negative effect "certain films could have on populations that were still little evolved, particularly the youth." Singled out as examples of films of which the commission should be wary and that it should greatly restrict access to were "Arab films" and "American westerns" for the reasons already noted.[79] Following the aforementioned guidelines, romances and films promoting "monogamous" familial relationships such as *L'amour toujours l'amour* (France), *Une histoire d'amour* (France), and *Room for One More* (United States) were routinely and without difficulty approved for general viewing, while other works like *La société du monde en action* (United States), *Los olvidados* (Mexico), and *Les statues meurent aussi* (France) were banned outright and listed along with such "unforgettable" productions as *Striporama* (United States), *Side Streets of Hollywood* (United States), and *Cinderella's Love Lesson* (United States) as undesirable for or offensive to West African audiences.[80]

Once constituted, the CFCC became a lightning rod for anyone interested in screening a film in West Africa or in objecting to what was available in the federation's theaters. Other groups and individuals in addition to the association of parents that had succeeded in changing the composition of the commission incessantly lobbied in an effort to influence the CFCC's decisions. By 1955 Catholic groups were active in trying to shape the outcome of the commission's deliberations through a systematic letter-writing campaign that protested against the "immorality" of certain types of films while framing their complaints as part of a federation-wide campaign against the spread of "alcoholism" that the Comité catholique du cinéma in Senegal associated with the "rapid expansion of the cinema" in the region.[81] This particular intervention in the field of motion pictures was reminiscent of the reaction of the association of movie theaters to lewd behavior in the 1930s, specifically the complaints about the poor hygienic practices attributed to film patrons. One early success of the Catholic lobby was the banning of *Le blé en herbe* by the CFCC on 18 August 1954. Based on the 1923 novel by Colette that centers on a love affair and betrayal, the film elicited the objections of a group based in Dahomey known as the Bons pères, who viewed the film as inappropriate for African audiences. The movie itself went on to modest international box office success, but significantly its banning in West Africa was cause for comment by the Catholic personalist François Mauriac in an article published on 25 October 1954 in *Libération*. He pointed to the incident as an example of the colonial government taking orders from special interest groups and silencing freedom of expression in West Africa.[82]

The CFCC met frequently after it was formed in 1954. From the start it had a standardized form for each film that was divided into three sections. On the far left was a list of the "members of the commission," starting with the representative of the general government down to the director of political affairs, all of whom had to check in as "present" or "represented" by someone in the specific agency selected for participation on the commission. The large and vacant middle section contained a space for "observations," which was followed by the third column at the far right for the signatures of those on the commission. Every film to be shown in West Africa that was made in the federation or that was about the region underwent the scrutiny of the commission. Each year the CFCC produced a lengthy list of "banned films" that was accompanied by their release date and country of origin. Moreover, the commission kept detailed information on the films that were being shown in the federation, including the dates screened, run time, which movie chain showed the films and when, as well as the country of origin of each film.[83] In other words, the CFCC not only became the nexus for the compilation of statistical information on the cinema industrial complex in French West Africa but also directly intervened to structure it in the waning years of France's rule in the region. The commission carried on the work of earlier government bodies that received requests from prospective filmmakers who wanted to film in the federation while taking on its new responsibilities to systematically regulate movies in West Africa.

The imperial administration did not confine itself to reactionary or censoring actions, though. Part of the new politics of film elaborated in the post–World War II period included a provision for the promotion of the film industry in Africa and the generation of what colonial officials defined as "positive images," images both directed toward Africans and about them. That involved the disbursement of funds to finance the production of certain kinds of movies, the purchase of equipment and film stock necessary for the making of motion pictures, and the distribution of the finished product. In 1951, François Mitterrand, minister for overseas France, issued a decree establishing a cinema commission within the information committee of the ministry to study "all questions relative to the development of the cinema in the territories relevant to the Minister of Overseas France" with the goal of using "the cinema as an instrument of information, education and the localization of technology." He ordered that the commission inventory what would be needed to achieve these objectives as well as report on the overall requirements in the fields of "production, distribution, and exploitation of films of all kinds useful for the attainment of the goals of education, information, and instruction in the Overseas Territories." The commission was also to study the means by which production and distribution in the colonies could be coordinated and controlled.[84]

Mitterrand's intervention in the cinema field followed very closely the lines laid down by his predecessors in the immediate aftermath of the Second World War. It is clear from the decrees of 1949 and 1951 that the French government was intent on fully developing a cinema industrial complex in the colonies and that with each passing year the perceived need for the state's direct involvement in determining that field's parameters became more urgent. Lemaire's 1949 memorandum spelled out what a fully articulated film system for the colonies would entail. It called for the appropriation of funds from FIDES, clearly positioning cinema as part of an overall development strategy. The notes to this memorandum specified the need for 25 million francs as "start-up capital" to build a movie industry in West Africa. Financing would be managed by a "mixed economic society" wherein half the money would come from private capital provided by the large African businesses and half would come from FIDES. FIDES would, in turn, be integrated within the existing government agencies specified in the document. Those included the Commission du cinéma d'outre-mer, the Cinémathèque de l'agence des colonies, the Commission du cinéma à l'assemblée de l'union française, and the governments of the overseas territories, in addition to any other relevant constituency of the imperial hierarchy. Lemaire's instructions then spelled out the "principal activities of the specialized society" he envisioned would finance the construction of a full cinema industrial complex in West Africa. His report asserted that the society "would have the power to provide to the territories all the material necessary for the organization of projections: projection trucks, projection material properly understood, generating sets, etc." The society should further have the capacity to organize "traveling projection services that would assure the distribution of films by organizing screenings in villages, aided by a program composed, for example, of the following elements: a recreational film, a documentary film on the metropole, a prophylactic propaganda film, an artisanal propaganda film."[85] Beginning in the 1940s the idea of mobile projectors or a cinema on wheels was considered integral to the system for the distribution of movie images in the federation. Later African filmmakers such as Sembène would also deploy the practice of a cinema on wheels to show their products to rural audiences in West Africa.

Lemaire's report followed on the heels of the first tentative steps taken by the colonial government to put in place its film politics. Money from FIDES had already been used to make a series of documentary films that were hailed as "examples" of the kinds of movies administrators deemed were the most appropriate in terms of advancing the purposes of the colonial mission. Some of those listed as triumphs of the new system were on the subject of "the evolution of Black Africa, following the economic and social plan, thanks to the introduction of the machine and modern methods that provide solutions to the big African problems." One production that was viewed as a significant success was *Paysans noirs,* which was made with the mixed funding scheme that Lemaire envisioned in his report as essential to a thriving cinema industrial complex in West Africa.[86] It had the added advantage of being based on the work of the same title by Robert Delavignette, one of the most prominent figures in the history of twentieth-century French colonial rule in West Africa.[87] The next chapter takes up the question of representation with an analysis of the kinds of images specifically generated as part of the cinema industrial complex and includes a more detailed look at *Paysans noirs.*

The colonial government also regulated the spaces wherein films were screened, removing the prospect that bedeviled officials in the 1930s of private individuals showing movies in their own homes. The visa system first implemented in 1919 and then systematized in the wake of the 1934 Laval decree became even more rigorous following the Second World War. Movies could only be screened in approved theaters, which had to report detailed information on what was being shown, the run times for each film, and the receipts generated at the box office. Theaters were placed in four categories based on size, which then determined the specifications of the building codes to which they had to adhere. Category 1 movie houses, the largest, could seat over 1,500 patrons, category 2 seated between 701 and 1,500 customers, category 3 held 301 to 700, and category 4 was reserved for those with 300 or fewer spaces. By 1956 the classifications became even more complex with the additional overlay of the types of films that each theater had the capacity to show. These were given letter designations with "G" for those screening 35 mm "inflammable" films, "H" for ones with 35 mm movies needing the "support of security," and "I" for all theaters displaying films on stock of less than 35 mm that all carried the designation "support of security." Thus, theaters were classed by size and type of film stock by the late 1950s. The designation was accompanied by specific guidelines concerning sanitary facilities, security requirements, fire codes, and other restrictions on construction.[88]

Such a deep level of involvement in the cinema industrial complex also implicated the colonial government in debates over the standardization of film stock to be used in West African theaters as well as the use of tax receipts from movie ticket sales in the federation. Initially the French government favored 16 mm film stock for films shown in the region. The primary reason for choosing that format was that it was much less expensive than standard 35 mm film in addition to being far more flexible because 16 mm cameras could be used in more environments. Since the government was largely interested in film because of its putatively educational virtues, this preference made sense. Already by the 1930s 16 mm film was the standard for educational, scientific, and documentary filmmaking, whereas 35 mm was typical for entertainment theaters showing major commercial releases. The imperial administration's predilection for the 16 mm format was even codified in the acts that created the quota system for West Africa through its demarcation of the length films had to be to meet the government's requirements. As notes from COMACICO and SECMA to the high commissioner for the federation repeatedly stressed, the equivalent length of film in 35 mm format for a standard thirteen-hundred-meter 16 mm film was between twenty-eight hundred and three thousand meters, "a very long film," as one letter put it.[89] Consequently, even the physical size of films became a matter of concern in relations between the distribution companies and the colonial government. In addition, theater owners and cinema companies objected to the new requirement, claiming that the cost to convert 35 mm theaters to 16 mm ones would be prohibitive. Many films shot on 35 mm film, the industry standard, would have to be redone to conform to the new format. It was much easier, although still costly, to blow up 16 mm film to 35 mm stock, a practice some postcolonial West African cineastes would later adopt.[90]

The colonial administration's concern with controlling every aspect of the cinema industrial complex in West Africa, though, did not stem from a malevolent attitude toward film. Rather, as I have suggested, moving pictures had been reconceptualized as integral to prevailing notions of development at all levels. With the renewed attention of French officials to the matter of building up their colonial possessions after World War Two the cinema was transformed from a place that lacked regulation and as such posed a potential threat to public hygiene and social order into a place that was at the nexus of cultural, social, and economic (re)construction in the metropole and overseas territories. Evidence of this new understanding of film in the empire is found in the way revenue generated from movie screening in the federation was to be used. The colonial government envisioned that the box office receipts could be taxed in order to finance the further development of the cinema industrial complex, which, in turn, would become a motor for the broader socioeconomic development of the region. As the Conseil économique de l'Afrique occidentale française put it during a 1949 meeting to discuss the formulation of "a politics of cinema," all aspects of the cinema industrial complex had to be brought together as an integrated whole in order to "aid in the development" of overseas France. That meant that "functionaries, producers, distributors, theater owners, and salaried professionals" at all levels should work together to further the colonial mission. The cinema, the commission concluded, would be "the best agent" for achieving those objectives.[91]

Thus, by the mid-1950s, after years of study and sporadic intervention, France had formulated a "film politics" as part of its strategy for maintaining and deepening French influence in West Africa even as political authority slipped to the Westernized elite. In the process, the cinema had become integrated with strategies of development. Socioeconomic development would aid the expansion of the film industry at the same time that the "revitalization" of motion pictures directly assisted economic progress. With those changes came an increasing interest in regulating the kinds of images available to and about Africans. The French strategy to project and construct images of itself through film to the wider world and especially Africa carried over into the postcolonial period and was taken up by the new Ministère des affaires culturelles and Ministère de la coopération, which preserved the colonial-era regulations through deals with the newly sovereign African States. I take up the postcolonial role of France in the emergence of Francophone West African filmmaking in chapter 5. Those agreements and the institutional groundwork prepared before 1960 constituted some of the toughest obstacles for Africans as they attempted to forge their own cinema tradition as a means to overcome the psychological, cultural, and structural legacies of imperial domination. In addition, they had to confront the legacy generated by decades of Western-constructed images of Africa and Africans. It is to the field of representation that the narrative now turns with a look at colonialist imagery aimed at extra-African and indigenous audiences during the period of imperial rule.

2 The Colonialist Regime of Representation, 1945–60

"BETWEEN THE PUBLIC and the screen," Robert Delavignette observed in 1948, "there is a space for misunderstanding that risks altering the knowledge of the world that the screen projects. It is for this mutual comprehension that the film is an irreplaceable and superior instrument."[1] Delavignette's concern centered on the potential for the distortion of meaning that the filmic image inherently allowed for. The "real" world captured by the camera somehow had to be "properly" understood by the viewer. The problem, as we have seen, was that the audience always brought to the space of the cinema certain cultural preconceptions, a universe of comprehension that structured the ways in which images were received. Motion pictures could fail if they did not take into consideration those who would be the consumers. Consequently, film was an intrinsically unstable device for transmitting "truth" and eliciting predetermined outcomes—the "space for misunderstanding" that troubled Delavignette. As Adorno notes, "The potential gap between ... intentions and their actual effect ... is inherent in the medium."[2] The articulation of a comprehensive "film politics" around the cinema industrial complex of the 1950s in French West Africa was, therefore, accompanied by a deep concern over what transpired in the realm of representation. While the materialist aspects of filmmaking were essential to the development projects the French imperial nation-state aimed at its overseas territories, which would also assist the metropole's postwar reconstruction, officials throughout the imperial hierarchy deemed the images projected to and about Africans to be of equal importance in their universal conceptualization of the cinematic field.

The new postwar film politics included a shift in colonialist film imagery, as government administrators expressed the concern that earlier tropes of the primitive African both failed to properly consider the "achievements" of the French civilizing mission and incited disorder in the colonies, since the indigenous population objected to the racist stereotypes propagated about them to extra-African audiences. Consequently, officials throughout the chain of command for overseas France found themselves having to become film theorists of a certain order. As Delavignette intimated, everyone from the minister for overseas France down to the local official in West Africa had to become cognizant of the relationship between the images projected on the screen and the "mentality" of the viewer in the theater. More than that, though, the administrators of the empire had to control that connection and manage the outcomes so that film could play the important role it was now deemed to have in the realization of France's ever-shifting colonial objectives.

As Slavin notes in his study of movies set in North Africa between the two world wars, "Colonial film reflected and reinforced the machinery of cultural hegemony, noncoercive social control, and the underlying politics of privilege."[3] However, the role film played within the larger project of sustaining and deepening imperial power was never straightforward or consistent over time. In his study of British film politics in colonial Zimbabwe, Timothy Burke cautions that "from the moment of its invention, film has provoked intense anxieties in every society exposed to it, and we should not suppose that white colonizers were any less anxious about the general power of cinema merely because they were colonizers."[4] With the explosive growth of the cinema industrial complex in West Africa, French colonial officials became increasingly unsettled about the images available to African audiences as well as those transmitted about Africa to outside viewers.

Thus, administrators in the federation suddenly found the prevailing racist representations of Africans and African culture that dominated movie screens before 1945 to be highly problematic if not subversive vis-à-vis their interest in sustaining French power in the region. This sentiment on the part of administrators did not alter the imperialist nature of the cinematic images produced or authorized in the late colonial period. The change in their perception was itself the product of a transformed political environment in the metropole and colonies after the war, but it reflected the continued desire to maintain the existing fundamental relationship between France and its overseas territories (formerly referred to as colonies). This subtlety is captured by Robert Stam and Louise Spence when they argue that "the insistence on 'positive images,' finally, obscures the fact that 'nice' images might at times be as pernicious as overtly degrading ones, providing a bourgeois façade for paternalism, a more pervasive racism."[5] This more pervasive racism reflected a general move by the colonial administration to fully articulate and control the cinema industrial complex in the 1950s in West Africa. Materialism and representation went hand in hand in the struggles that defined the field of film production.

"Colonial cinema" has been the subject of scholarly attention for some time and has become a subgenre of research in its own right. Researchers across a variety of disciplines have enhanced our knowledge of empire, how images of the exotic participated in sustaining colonialism, and the ways in which representations of the colonized informed the articulation of imperialist identities. The consensus that has emerged from such studies generally follows the lines sketched by Pierre Boulanger in *Le cinéma colonial*: "This cinema conveys several myths that are [ultimately] more damaging than the [initial] aggression [of the conquest]. It makes an apology for the conquest, of murder, engenders ignorance, abasement [of the colonized,] and hatred. It [either] ignores the autochthonous populations or depicts them, with very few exceptions, as possessing the most malevolent of traits."[6] As Stam and Spence note, "Since the beginnings of the cinema coincided with the height of European imperialism, it is hardly surprising that European cinema portrayed the colonized in an unflattering light."[7] Despite the seeming convergence of interests between colonialism and colonial cinema, though, there was not often an overt relationship between those who made such films and the imperial state. In other words, the absence of a coherent film politics until the 1950s, at least in the case of French West Africa, meant that filmmakers were independent agents who operated in a specific hegemonic cultural environment, and their work largely reflected prevailing tropes that reproduced the power relations that inhered within the imperial context. Moreover, the colonial state was not overly concerned with the images purveyed by those products as long as they did not lead to social disorder in the colonies. Prior to the Second World War the only films that consistently provoked the ire and censure of the imperial officials were those that explicitly challenged the legitimacy of colonialism or the specific practices of the overseas administration, including any movie that expressed the slightest sympathy for socialist politics or the Russian Revolution. As discussed in the previous chapter, it was the appropriation of screen images (and even films) by Africans for (potentially) subversive ends that prodded government officials in West Africa and Paris to begin to take seriously the kinds of portrayals available to cinema patrons, both licit and illicit.

Paul Landau explains that Western images of Africa have a very old pedigree. Twentieth-century cinema became merely the latest vehicle through which some well-entrenched tropes of Africanity were made available to consumers around the world. The impact of photographic and cinematographic technology, though, did influence those representations in some profound ways. What Landau calls the "image-Africa," a "collage" of Africa fabricated in the nineteenth century from "a shallow archive of reports, glimpses, and rumors accumulated over past centuries" became "even simpler and flatter in its resonances" with the new machinery of mechanical reproduction: "Items of visual media were . . . critical to the image-Africa. Colonial-era cinema, stereoscopic slides, tobacco-package inserts, Senegalese postcards, *Tintin* comic strips, half-tone news photographs, colonial exhibitions, *Natural History Magazine,* animal trophies, and mounted spears and shields all informed it."[8] Thus, by the time French rulers instantiated a film politics in West Africa they found themselves confronting a preexisting hegemonic image-Africa that many officials in the region suddenly found troubling and potentially destabilizing of their power.

Kenneth Cameron sees this same flattening of the image-Africa in colonial cinema from the 1890s to the 1950s. However, he raises the question of whether the flattening is the product of the films (and filmmakers) or of the tradition of film criticism that has taken motion pictures about Africa as its subject. He asks, "Is racism the only thing to be seen in these films?" Cameron does not deny the prominence of racist images and racial tropes in colonial cinema about Africa. However, he wants to broaden the field of vision to include an interrogation of the role of class and gender and an interrogation of how these "films reveal things other than racism in the societies that produced them."[9] This is a good place to start for the discussion of representation at the center of this chapter. It leads back to the fundamental issue of the relationship of the cinema industrial complex and the colonial state, for it was concern over the specific images conveyed on the screen and the manner in which they were interpreted by indigenous West African audiences that led French officials to inaugurate the process of elaborating a film politics for the empire.

Much of the scholarship of colonial cinema has centered on the convergence of interest between imperial power and the screen images in films about the colonized peoples and territories. Slavin's analysis of the "overall role of colonial cinema as an expression of the interaction of cultural hegemony and political power" focuses on the impact that the motion picture genre had on the French political left and its base among the European working class. He argues that colonial cinema "legitimated the racial privileges of European workers, diverted attention from their own exploitation, and disabled impulses to solidarity with women and colonial peoples." While the subject of his research is colonial cinema, the study itself is anchored to the metropole in an attempt to unpack the seeming ineptness of the radical left when it came to articulating a line of solidarity with colonized peoples or women prior to the Second World War. Slavin concludes that this debilitation resulted from their being "transfixed by exotic images and [being] blind to colonial and sexual realities."[10] Slavin's analysis reflects the flattening that Cameron mused might be more a product of the critic than the films themselves. His pessimistic conclusion about the manner in which the French left was influenced by the racial and gender fantasies propagated by colonial cinema assumes that the images themselves could only be singularly interpreted and that the audiences came to the space of the theater with a monolithic interpretive framework. Was there no possibility that the images projected on the screen might disturb as much as reinforce audience perceptions of themselves or their society? It seems Slavin does not pose the same order of questions in his analysis that colonial officials certainly posed in their debates over a film politics for the empire. Ironically, they were more open to the idea (even danger) of multiple readings of a film than Slavin is as a critic of the nefarious influences colonial cinema had on European society.

While Slavin offers important insights into the limitations of leftist solidarity with colonized populations induced by the cultural blind spots captured so well in colonial cinema, he does not venture too far into the colonies to gauge potential reaction among the subjugated populations to those same films. It is Boulanger who brings the analysis to the colonies—in fact to the same region of French-ruled North Africa that is Slavin's focus. However, he flattens the indigenous audience in their reception of the colonial films by assuming that they universally reject the images made available to them on the screen. He appeals for more "honest" portrayals of Muslims in the region and for a truthful representation of the colonial condition.[11] His concern for a postcolonial correction of the cinematic record about Africans' reality was taken up by the African filmmakers at the center of this study and is discussed in chapter 4.

Cameron's interrogation of the ways in which Africa has figured in the history of cinema from its invention in the 1890s to the 1990s begins to move more firmly to the site of the colonies. Agreeing with Slavin and Boulanger, he notes the close structural interdependence of the colonial state with filmmaking that took the colonies or Africans as its setting/subject. This symbiosis of choice and stricture led to a constrained cinematic practice. Cameron concludes that "while the appeal of the mass audience led them [filmmakers] to turn their cameras on the exotic and the shocking, their reliance on colonialism led them *not* to turn their cameras on colonialism. Africa was greatly modernized in the thirty years after Keaton's first effort, but film ignored the changes; rather, it had increasingly to seek out the primitive and the exotic, ultimately paying Africans to stage events and ceremonies and to wear costumes." As I have noted, this was a complaint voiced by colonial officials (for very different reasons) in their discussions of film in the empire. Cameron is certainly sensitive to the fact that despite the convergence of interest between colonial cinema and imperialism, officials were concerned that "the Empire was . . . particularly vulnerable to the effects of motion pictures."[12] Because his timeframe extends beyond the interwar period that is the context for Slavin's work, Cameron is able to note the shifts in the nature of colonial film through different historical eras and to document the way in which cinema responded to and helped to shape the changing power dynamics of the colonial field.[13] That alteration in the presentation of the African, noted also by Stam and Spence, is significant for grasping the complexity and instability of representation on the screen that Delavignette and others in French West Africa wanted to contain in order to harness the power of the moving image to the imperial project. To echo Cameron, the films produced in the late colonial and early postcolonial era may have appeared to be less racist than those generated in previous era, but the "structure and intent behind them" had not significantly changed.[14] What was an informal, even abstract, convergence of interest between filmmakers and the colonial state during the interwar period was transformed into a tightly controlled system that called for cineastes to submit their vision to the interests of imperial hegemony. Ironically, this requirement often found colonial censors demanding that movie directors tone down their racism and make it more subtle.

Despite the growing literature on colonial film, this important pivotal period in the history of cinema in West Africa has been largely overlooked by scholars or glossed over in a rush to get to the works of postcolonial African filmmakers who sought to "correct" the record in the representational arena. Femi Shaka's analysis of the ways in which cinema figured in the constitution of modern African identities goes some way toward acknowledging the fluid nature of representation in the context of colonial film. He notes the dialectical relationship between "colonialist films" and postcolonial African cinema. In his view, the works of Sembène, Hondo, and others are "counterdiscursive" in incorporating the heritage of the "Euro-African encounter," but their films also transcend that encounter and contribute to the adumbration of an African modernity. The colonial rulers actually prepared the ground for the antithetical position occupied by West African cineastes through their intervention in the medium of film. Specifically, Shaka finds the introduction of "instructional cinema" in the colonies to be a key moment in the subsequent development of African motion picture production: "The practices of colonial instructional cinema instituted a different regime of representation of Africa and Africans that stands in direct contrast to that of films of colonialist African cinema." Shaka finds that, generally, the images conveyed through instructional cinema were "positive," contributing to African modernity, while those from colonialist cinema were "negative," representing an "arrested form of knowledge and perception." The main problem that arises from instructional cinema for Shaka is its tendency to absolve the imperial government of any responsibility for the African condition by promoting the idea of "self-help" among the colonized populations.[15]

However, Shaka's analysis still does not take into consideration the specificity of the developments in the 1950s. Partly that is the result of his choice to center much of the analysis of colonial film on the British Empire and then to shift to a study of mostly Francophone West African filmmakers in the postcolonial period. Dina Sherzer and Jean-Pierre Jeancolas highlight the first decade after World War Two as crucial to the history of film in the Francophone world, especially with respect to the relationship between France and its colonies.[16] However, the essays in Sherzer's edited volume are almost entirely devoted to an examination of how French films reconstruct the colonial experience for French audiences. Sherzer argues that later films (mostly from the postcolonial period) seek to "sensitize French viewers to the colonial past, and they have an impact on the formation of a common collective memory of the colonies." They are, she concludes, "the only [real] colonial films."[17] As with Slavin, the question remains: what about African audiences? The consumer of film images is here strictly French and the subject to be represented is "France" in the colonial context. Jeancolas follows this same trajectory back to the metropole, despite his more explicit focus on the role of the French state in promoting cultural cooperation (including the cinema) with the former colonies. He sees postcolonial French filmmakers as taking "over the role of agitators" by calling into question the received knowledge of France's colonial past.[18] Thus there is an acknowledgment of the important moment of the 1950s in the history of cinematic practice in the colonial context without an analysis of the actual shifts in representation and their impact in the colonies, such as in French West Africa. As I argue in chapter 1, the imperial government in the federation was increasingly concerned with and involved in constructing the kinds of images that circulated to Africans and about Africa to the outside world. The story now ventures into the prewar period to look at the kinds of portrayals that began to agitate colonial officials after 1945 and that generated a changed mandate in the representation of/to Africans.

Colonial Cinema in the Colonies

The 1934 Laval decree that for the first time erected the scaffolding around which a film politics for the empire would be constructed provided the grounds on which the colonial state could first venture into debates over representation on the screen. Part 4 of the decree instructs the various censorship boards the act called into being to ensure that their deliberations take into "consideration the entirety of the national and local interests at stake and especially the interest of the preservation of the national and local mores and traditions."[19] This broad mandate meant that colonial officials would have to submit the entire range of images available in the colonies to close scrutiny and judge their appropriateness on the basis of a delicate and unspecified balance between national (French) and local (indigenous) interests. If such an approach were successful, it would invariably lead to a hybrid visual field that was neither/both French and African, sustaining the interests of both communities. In other words, the censors would achieve through their actions the goals of the civilizing mission at the time—to impart French values in a manner that enhanced and preserved the essential cultural attributes of Africans without making them into poor imitations of Frenchmen lacking a moral anchor in their traditions.[20] Film was imputed with the power to both represent and call into being the truth of the African condition regardless of whether the motion picture in question was "entertainment" or was "instructional" in nature.

The line of thinking embedded in the Laval decree recalls André Bazin's theory of cinema. In discussing the role of photographic and cinematographic technology in altering the way viewers understand images Bazin writes, "All are agreed that the image helps us to remember the subject and to preserve him from a second spiritual death. Today the making of images no longer shares an anthropomorphic, utilitarian purpose. It is no longer a question of survival after death, but of a larger concept, *the creation of an ideal world in the likeness of the real*, with its own temporal destiny." Finally, he notes with regard to cinema's specific impact that "viewed in this perspective, *the cinema is objectivity in time.*"[21] The astonishing claim that creating the ideal world in the likeness of the real amounts to a greater accomplishment than survival after death aside, Bazin's notions mesh perfectly with the trajectory of colonial officials' thinking about the role of film in the empire. The kinds of images that were to be made available on West African screens had to reflect the truth of the material world but also go beyond it to a future reality that the film would call into existence in the minds of the audience. Harris and Ezra find this same process of portraying and adumbrating reality to be central to French leaders' conceptualization of cinema within postwar French reconstruction: "What is certain is that the French recognized earlier than most the importance of cultivating a national image—'une certaine idée de la France,' as de Gaulle famously put it; and they also recognized the central role of cinema in constructing and disseminating this image."[22]

The outcome it was hoped would follow from carrying out the process sketched in the Laval decree was a Franco-African identity that was essentially rooted in African traditions but inflected by French modernity; the perfect embodiment of the notion of *la plus grande France* that Wilder explicates in his study of colonial humanism and *négritude* in interwar France.[23] On the heels of the Laval decree's enactment, government officials had to determine what exactly conformed to these ideals and what representations were antithetical to the goals of France's mission in West Africa. That determination was to be made through their examination of cinematic images circulating in the federation. One report on the movie-going practices of African audiences found that most viewers were young and therefore more susceptible to being influenced by the kinds of images they consumed from the screen. However, Marcel de Coppet, the governor general of French West Africa at the time, also noted that most "theatrical films do not touch the essence of the indigenous soul." This was both good and bad. It was good because it indicated that Africans were sophisticated connoisseurs of the cinema and could distinguish between fantasy and reality. It was bad because it suggested the paucity of films available to African audiences that could contribute to their further "evolution" along the path of modernity laid out by France. After all, motion pictures had to be able to affect Africans at some level if the use of cinema in the manner being discussed among colonial officials was to be successful. Evidence this strategy could still work was found in those movies that did resonate among indigenous audiences. Most of those fell into the categories of "police shoot-ups and gangster" films. Those offerings tended to "wound their beliefs or their traditions," as well as presented a troubling image of the forces of order being shot up on the screen by street rebels, and had to be proscribed.[24]

Much of the work on this front, though, remained at the level of interministerial and administrative exchanges of reports and letters. In reality little action was taken with regard to banning films, censoring those movies that were still being shown on West African screens, or even in making the kinds of educational films high colonial officials had advocated since at least 1932. Even the frequent requests by independent filmmakers and production studios to make educational and propaganda films for France were not acted on during the 1930s.[25] Finally, an observation from the director of colonial education in French Equatorial Africa that entertainment films available to African audiences would achieve great success if they put in "a certain number of actors of color" failed to go any farther than the desks of the colonial ministry.[26] The main barriers to real movement in the realm of representation in cinema prior to the Second World War seemed to be a lack of personnel due to cutbacks during the Great Depression, a lack of financial resources, and French leaders' understandable preoccupation with the gathering war clouds in Europe.

Despite the propaganda initiative undertaken by Vichy France during the war, the terrain of representation was not significantly impacted. The national revolution's ideology in the field of cinematic production hardly ventured beyond what prewar colonial officials had already sketched in their internal memoranda, and its influence was quite limited in West Africa.[27] The only noticeable shift in the pattern of those films permitted, censored, or banned related to the perceived political orientation or usefulness of the films in question. The fate of two movies was emblematic of the changes from Third Republic France to Vichy to the Fourth Republic. One is *Der Rebell*, a German film released in December 1932 and starring Luis Trenker as a medical student who returns home in the Tyrol region only to discover that his mother and sister have been murdered by Napoleon's invading troops. Trenker's character, Severin Anderlan, becomes a resistance fighter in the war against foreign occupation. The film is a classic tale of heroism in the face of immense odds that celebrates the ideals of liberty and action against oppression. Ironically, it was first shown in Berlin on 17 January 1933, just thirteen days before Adolph Hitler, the very antithesis of the virtues extolled by the movie, was named chancellor.[28] COMACICO immediately picked up the film and showed it throughout its theaters in West Africa during the 1930s, where it managed to pass the scrutiny of censors despite its conceivably anti-French theme. Perhaps it survived owing to both neglect (I have noted the paucity of structural support for the regulations promulgated at the top of the administrative hierarchy) and the fact that Anderlan's stance accorded with the putative values of the Third Republic. Napoleon could be read as a monarchical tyrant who subverted the republican ideals of the revolution. Amazingly, colonial officials did not appear to worry about how the overriding plot of the story—resistance to foreign occupation—might be interpreted by African audiences chafing under French imperial domination.

While the Third Republic may have missed the film's main message (or deemed it to be nonthreatening), Vichy officials did not. In 1942 the collaborationist government ordered *Der Rebell* banned. One can reasonably surmise that officials within the colonial administration under Vichy realized a film celebrating resistance to foreign occupation would not only arouse anticolonial passions but could also complicate the government's relations with Nazi Germany. Moreover, the republican ideals embodied in Anderlan's actions ran counter to those now embraced by Marshal Henri Philippe Pétain's regime. Not surprisingly, then, in 1943 after the general government for French West Africa switched sides to back Charles de

Gaulle's Free France government in exile the ban was lifted. COMACICO immediately began screening the film to wide approval among audiences throughout the federation.

Only in 1947, with the escalation of Cold War tensions that was reflected in a major shuffle within the French government, including the removal in May of the Communist Party from the resistance coalition that had governed since 1946, did the film once again become a source of controversy. On 3 May 1947 Georges Poirier, the acting lieutenant governor of Mauritania, fired the first salvo in a letter to the high commissioner of the general government for French West Africa. He called for the movie to be banned because it elicited "diverse reactions": it was "booed by many of the French" and "applauded by a lot of the Africans, who, perhaps, don't see the anti-French tendency because of the anachronistic uniforms that they don't know about."[29] Interestingly, Poirier's objections followed the lines laid down by Vichy when it banned the film. Specifically, the problem with *Der Rebell* was its anti-French message—Germans valiantly struggling against France—and not the more universalist message of resistance to foreign domination as such and the struggle for the human right to self-determination, enshrined in the recently installed United Nations. The reason for banning the movie, besides its anti-French message, was that the African audiences did not get it. The use of costumes from the Napoleonic age confused Africans because they could not recognize that the villains portrayed on the screen were French soldiers. Following Poirier's logic, if contemporary uniforms had been used and the Africans recognized they were French the indigenous viewers would have had a different reaction, one more akin to the negative response of the French in the audiences. This was the "misunderstanding" between the objective reality displayed on the screen and its reception by the viewer that troubled Delavignette. It did not occur to Poirier that Africans could be skilled and experienced readers of cinematic texts and that they applauded precisely because they got the universal message of the fight for liberation and vengeance against one's oppressor that the French colonial officials seemed to be missing. It is unclear what the film's fate was at the time, but the first postwar systematic list of authorized movies, published in 1949, does not include it.[30]

Another film that received contradictory treatment from the 1930s through the postwar period was *L'esclave blanche*, a 1939 French film directed by Marc Sorkin and Georg Wilhelm Pabst starring the American actor John Lodge as Vedad Bey and the French starlet Viviane Romance as Mireille. The plot centers on a Turkish politician (Vedad Bey) and a French woman (Mireille), who get married in France and then return to Turkey and settle into a highly orientalized version of Turkish life. Mireille expects to enjoy the exoticism of life in the Orient and the privilege that comes with being wed to a prominent figure in society. However, she soon discovers as she is subjected to the harsh regimen of harem life that wives in the Turkish tradition are "slaves" (hence the film's title). Mireille's fate is made worse because she is the kind of "modern woman" that emerged after the First World War, an identity that is utterly incongruous within a Turkish setting, locked as Turkey is in an eternal medieval culture, according to the film's portrayal.[31]

L'esclave blanche was an instant box office success. It easily passed the scrutiny of censors in West Africa and continued to be shown all through the Second World War. As one colonial official noted, the movie was shown with "the greatest success" in France, the colonies, and foreign countries alike (the U.S. release date was April 1942).[32] However, the shifting sands of approved images in the area of representation during the late colonial period were such that previously acceptable portrayals often came to be regarded as no longer consistent with the types of messages French officials wanted to convey to African cinema audiences. In 1949, after ten successful years of uncensored viewings in the federation, the film was banned. In explaining its decision, the Commission du cinéma d'outre-mer noted that in its opinion the film "was of a nature to offend the mores and traditions of the Islamicized populations" of the French territories."[33] This was an early indication of the colonial government's concern with Islam as a potent anticolonial force. It is even more surprising when one considers the ban occurred amid the massive repression of the RDA for its supposed "communist" sympathies.

The fate of *L'esclave blanche* reflects both a more concerted effort on the part of the colonial administration to control the range of representations available to African audiences in the cinematic field and a shift in the understanding of the kinds of images deemed acceptable as part of the changing mission of French imperialism. As we have seen, the colonial apparatus erected a dense structure of control over the distribution of films after 1945, at the center of which was the CFCC, founded in 1954. However, in addition to censoring films produced by independent cineastes (the reactionary dimension to film politics embodied in the Laval decree of 1934) the colonial state also ventured into the realm of proactive measures, generating movies that carried the "truth" it wanted to reach African spectators as well as extra-African consumers of motion pictures. The year *L'esclave blanche* was removed from screens across West Africa, *Paysans noirs*, the film based on the 1931 novel of the same title written by the colonial administrator and ethnographer Robert Delavignette, was released to wide acclaim up and down the imperial hierarchy as a model for the kinds of motion pictures that should be made and supported by the cinema industrial complex in the federation.

Reality and Representation on the Screen

In the early 1950s, the period during which France developed a film politics for the overseas territories, André Bazin made the observation that "the image is evaluated not according to what it adds to reality but what it reveals of it."[34] This statement could just as well have been uttered by colonial officials, who sought to use film as a truth-telling (and truth-creating) form for validating the metropole's imperial mission as well as advancing it along centrally prescribed lines. As I have noted, the decision by colonial administrators to engage directly, deeply, and systematically in the cinematic field meant that at a certain level they had to assume the role of film theorists. Consequently, it is important to discuss the relationship between prevailing accounts among film theorists and critics about the nature of the cinema and representation as it was constructed and contested in West Africa. Specifically, how the relationship between the image projected on the screen, the meaning attached to it by the spectator, and the intentions of the filmmakers or producers was understood at the time is central to elucidating the dynamics at play as the cinema industrial complex developed in the region during the 1950s.

At the center of France's imperial film politics in the 1950s was the notion of reality and its relationship to moving pictures. Even if the movie being viewed was pure "entertainment" and lacked any explicit political content, officials understood by the 1930s that films had real-world consequences whether they simply facilitated poor hygienic practices and social disorder of a juvenile nature or morphed into a threat to French rule. Maya Deren's work on the "creative use of reality" is particularly useful for understanding what was at stake for government agents as they grappled with representation on film as French power waned in West Africa. In discussing documentary filmmakers, she writes, "They operate on a principle of minimal intervention, in the interests of bringing the authority of reality to the support of the moral purpose of the film."[35] This is an important point of departure, because colonial officials viewed the documentary (or documentary technique) as the most appropriate form of filmmaking for revealing a truth about African audiences and about Africa to external viewers as well as for forging a truth for African viewers, a point also made by Shaka in his study of modernity and film in Africa.[36] Starting from the photographic image—a snapshot of reality—film moves the observer even closer to a replication of the objective world. As Deren notes, "The creative action in film, then, takes place in its time dimension; and for this reason the motion picture, though composed of spatial images, is primarily *a time form*. A major portion of the creative action consists of a manipulation of time and space." "By manipulation of time and space," she concludes, "I mean also the creation of a relationship between separate times, places, and persons."[37] The coupling of temporal movement with photographic images approximates the lived reality of the viewer who exists in time and to whom motion is central to the way in which life is conceptualized. Thus, film marked a significant advance in the capacity of the artificial machine to reproduce reality, blurring the lines between the objective world and the subjective imagination. Motion pictures made it possible not only to preserve the real and present it back to the spectator but also to call into being a certain reality that was the product of the filmmaker's imagination combined with elements from the actual material world. This dimension of cinematic representation had been central in colonial officials' thinking about the potential for cinema to either negatively or positively shape objective conditions in West Africa since at least the 1930s.

A precursor of Deren's ideas about motion pictures and reality is Siegfried Kracauer's "theory of film": "In establishing physical existence, films differ from photographs in two respects: they represent reality as it evolves in time; and they do so with the aid of cinematic techniques and devices."[38] Interestingly, to make his point about the role that cultural predisposition plays in constructing meaning from the film image, Kracauer uses African audiences as an example of the "miscomprehension" that may result from the cinematic experience. "The role which cultural standards and traditions may play" in situations in which audiences fail to notice certain things portrayed on the screen, he argues, is "drastically illustrated by a report on the reactions of African natives to a film made on the spot. After the screening the spectators, all of them still unacquainted with the medium, talked volubly about a chicken they allegedly had seen picking food in the mud. The filmmaker himself, entirely unaware of its presence, attended several performances without being able to detect it." Only by detailed examination was the filmmaker able to find the chicken in the film.[39] This tale relates a double miscognition. The filmmaker shot something of which he was utterly unaware, presumably due to his attaching little importance (culturally) to chickens grazing in public spaces. The African audience focused on the scene of the chicken eating while missing the larger film and, presumably, the meaning that the filmmaker wanted to convey to his erstwhile viewers. The task of the filmmaker, then, is to become more self-conscious of his/her own cultural blind spots in the production of the representations to be projected and more aware of the system of meaning the spectator will draw from in consuming those images. A double cognition has to be brought to bear in order to limit the possibility for misunderstanding. Again, this was the fundamental problem that vexed colonial officials in West Africa, including Delavignette. They wanted to shape a film culture that followed Kracauer's vision for cinema: "The cinema, then, aims at transforming the agitated witness into a conscious observer."[40] Even further, administrators in the federation wanted the viewer to become a conscious participant in actualizing their imperial vision.

The model that became the gold standard for what film should be in West Africa was, ironically, the 1948 screen adaptation of Delavignette's novel *Les paysans noirs*. It is telling that a novel should be the basis for the presentation of reality in the region. The film was shot entirely in French West Africa during 1948 and released in France on 6 May 1949 to effusive praise from the entire colonial government. Delavignette offers the following assessment of the process: "The film became a collective work, where Whites and Blacks served together the truth and the beauty of Africa."[41] In a presentation of the film to an audience in the Salle du musée social in 1953 he further added that the Africans [were] going to see themselves on the screen," fulfilling one of the goals of officials in the 1930s who sought to encourage the making of films that would be well received by local audiences.[42] The process of making the film, in Delavignette's presentation of it, embodied at a fundamental level the myth of Franco-African cooperation in the making of modern Africa that was the ultimate objective of the colonial mission in the postwar years. This supports Burke's contention in discussing the experience of motion pictures in Zimbabwe that "anxieties about the cinema have centered on its technologically driven capacity to make the imaginary come to life."[43] In the case at hand, participants actualized the imaginary in the real-life construction of a movie meant to project a "true" representation of African experiences that modeled behavior to be emulated by the consumer of the finished product. It demonstrates what Paul Stoller describes as film's ability to construct and transform.[44]

Remarkably, there is not a single extant print of *Paysans noirs*. Therefore, we must rely upon the records of colonial archives, published reaction, and Delavignette's own personal papers (including the film treatment) in order to reconstruct the movie's representational range and impact as well as the degree to which it faithfully reproduced his novel. From Delavignette's own detailed commentary on the movie, we know that he and the filmmakers viewed the "authenticity" of the representation of African reality and faithfulness to the book as paramount in the cinematic process. The events of both the film and the novel transpire in the region of Banfora (present-day Burkina Faso). Consequently, the action is situated in a real place, inhabited by those who are said to be the subject of the film. Delavignette asserts that because of the temporal and spatial situatedness of the film, the "greatest question" connected with making the movie was "to understand to what degree authentic Africa is communicable to other men than the Africans, in what measure the sensibility of the spectators of the cinema relates to the life of the Black Peasants. I say that this is a very big question. These Cinema spectators, you know them. We are among them. And as such, we are brothers of all Europeans, of all Americans, of all the men of every color who go into the darkened room to search for the unusual, for excitement, for diversion from daily life, for an enrichment of their personality." Delavignette then rhetorically asks, "What is it that *Les paysans noirs* brings to us, which is that part of ourselves that will be given satisfaction, and with which aspect [of the film] will there be established a mysterious accord?" His answer is "I don't know anything. It is the public who will respond." But, he adds, "it appears essential to me that such a question be posed. And it is [a testament to] the social merit of the film to have posed it."[45]

From Delavignette's own assessment and his prominence within the colonial government as an official and moral force for influencing policy decisions, it is clear that filming his book was a major undertaking designed to fulfill the representational aspect of the new film politics taking shape in West Africa. That is, it was intended to (re)construct images of Africa that would resonate with African audiences and also challenge the prevailing tropes of Africa and Africans circulating among external audiences. Interestingly, Delavignette assumes that local audiences in the federation would not find anything troubling about what was conveyed on the screen. They would recognize the truth of the images projected back to them. For African audiences, *Paysans noirs* was to function as a validation of their lived experiences and their essential reality. The real mystery lay with how non-African audiences would respond to the film. However, it was vital for the film's success in terms of structuring the representational framework within which notions of Africanity circulated that European, American, and all other non-African audiences connect with the movie at some level. That connection would be the circuit through which France would relate the beneficent impact it had had in shaping African modernity as well as restore humanity, which Delavignette and others in the French overseas administration claimed was in sore need of restoration, to the globally consumed image-Africa.

Consistent with established French colonial praxis, Delavignette and his collaborators on the film asserted they had captured aspects of "authentic Africa" and were expertly positioned to project them back to African and non-African spectators alike in a way that would reveal the essential truth of the material and abstract existence of the local population, even if the locals may not have been fully aware of it.[46] This is part of a long-standing practice in the convergence of imperialist ideology and cinematic practice identified by Stam and Spence: "colonialist cinema produces us as subjects, transforming us into armchair conquistadores, affirming our sense of power while making the inhabitants of the Third World objects of spectacle for the First World's voyeuristic gaze."[47] Delavignette's efforts to "correct" the cinematic record with regard to representations of Africa and Africans did not alter this fundamental relationship of power between the Western world and the colonized populations. In fact, the film deepened this structure through its masking of the racism at the core of the imperial system. Moreover, the African spectators of *Paysans noirs* did not even have the privilege of being transformed into subjects by being consumers of the images projected back at them. Their ideal selves were in fact the subjects that were objectified on the screen and returned to the spectator in an objectifying process that reified preconceived Western notions of what it meant to be authentically African.

Stam and Spence add, in discussing the mode of interrogation of colonialist cinema, that "a comprehensive methodology must pay attention to the *mediations* which intervene between 'reality' and representation. Its emphasis should be on narrative structure, genre conventions, and cinematic style rather than on perfect correctness of representation or fidelity to an original 'real' model or prototype."[48] A more systematic interrogation of the film and novel teases out the mediations at work that constituted the links connecting filmmakers, colonial officials, the film, and audiences in ways that reinforced French power in West Africa and that called into being an altered representational universe within which Africans were asked to locate their identity. Delavignette understood what was at stake in making a film such as *Paysans noirs*. He observed that "the French Union contains many diverse peoples of whom we have a need to understand. On one side are those who possess a scientific and literary culture that is written and tends toward the universal but which must not forget the ancient truths acquired by oral tradition. On the other side are those who do not yet have a written culture, but they powerfully bring to life their customs from where they get their . . . sustenance." A film like *Paysans noirs*, he concluded, helps us to affirm "these relationships and these affinities."[49] Significantly, the two groups about whom Delavignette was writing were both located in the colonies. The people who had acquired a "scientific and literary culture" but remained attached to their roots in oral culture were the French-educated elite in the colonies. According to Delavignette, who merely reiterated what had been the hegemonic framework for articulating imperial policy since the 1920s, educated Africans should not have the link severed with their "source," as that would lead to disorder in the colonies and would undermine local culture.[50] The other group was comprised of those not yet profoundly touched by French civilization. The film was to mediate the rift between those two groups and become a bridge suturing the empire together in a harmonious relationship based on mutual comprehension and respect. Delavignette and his contemporaries in the administration of West Africa positioned the cinema industrial complex in its materialist and representational dimensions at the core of the colonial power structure. The images projected through *Paysans noirs*, then, constituted a potent force promoting colonialist power relations, as Africans struggled to jettison the imperial yoke in the 1950s.

As Delavignette hoped, the 1949 movie faithfully followed the contours of his 1931 novel. It is a semiautobiographical novel that has the air of documentary filmmaking, which is perhaps one of the reasons the Commission du cinéma d'outre-mer extolled it as an "example of how to produce useful films with mixed funding" at its 15 June 1950 meeting.[51] *Paysans noirs* centers on the travails of a newly appointed administrator, Guillon, sent to Banfora following the assassination of the previous official. Consequently, we know from the start that this is going to be a difficult posting that requires the steady hand of an agent of the colonial state who can navigate the complex divisions of native society. Guillon's ideas very much reflect those held by Delavignette. Emerging from a leftist tradition and embracing what Wilder and others have described as a "colonial humanism," Delavignette embraced the diversity and legitimacy of indigenous traditions while also holding to the idea of French colonialism as a modernizing force for Africa/Africans.[52] Consistent with prevailing notions of the civilizing mission in the 1930s Africans' modernity was rooted in the fundamentally agricultural/peasant nature of their cultures. Consequently, France had to modernize Africa without destroying the essential aspects of Africans' traditions.

This is the delicate position into which Guillon, played in the film by Louis Arbessier, is thrust as he takes up his post in Banfora. Once there he immerses himself in the local culture and works with the resident engineer and doctor as well as traditional elites to forge a consensus in favor of modernization while conserving the extant culture. This process is bitterly opposed by a caste committed to archaic practices that tyrannized the people. In the end, the understanding Guillon has forged with the elders as well as his ability to serve as a bridge between the French and the Africans produces the formula that overcomes oppression and opens the door to a truly African modernity that is exemplary of the potential resulting from Franco-African cooperation.[53] As William B. Cohen summarizes, Delavignette "showed the Africans to be peasants, black peasants. He did not deny Africans their own personality, portraying them as inferior versions of French peasants.... [T]hey, too, had local traditions and beliefs that deserved respect.... Delavignette thought of change as a means of saving the village life while auguring a new era.... Humane administration would permit traditional societies to preserve much of their structure, but it was also creating a new Africa."[54]

As Delavignette explained at a screening of the film at the Conférence d'Angers held 10 March 1953, the film version closely followed the novel in its structure and dialogue.[55] It was important that the "colonial realist novel" of 1931 be translated into celluloid format as exactly as possible not only to preserve the naturalist effect of the original but most importantly to create the kind of film that would be well received by African audiences as well as present to external viewers the positive impact French rule had had in shaping African societies. While there is no known extant print of the film, its scenario (approved by Delavignette) survives in Delavignette's private papers currently held at the Centre des archives d'outre-mer in Aix-en-Provence, France. If the film version followed the treatment and scenario it would have closely resembled the novel, a point attested to by colonial officials and Delavignette after they viewed the finished product.[56] The "regime of representation" contained in *Paysans noirs* was meant to convey an extant reality while also actualizing it in the process of articulation.[57] The film was the archetype of what cinema was to be in the late colonial period. It set the bar for what was acceptable in the area of representation and at the same time demonstrated, through the very process of its production and its message, the role of film in the materialist dimension of the cinema industrial complex.

However, French administrators were not alone in the way they conceptualized African modernity. Some Africans who had been trained in French schools also saw Franco-African cooperation as the only path toward formation of an African culture worthy of the twentieth century. In the spring of 1945, officials in West Africa discovered an essay published by a medical student, Conte Saidou, in *Clarté*, which they preserved as evidence the civilizing mission was being accepted by their subjects. Titled "Une culture africaine," the essay explores the basis for an emergent African identity that would enable economic and social development while preserving the African essence. Saidou explains that "the French school has perfectly realized the cohesion of the elements (French and African) and has begun the process of creating a federation that begins to understand and centralize their interests, that implies a community of culture and a homogeneity of aspirations." The basis of this new formation is "a synthesis of French and African cultures." He then cites a recent article by Mamadou Dia in *Dakar-jeunes* in which he had proclaimed that "it is really audacious to dream of a cultural renaissance in French West Africa that is accomplished (only) with the specifically African elements, untainted by any admixture."[58] This essay fit within the developing philosophical tradition called "négritude" that is best exemplified in the work of Léopold Sédar Senghor, who would become Senegal's president in 1960. His vision for a distinctly African modernity involved not only a rediscovery of the essential nature of the African as an existential being but also the incorporation of aspects of French civilization that would enable Africa to meaningfully contribute to the further enhancement of the human condition.[59] Senghor's ideas and those expressed in Saidou's essay reflected what Shaka describes in his study as the historical and dialectical basis of African modernity.[60] Thus, by the late colonial period there was a growing convergence of interest between the aspirations of the West African educated elite and French rulers of the federation that together, but for different ends, helped to delimit the regime of representation informing cinematic practice in the transition to independence.

The Regime of Representation in 1950s West Africa

In his examination of sound in the cinematic experience John Belton writes, "Images attain credibility in the conformation to objective reality; sounds, in their conformation to the images of that reality, to a derivative reconstruction of objective reality." He adds that "in the cinema, there is always present, in the positioning of the camera and the microphone(s), a consciousness that sees and (in the sound film) hears and that coexists with what is seen or heard. . . . The cinema remains the phenomenological art par excellence, wedding, if indeed not collapsing, consciousness with the world."[61] Following the success—in the perception of colonial administrators—of *Paysans noirs,* imperial officials set to work more aggressively defining the parameters of the representation of the image-Africa that would be acceptable within the film politics of the age. They did so by financing or permitting films that replicated the model provided by *Paysans noirs* as well as by restricting those movies that violated the principles the colonial state set forth as the basis of its program for the federation. In the process, as a colonialist regime of representation took form in the latter years of French rule in the region, the language of the films' dialogues and the cinema as a way of speaking became important considerations.

Sergei Eisenstein, writing at the threshold of cinema's transition from the silent to the sound era, asked rhetorically, "Why then should cinema in its forms follow the theatre and painting rather than the methodology of language, which gives rise, through the combination of concrete descriptions and concrete objects, to quite new concepts and ideas?"[62] What French rulers in West Africa did in the 1950s was to push along and structure a process whereby a certain film language emerged that became the representational pole against which future African cineastes would have to struggle in order to forge a postcolonial image landscape. More than that, though, the actual language spoken by the performers in the movies was crucial in the colonial state's considerations of what films were allowed to be screened for local audiences, as well as in its deliberations about those films it wanted to promote beyond French borders. Officials went so far as to engage in protracted discussions about the usefulness or not of dubbing and whether films performed in non-French languages could obtain the censors' approval once they had been dubbed into French. The remainder of this chapter considers the dual meaning of cinematographic language and its place in the adumbration of a colonialist regime of representation.

From the earliest days of French officials' efforts to formulate a film politics for the colonies there existed among them a bias in favor of what they considered realist motion pictures. While documentaries represented the pinnacle of the genre, fiction films done in a naturalistic manner that accurately portrayed African cultures and their experiences under French rule were also acceptable. In fact, some argued those movies were even better vehicles for achieving colonial objectives in the cinematic field because they had the advantage of being educational and entertaining at the same time. Officials placed great emphasis on films that would provide "a benefit to the African" and argued that movies that were "poorly adapted to autochthonous intelligences" should be avoided.[63] As the debates unfolded among colonial administrators in West Africa and France, the outlines of a colonialist film language took shape that privileged French understandings of authentic African culture that also strongly emphasized the positive impact the imperial encounter had in moving traditional societies toward modernity. However, it was vital that in the process the Africans be portrayed on screen as being agents of their own transformation, willing collaborators in the civilizing mission but nevertheless maintaining their ontological essence. The specific colonialist film language of such movies, though, also had to be true to emerging cinematic discourse in general so that experienced motion picture audiences would be able to grasp the film as such. In other words, the successful movie had to register on Metz's two levels of "*cultural codes* and *specialized* codes": cultural codes " define the culture of each group; they are so ubiquitous and well 'assimilated' that the viewers generally consider them to be 'natural.' . . . On the other hand the codes I have called 'specialized' concern more specific and restricted social activities." Metz further reminds us that "the cinema, which could have served a variety of uses, in fact is most often used to *tell stories*—to the extent that even supposedly nonnarrative films (short documentary films, educational films, etc.) are governed essentially by the same semiological mechanisms that govern the 'feature films.'"[64] Consequently, the dichotomy established by Shaka in his study of African cinema between "instructional cinema" and "colonialist African cinema" does not hold in our current analysis of French cinematic practice in West Africa during the late colonial period.[65]

If *Paysans noirs* set the standard for colonialist film in West Africa, the imperial state supported a variety of other motion pictures that built on that foundation and solidified its preferred cinematic language. The typical movie that gained the approval of or was financed by the colonial government deployed certain tropes that established its identity as "African" and connected it to the process of modernization. The films used grounding shots of the natural environment, animal life, and the indigenous population situated in those contexts. Once those associations had been fixed, the European element was introduced usually around some specific project or dilemma in need of resolution. Those objectives or problems were cast across a wide spectrum encompassing conservation (of wildlife and land), facilitation of Western education, improvements in health, infrastructure development, political maturation, and so forth. The resolution to any problem centered on the coming together of Africans and Europeans in a manner whereby the outsider accepted the humanity of the indigenous people as well as the legitimacy of their culture and the African embraced modernity as defined by the European. The narrative usually concluded with a harmonious movement into the future where only benefits awaited both Europeans and Africans. The composition of the scenes generally involved long shots allowing the viewer to absorb the specificity of the tale that was unfolding as well as the majesty of the subjects who enacted the drama. Unlike earlier films (such as the Tarzan movies) that were discouraged in the 1950s, the new colonialist cinema favored bright lighting, open spaces, and slower plot development that allowed for greater character development (within imperially determined limits).[66] It was crucial that African and extra-African audiences could each relate to the regime of representation projected on the screen while at the same time absorbing the message embedded in the narrative structure. The product had to speak an intelligible cinematographic language or it would fail in its purpose and risk sowing the kind of confusion in film viewers that Delavignette warned against.

One film that received the support of the high commissioner's office in French West Africa was a production by the Swiss firm Studio Realizzazioni industriali fotocinematographiche (RIF) for their treatment "Civilisation européenne en Afrique." In presenting its argument as to why the colonial government should support the making of its film (with financing as well as the use of locals and permission to shoot it on location) the company declared that "the Europeans who live in Africa have a mission to accomplish and a program to complete. The conditions of life among the primitives subsisting in the interior of the territory justifies completely and morally this mission." The tenor of this introduction, while perhaps pleasing to French officials in the federation, was nonetheless archaic when viewed in light of the shift in the direction they had taken with regard to representation in films. However, the fuller elaboration of the proposed film converged with those redefined image parameters. Studio RIF's proposal went on to observe that "it has become commonplace to say that the European has not done anything but 'exploit' the local populations: On the contrary [the European] has made more useful the treasures held in the forests or buried in the desert; the European also has ameliorated the way of life of the primitive populations, this manner of living which was incompatible with the social morality of the twentieth century." For the coup de grace, Studio RIF summed up its objectives as follows: to make a film that would show "the aspects of primitive life that survive in the interior of the territory," "the public works achieved and others that are in the process of being executed," and "a modern village with its school, its hospital, its organizations of social assistance." The CFCC reviewed the treatment and granted its permission on 19 December 1957.[67] I could not determine whether the film was actually shot, since the archival record goes cold in the following year. Moreover, movie databases do not contain any reference to a film by that title released in those years. Likely the proposal came too late in the day to be realized, as just over two years later the federation's territories gained political independence.

What is important for the current purposes is the manner in which such proposals were handled by the colonial state in comparison with other films that it banned or censored in the same period. A treatment such as the one advanced by Studio RIF fit within the cinematographic language favored by French officials in the federation while at the same time calling it into being through the production and distribution process. Significantly, the film was to be set in the village life of some unnamed community in the interior of French West Africa. The backdrop enabled the kind of "authentic" shots necessary to validate it as an "African" film portraying the "reality" of life among the local population. Such a setting would contain nature shots, landscapes, shots of daily life, and most importantly shots of the interaction between Europeans and Africans as they navigated the complexities of the transition from primitive to modern, or the entrance to the twentieth century as Studio RIF's proposal put it. Finally, the film was to follow the favored story logic detailing how the initial resistance of the Africans was overcome by the establishment of mutual comprehension and led to the formation of a "modern village" that had all the accouterments of "civilization" but that remained firmly "African" in its essence. Such a film, had it been made, would have fulfilled the requirements sketched by colonial officials that the films it sponsored be intelligible to African and non-African audiences alike. It would have "corrected" the prevailing image of an Africa as backward as ever after half a century of French rule while also showing the subject population that an African modernity was possible and desirable, under European direction.

Another proposal acted on favorably by the CFCC, but very late in the colonial period, was that put forward by Films Pierre Cellier Dakar on 2 January 1959. Beginning with the same premise as the earlier film treatment by Studio RIF, this company explained that "with regard to our modern world and of the effects of its civilization, Africa still remains in our century one of the continents where one finds the ageless life of eternal nature.... One still finds some tribes with primitive morals. All this beauty of nature, concretized by the life that takes place within it, gives to Africa an attraction such that some spectators go there from all points of the world to play with the spectacle that it offers to them." Films Pierre Cellier Dakar wanted to make a movie that centered on a "hunt" during which Westerners battled "great beasts." However, lest the colonial authorities thought this was to be a typical colonial film from the interwar period the treatment's authors reassured them that this story cast the Westerners as dilettantes who threatened Africa's future by indiscriminately killing off the wildlife and thereby disrupting the natural way of life of the locals, actions that consequently undermined the civilizing mission by causing disorder as well as discredited the work of "good Europeans" in Africa. The film's ultimate message was about the need to "safeguard" Africans' way of life (and the civilizing mission) as well as to "conserve" the natural world that was the context within which local cultures had been shaped and modernity must develop.[68] As with the Studio RIF proposal, it is unlikely this film was ever made, given that it came at a time of tremendous upheaval in the federation as well as in France itself. Nevertheless, it confirms that the colonial state had effectively articulated a film language it found appropriate for its purposes in the region.

Beyond viewing cinema as a language and developing a particular colonialist movie grammar, the federation's government took the idea of language in film literally and wanted to make sure that French was promoted through the cinema industrial complex as the lingua franca of the region. Thus the idiom of the dialogue became a major point of concern for colonial officials as they engaged in the cinematic field during the late colonial period. In fact, this dimension of the regime of representation constructed as part of the cinema industrial complex in the 1950s formed one of the most important structural barriers to the development of an independent African cinema in the postcolonial period. According to a statement published in 1949 by M. Bouruet-Aubertot in the *Bulletin du Conseil économique* for French West Africa, "The cinema serves, notably in the Overseas Territories, as a means for the expression and the diffusion of the French intelligence and thought." Film should be used, he wrote, as a force "uniting the French people and those of the territories of the French Union."[69] The primary means through which French thought would be spread and the unity preserved between the metropole and its colonies was in the promotion of the French language as a vehicle of culture and a mode of communication defining the parameters of a Francophone world.[70]

The colonial government's concern with the language of the dialogue in films screened throughout West Africa went beyond the mere censorship of films in

Arabic (perhaps the most dangerous language from the perspective of those officials) to the actual promotion of cinema as a means of drawing larger sections of the population into the French-speaking universe. Through such a development, the modernizing projects envisioned by the administration could be surreptitiously promoted and Africans would come to see those processes as their own, a basic tenet of the reconceptualized imperial mission with regard to the cinema in the 1950s. As the French West African economic council stated days after Bouruet-Aubertot offered his assessment, "The cinema will be for [France] the best agent for propaganda and for the expansion of French thought." The council even outlined the full scope of the representational framework that the colonial administration was on the path to articulating, suggesting that "First of all, the production of films must be established according to the principle of converging with the mentality of the different populations. There could be envisioned certain productions with the participation of the ... autochthonous populations, on the [subject of] local history, art and dance, singing, the [daily] activities of the populations, etc."[71] That explication of the representational aspect of the cinema industrial complex could just as easily have been uttered by Delavignette, and coming as it did in the year that *Paysans noirs* was released, it constitutes an endorsement of the type of motion picture officials throughout the imperial hierarchy embraced as a model in their film politics.

However, merely dubbing foreign language films into French was insufficient to achieve the objectives envisioned by the government in the federation. In fact, dubbed films often aroused the suspicion and approbation of the CFCC. John Belton discusses the epistemological problems of dubbing in his analysis of the impact of technology on the aesthetics of filmmaking, noting that " dubbing, and especially the dubbing of foreign films in which one language is seen spoken but another is heard, is 'read' by audiences as false. . . . The rather obvious intervention of technology involved with dubbing severely circumscribes our faith in both sound and image, provoking a crisis in their credibility."[72] For French officials, dubbing failed to achieve the double objectives of promoting the French language and preventing the spread of surreptitious and potentially seditious speech through the nuances contained within other vernaculars. In dubbed films, the overlaid language often appeared alien and inauthentic. Moreover, viewers could still follow the original language by reading the lips of the actors on the screen, if they were versant in that idiom.

Particularly troubling to many officials charged with regulating the cinema was the problem of dubbing Arab language films into French. This was especially vexing because "commentaries in the Arab language" often contained allusions that were "hostile or at least unfavorable to the cause of countries which, like France, administer Arab populations."[73] French colonial rulers and their metropolitan counterparts imbued language with almost mystical powers. The words not only carried culturally specific meanings; the linguistic structure conveyed the national spirit as well.[74] Consequently, the superimposition of French narration over a foreign (in this case Arabic) dialogue created a double alienation—the overlaid dubbed language came off as artificial and disconnected from the action on the screen, while the original idiom remained decipherable for knowing audiences (even if silenced in the unfolding scenes) and manifested itself as the antithesis to the imposed mode of expression. A dialogic cinema text was forged that enhanced the resistance credentials of the feared language at the same time that it diminished the authoritative voice (literally in this case) of the added dialect.

Mikhail Bakhtin offers an explanation of the dialogic nature of language that is useful for the current discussion: "Images of language are inseparable from images of various world views and from the living beings who are their agents—people who think, talk, and act in a setting that is social and historically concrete."[75] The dialogic nature of language for Bakhtin results from its temporal conversational essence. Language is a dynamic element of human consciousness in that it is shaped by the past while also shaping the past through interpretive acts ensconced within the meaning of specific words. Language contains within it the experiences of the linguistic community and simultaneously gives meaning to the present. The problem that confronted colonial officials in West Africa was that the superimposition of French over another language brought together two different cultural frameworks in an oppositional context masquerading as a synthesis. The audience was made conscious of the artificiality of the French dialogue, which thus exposed the fraudulent claims of the civilizing mission. The dubbed film became a realistic representation of the fundamental imperial relationship in which French power and culture were overlaid on indigenous cultures in a manner that sought to erase the local traditions but in so attempting only reified them in an oppositional manner.

French administrators in West Africa could not ban the screening of dubbed films in any practical sense. Dubbed movies at least offered the possibility of exposing audiences to the imperial language, even if it was a poor substitute for having original French films. Censors in the federation routinely authorized dubbed movies from Hollywood and Europe. However, officials took a jaundiced view of dubbing Arab language motion pictures and generally concluded the dangers far outweighed any potential benefits in showing those films, no matter how innocuous the subject matter.[76] Throughout the late colonial era French rulers in West Africa feared Arab and African nationalism more than any other political force that could challenge their hold on the region. The promotion of French cultural values through the language and images that constituted the representational framework of the cinema industrial complex became the main antidote to such threats.

During the late stages of colonial rule officials in French West Africa and the metropole had struggled to articulate a new regime of representation that accorded with the altered imperial mission following the Second World War. From Delavignette to Pinay, and from Mitterrand to the members of the CFCC in the federation, agents of the imperial nation-state sought to harness the power of moving pictures to the project of image/reality construction both in the overseas territories and in the wider world. The racist tropes of the image-Africa that permeated films prior to 1945 subverted French rule in the region on two levels. First, their pervasive portrayal of Africans as stuck in a primordial past denied the "progress" wrought through the civilizing mission, thereby undermining the legitimacy of the colonial project. Second, such images fueled opposition among the subject population, who sought to wrest control of their own image construction from the imperialist rulers. French officials wanted to articulate a new representation for Africa and Africans that spoke to the beneficence of colonial rule while also imbricating the colonized in the project of the construction of their own Francophone African modernity. In their search for a representational model for cinematic practice administrators in West Africa embraced *Paysans noirs*. The film not only encapsulated the imagined reality of the situation in the region but called it into being through the action portrayed on the screen. In addition, the movie had the advantage of exemplifying the materialist component of the cinema industrial complex through its funding mechanisms, the manner of the film's production, and the use of locals as actors.

The African modernity French rulers sought to shepherd into existence depended on the articulation of a cinematographic language as well as the promotion of French as the lingua franca of the federation. The idiom of colonialist cinema involved structuring the film through extensive shots of African scenery and daily life, close-ups of indigenous people, and deliberate (even slow) pacing. The narrative typically progressed from an idyllic moment disturbed through the imposition of tyranny or the violation of tradition that led to disorder and oppression and that precluded the further development of the local culture. Subsequently, a French official arrived, who conveyed the sense that his being there constituted a moral sacrifice on his part and who was determined to *really* understand the indigenous community. In the course of such careful investigation, the official often found collaborators among the autochthonous group, and together they overcame the forces constraining the culture. In terms of the actual dialogue, where possible use of French was encouraged as a vehicle through which the ideas, values, and practices associated with modernity could be transmitted to the indigenous population. Consequently, by the late colonial era French officials had elaborated a regime of representation and materialist context that structured the cinema industrial complex in a manner designed to preserve the metropole's power in the federation. Simultaneously, those parameters were shaped by the engagement of African cultural activists and moviegoers who sought to reclaim their sovereignty in both representational and materialist terms. The story now turns to the elaboration of that anticolonial African film politics in West Africa during the 1950s.

3 West African Anticolonial Film Politics, 1950s–60s

In 1959 at the Second World Congress of Black Writers and Artists, convened in Rome, Italy, Paulin Soumanou Vieyra issued a bold proclamation: "We want a cinema in the service of the people." For Vieyra, the appropriation and adaptation of the cinema industrial complex in West Africa was crucial for the region's (and Africa's) economic and cultural development. "Film, in this domain," he explained, "has some enormous responsibilities in our land." Vieyra conceived of the production of African motion pictures as a "motor" for economic progress, a means for allowing "the African people to acquire a more just notion of their own condition" and as a way, through the export of those commodities, "to represent the true face of Africa" with "authentically national films."[1] In other words, Vieyra led the call for Africans to articulate an anticolonial film politics that would transform the region's emergent cinema industrial complex into an agent for the emancipation of subject peoples and the construction of modern African societies. In the mid-1950s he became one of the founders of West African cinema, and by the late 1960s he had clearly emerged as a central figure in the adumbration of African film practice and theory.

Vieyra can be viewed as occupying the countervailing position in the postcolonial period to Delavignette's in the colonial period with respect to the elaboration of a colonialist film politics. He became such a force in the definition and building of the tradition of West African filmmaking that the journal *Présence africaine*, which had played an important role in galvanizing resistance to French rule in the late colonial period, devoted an entire issue in 2004 to him in celebration of half a century of African cinema. Vieyra captured the spirit of the age and had the prescience to locate cinema at the center of the anticolonial struggle as well as to identify its potential as a key component of (re)constructing African cultures and economies after independence. Vieyra conceived of the cinematic field as structured around the conjoined notions of materialism and representation, and he argued that Africans had to offer a counterpoint to the extant practices instantiated by the imperial nation-state. A cinema in the service of the people had to be the antithesis to a cinema in the service of empire and in so doing transform the cinematic field of engagement along with African societies.

In this chapter, the focus shifts to the strategic counterhegemonic film politics that African cultural activists elaborated in the transition from the late colonial to the early postcolonial period. Commenting on this formative age for African cinema, Françoise Pfaff observes that "in order to challenge hegemonic Western iconography and assert their African identity, committed Black directors set out to emphasize Africa's cultural worth and diversity—historical, political, social, ethnic, cultural, ideological, and geographical."[2] However, it was not at all clear at the time what an African cinema aesthetic would look like or on what it would be based. Throughout the late 1950s and 1960s African theorists and cineastes debated what an African film and cinematic practice would and should be, just as French colonial rulers had debated the essence of their film aesthetics.

African practitioners of the seventh art originated their tradition within the existing parameters of the cinema industrial complex as it was forged during the colonial period on materialist and representational grounds. Those boundaries constrained the range of possibilities for filmmakers like Vieyra and Sembène and also provided the markers against which change to the field could be measured. For the African cineastes of the first generation engaging with the repressive structures of the materialist element of the cinematic experience was inseparable from transcending the derogatory (mis)representation of the image-Africa that dominated movie screens around the world. To forge a film praxis that could contribute to the fight of overcoming the colonial legacy and contribute to the development of an emancipated Africa, those cultural activists involved in motion picture production had to question the extant cinema industrial complex as such.

In examining the elaboration of an anticolonial film politics in West Africa, the insights of the cultural critic and theorist Theodor Adorno are particularly useful. According to J. M. Bernstein, Adorno approaches the culture industry from "the perspective of its relation to the possibilities for social transformation. The culture industry is to be understood from the perspective of its potentialities for promoting or blocking 'integral freedom.'"[3] Adorno posited the concept of "integral freedom" in a 1936 letter to Walter Benjamin wherein he discussed the fragmenting and alienating aspects of capitalist modernity as manifested in cultural practices, specifically with reference to the divide between "high art" and "industrially produced consumer art." The "freedom" produced by this fragmentation generates structures of "integration and domination" that undermine the existential and epistemological liberty that Adorno, Benjamin, and other cultural critics in the Frankfurt school believed was vital for transcending social inequality and realizing the capacity for the development of the person.[4] With regard to the specific place of motion pictures in this process Adorno states, "Film suggests the equation of technique and technology since, as Benjamin observed, the cinema has no original which is then reproduced on a mass scale; the mass product is the thing in itself."[5] Cinema, accordingly, is unique among the modern arts in that it is simultaneously industry and art. Unlike other expressive forms of the modern age, cinema is by its nature a transcendent art in the sense that it can bridge the divide between high and consumer art as well as between materialism and aesthetics. Following the Second World War, colonial officials grasped this essential dimension to filmmaking; it formed the basis for the elaboration of their film politics, which was designed to perpetuate imperial rule by constraining the emancipatory potential of filmmaking. It was also something identified by Vieyra, thereby making cinema an important component of the unfolding liberation struggle in West Africa.

On the special character of film Adorno further notes that "there can be no aesthetics of the cinema, not even a purely technological one, which would not include the sociology of cinema." As has been suggested in the previous chapter with regard to Delavignette's analysis of the process whereby films are consumed by their audiences, in the making or examination of motion pictures the viewers are elemental to the product's construction. One must take into consideration the audience as a component of the cinematic experience. That interaction between the movie projected onto and from the screen and its reception by the patrons in the theater, though, becomes a constitutive space of specific discursive practices. This brings the analysis back to the discussion of "film language" and film as a linguistic form. As Adorno again observes, "Technology in isolation, which disregards the nature of film as language, may end up in contradiction to its own internal logic."[6] Consequently, cinematic practice had to involve a conscious attention to celluloid syntax as articulated through the interaction of the conveyance of the author and the interpretation by the end users. Just as colonial administrators sought to control the space between projected image and audience in order to direct interpretation toward goals that would sustain the existing power relations within West Africa and between the region and France, so too anticolonial activists wanted to seize that zone and reorient the cinematic experience in such a way that it contributed to the liberation of Africa/Africans and by extension humanity in general.

In recent decades scholars have paid more attention to the centrality of culture in the decolonization process, especially with regard to Africa. However, that turn has often occluded film, seeing it only as an aspect of the postcolonial period. Diawara argues that Francophone African film production was completely precluded during the period of French rule through the restrictions that can be traced back to the 1934 Laval decree. Thus, according to him, Vieyra's work in the 1950s, serves as an indication of the degree to which cinema was marginalized as an aspect of the struggle to end colonial rule.[7] Ukadike draws more explicit connections between the advent of African cinema and the colonial era, but in doing so he preserves the barrier between the colonial and postcolonial periods, arguing that black African filmmaking emerges "out of the excitement of nation-building and a quest for the revivification of Africa's lost cultural heritage and identity, a quest that has inspired innovative and creative diversification in the cinema and the arts."[8] This was certainly one of the critical aspects to the development of African filmmaking. However Ukadike's approach rests on a unidimensional reading of the cinema that confines it to the plane of representation and makes no reference to its materialist underpinnings. Moreover, the connections he finds between independent African cinema and that of the colonial era are sequential; independent African cinema followed on colonial cinema and challenged colonialist conceptions of the image-Africa *only* after independence was realized. According to this logic, African filmmakers' articulation of an anticolonial film politics, ironically, takes place entirely after colonialism has formally ended. Cham offers the same perspective when he argues that "African film-making is in a way a child of African political independence. It was born in the era of heady nationalism and nationalist anticolonial and anti-neocolonial struggle."[9] None of these perspectives account for the emergence of an anticolonial African film politics in the 1950s that provided the conceptual context within which some of the first African films were actually produced.

Recently, Kenneth Harrow has put forward a radical rethinking of this early period of African cinema that not only retemporalizes the history of African film but also challenges the very foundations of the film politics at the heart of that production. In arguing for a revisiting of "the beginnings of African filmmaking" he suggests that "we may now ask what limitations these beginnings might have contained, what price was paid for the approaches then taken, and whether we are still caught in those limitations (if not traps) today." All are worthy points of entry into the analysis of the origins of African cinema. However, Harrow's approach posits the source of the "traps" in which African filmmaking is caught as being the first generation of cineastes like Sembène and Hondo. But the choices made by West African filmmakers in the 1950s and 1960s cannot, I argue, be divorced from the materialist and representational context within which they were made. Thus, the colonialist film politics that dominated cinematic practice in the late colonial era had to be explicitly referenced and combatted if any alternative tradition of motion picture production was going to be possible in West Africa. This was precisely what Vieyra, Sembène, Hondo, and others of the period attempted to do, contra Harrow, who argues that their work "has to be understood as continuing . . . the incomplete project of colonialism, which is still felt in issues concerning race, the normative dominance of so-called modern values, and Eurocentric definitions of self and other along lines of modern and primitive, or modern and traditional."[10] Harrow's account of the founding of African film, misunderstands, I suggest, the nature of the project undertaken by those active at that time. It undervalues the real contribution that they made to film practice generally as well as to the fight for an independent African cinema against intractable forces determined to prevent it, as Diawara points out in his study.[11]

This chapter maps the anticolonial African film politics that cultural activists devised amid the struggle to achieve political independence and to launch a process of social, economic, and cultural development that would serve the interests of the people in West Africa. Figures such as Vieyra and Sembène worked within extant materialist and representational structures constructed to benefit the imperialist system. Consequently, they had to articulate a vision that convinced others in the struggle for liberation that the cinema could be a vital mechanism for reaching their aspirations of situating a free Africa in the modern world as well as for shaping a distinct African modernity. This entailed a willingness among Vieyra and his cohort to engage with France on a terrain the metropole had worked systematically to define, constrain, and direct. They had to do so without the benefit of state power, ready access to technology, capital, and experience and in the absence of any prospect the monopoly distribution chains would screen their films. In other words, the pioneers of West African filmmaking functioned in a guerrilla environment with the odds stacked decidedly against them. What they lacked in material they compensated for with vision and tenacity. Not surprisingly, they found inspiration and support in the emergent cinematic schools of Italian neorealism, Latin American Third Cinema, and the established tradition of Soviet cinematography. However, African anticolonial film politics was not a copy of any external cinematic practice. Vieyra, Sembène, Hondo, and others of the first generation forged a distinct foundation for African cinema that engaged with wider global trends while drawing explicitly on local experiences. First, though, the story turns to the struggle within the anticolonial movement in West Africa to elevate the cinema industrial complex to a central position of consideration in their struggle.

From Literature to Film

"For the first time in history, the black writers and artists are going to take the initiative to meet each other and to appreciate their situation and their specific responsibilities in the world." With those words Alioune Diop and the editorial board of *Présence africaine* launched an appeal for an international congress of cultural activists from throughout the African diaspora to gather in Paris in 1956 to discuss their role in the unfolding drama to end colonialism and racism around the world. What was, the announcement asked, "the responsibility of the man of culture[?] He is the animator of modern society, seeing that he has the mission of clarifying the cultural vocation of each man, that is to say of revealing and developing in each one the sense of solidarity with the men of the world." Diop added that "the task returns to them of describing and defining the genius of their people."[12] For nearly ten years the circle of West African intellectuals associated with the journal *Présence africaine* had been organizing resistance to the colonial state's efforts to articulate an imperialist regime of representation. Through the pages of their journal, the publishing of African writers (poets and novelists), and the sponsorship of conferences (such as that called for in 1956), intellectuals like Diop had been seeking to forge their own counterhegemonic image-Africa and to wrest control of its adumbration from the French imperial nation-state. However, until the late 1950s, cinema had been largely absent as an identified terrain of anticolonial struggle. It took Vieyra's intervention to begin to change that situation.

Throughout the period during which the French imperial nation-state honed its film politics in West Africa, the contributors to *Présence africaine* centered their fight on defining the essence of an emergent African literary tradition. Almost all of that conversation dealt with the regime of representation and the kinds of genres that would be consanguineous with African cultural practices. Materialism entered the equation almost exclusively in discussions about classical economic development—promotion of heavy industry, infrastructure, and so forth. Rarely did these conversations consider representation and materialism together. Moreover, materialist questions were often relegated to secondary importance on the assumption that reclaiming one's cultural identity was a necessary precursor to meaningful economic development, which could only follow on the attainment of political independence. Thus, issues concerning the manner in which Africa and Africans were portrayed in literature were paramount in the debates published in the pages of *Présence africaine*.[13] As the statement of purpose in the inaugural issue of the journal explained, of the three dimensions at the core of its mission, "the second, the most important in our eyes," was to be "constituted by African texts (novels, news, poems, theater pieces, etc.)."[14] The overarching concern of those running the journal was dealing with the regime of representation that until then had largely demeaned or ignored the place of Africans within the human patrimony.

The direction in which Diop and his cohort wanted to move the image-Africa within that field was similar to the one promoted by Delavignette at about the same time. As the editorial board of *Présence africaine* outlined it, "Incapable of entirely returning to our original traditions or of assimilating to Europe, we had the feeling we were forming a new race, mentally mixed, but which was not aware of its originality and had not become self-conscious. Uprooted? We were precisely to the degree that we had not yet defined our position in the world and [because] we were stranded between two societies, without recognized meaning in either one, foreigners to both."[15] What Diop and his associates proposed was the pursuit of an African modernity that drew inspiration from their own roots and blended in aspects of European society to create something new. They were to be the architects of their own development, with contributions from the outside. This closely approximated Delavignette's approach outlined in chapter 2 with the important qualifier that Diop's objective was not to maintain the existing relations of power between France and West Africa but to overturn them and fully restore sovereignty to Africans. The autochthonous population would completely direct the construction of their unique form of modernity without the paternalistic guidance of France.

However, while Delavignette and his colleagues within the imperial hierarchy embraced film as the most appropriate medium through which to promote their project of African modernity, Diop and *Présence africaine* advocated the development of an African literary tradition as a marker of the continent's entry into the modern world. It was, in the end, an effort to replicate the presumed process whereby European national identities formed in the modern period.[16] Guided by that idea, the journal played a crucial role in promoting the literary work of African writers and can be credited as a major force in the rise of the West African novel in the 1950s. Many writers first appeared in print in the pages of *Présence africaine* or saw their books published by its publishing house. As V. Y. Mudimbe notes, "*Présence africaine* succeeded in organizing a new literary and intellectual space for a 'surreptitious speech.' . . . [The journal] could appear to signify the unthinkable: an otherness spatializing itself from a nowhere which cannot be but a utopian project. In effect, its surreptitious voice faces Western culture in the name of an absolute alterity; yet this very alterity seems to spring from the Western space."[17] Conceptually, that was not far removed from Delavignette's idea for an effective film. It had to both embody an extant reality while actualizing a desired reality in which viewers were to locate themselves. The audience was expected to both recognize themselves in the portrayal on screen and also become the altered image projected to them. Similarly, the literary images promoted by *Présence africaine* reflected a "real" Africa while also offering an idealized modern Africa to be brought into being through the act of writing and the interaction of a literary public with the printed text.

For Diop and his associates at *Présence africaine* the promotion of a West African literary tradition was a central marker of Africa's modernity. The movement from orality to literariness as its form of cultural expressiveness signaled Africa's assumption of its place among the modern societies. As I have argued elsewhere, the advent of the West African novel in the 1950s coincided with and reflected the rapid urbanization of the societies in that region, along with all the social changes connected to that process.[18] Consequently, many of the themes expounded on in the early West African novels focused on urban struggles (labor strikes, education, assimilation, migration) and the conflict between tradition and modernity. These same issues were prominently debated in the pages of *Présence africaine* throughout the 1950s. The objective of many writers, among them Sembène, was to create the "new" Africa by translating their heritage into a modern form that also borrowed from the outside. There would still be a place for traditional expressive forms, but they would no longer occupy a centrally determining role in the articulation of prevailing cultural values and in the projection of the trajectories for future development. As Bogumil Jewsiewicki observes, "Narration and its written form distinguish it from the 'recited' and oral history, and make literate intellectuals out of the modern griots of the new nations (who pride themselves just as much on their being guardians of tradition), thereby leaving to the traditional griots only the archival role, only the technicality of positive history vouching for objective truth." He adds that the crucial move undertaken by the intellectuals around *Présence africaine* was to translate "the oral into the written."[19] However, the *Présence africaine* group did not simply substitute the literary for orality. Mildred Mortimer notes that "in Africa, orality and literacy often inhabit the same space." African writers like Camara Laye or Sembène often described themselves as writers who were reinventing expressive traditions in modern forms. The link between orality and literacy was, consequently, a distinguishing feature of the West African novel, helping to mark off its cultural specificity. In her work on the Francophone West African novel, Mortimer highlights "the importance of cultural blending in a literary tradition that owes a great debt to the spoken word."[20]

However, the strategy of promoting literary forms as the vehicle for engaging with colonialism on the terrain of representation had fundamental weaknesses that the imperial nation-state had already identified when it decided to articulate a film politics for West Africa. Sembène and other writers in the 1950s produced original works that valued African contributions to the forging of their own destiny and that countered prevailing negative tropes of the image-Africa, but they did so in the idiom of the colonizer. Moreover, their intended African audience—those expected to recognize themselves in the text and be motivated to take on the identity projected in print—was largely illiterate and would not actually constitute the readership for the works published through *Présence africaine*. The real consumers of those products were either those handfuls of Western-educated Africans living in Paris or in West Africa, many of them working in administrative jobs or as teachers in French language schools, or French intellectuals who had come to identify themselves with the anticolonial cause. Such an audience was, by definition, extremely limited.

Moreover, the linguistic divide between the idiom of the published text and the vernacular of everyday life in West Africa was enormous. As Bennetta Jules-Rosette explains it, "The preference for written literary expression (as opposed to representations in the visual or plastic arts) is a further indication of the tension between conventional artistic strategies and innovative cultural content in the *Présence africaine* movement."[21] While the novel was a new form of cultural expression for West Africans during the late colonial period, it was nonetheless a well-established genre in the Western world and was "conventional" in the sense of not marking a rupture with extant expressive means. It was directly borrowed from the colonizer and even used the language of the imperial power to convey its content. The image-Africa presented within the texts, however, did signal a major intervention in the struggles that had unfolded within the regime of representation and that were intensifying as French power waned after the Second World War. The literary work promoted by *Présence africaine* as well as that inspired by it was an important step in the process of Africans reclaiming their voice from the colonizer and demanding their right to speak on behalf of themselves. No longer would the image-Africa be a construct of exogenous actors alone, if it ever really was. The French would have to contend with their colonized subjects interjecting notions about Africa and Africans that challenged or contradicted those espoused by officials within the imperial hierarchy. In fact, the images of an urban and proletarian Africa permeating the pages of

Sembène's early novels *Black Docker* (1956) and *God's Bits of Wood* (1960) directly refuted the rural and peasant Africa of Delavignette's *Paysans noirs* (both the novel and the film versions).

The problem for West African cultural activists connected with *Presence africaine* was that their interventions in the area of representation did not reach the desired audience. It, therefore, largely failed to convey the African modernity presented in the pages of the novels to West Africans, even if it introduced that alternative image-Africa to extra-African audiences, thereby challenging their preconceptions of Africa and Africans. Not only was the idiomatic language of the narrative inaccessible to most West Africans, but novelistic language was also alien to the experience of most people in the region. As Bakhtin argues, the novel is itself a linguistic structure (much as filmic language is). It is its own means of communication that is distinct in that it arises in specific cultural times and contexts while also calling into being certain ways of being and understanding. Bakhtin writes, "We speak of a special novelistic discourse because it is only in the novel that discourse can reveal all its specific potential and achieve its true depth."[22] I suggest that the specificity of novelistic discourse should not be read as exclusive in its ability to actualize its inherent potential or depth, since, as we have seen, the same argument has been made by Bazin and others with regard to the language of the cinema.

Nonetheless, this does not detract from the argument for a distinct novelistic discourse. As in film, "images of language are inseparable from images of various world views and from the living beings who are their agents—people who think, talk, and act in a setting that is social and historically concrete."[23] The reality portrayed in West African novels like Sembène's *God's Bits of Wood* was deliberately constructed from the raw material of lived experience and repackaged to project and actualize the emergent reality of modern Africa. By taking a historical event like the Dakar-Niger rail strike of 1947–48, a seminal event in the decolonization process, and transforming it into a dialogue about the relationship between tradition and modernity, the urban and the rural, the place of women in the new Africa, foregrounding the role of technology and the machine in that transformation, Sembène effected an important shift in representation that placed Africa and Africans within the temporal space of modernity and decultured the artifacts of industrial society.[24] However, he did so in the idiom of the colonizer. In this case French stands as the "sacred language," in the words of Bakhtin, that is valorized in its deployment by the colonized and consequently instantiates a distance between the expressive dimension of the text and the reality portrayed in its content.[25] The attempt to translate orality into literacy was circumscribed by its translation into an alien language that disturbed orality's function in African society and separated the story from its origin, potentially delegitimizing it among the presumed domestic consumers/producers of the tale.

As Bill Ashcroft, Gareth Griffiths, and Helen Tiffin observe, "One of the main features of imperial oppression is control over language."[26] As I have argued, language in this context designates both the spoken idiom, in this case French, and the syntactic structure of the specific genre, in this instance the novel. Thus, the French-African novel of the late colonial era was doubly constrained in its attempt to fulfill the representational objectives sketched by the authors. Only the elite communicated in the colonizer's idiom, and the syntax did not resonate within the traditional interpretive structures wherein meaning was determined. Thiong'o identifies the problem in the following way: "Unfortunately writers who should have been mapping paths out of the linguistic encirclement of their continent also came to be defined and to define themselves in terms of languages of imperialist imposition." He adds, "Even at their most radical and pro-African position in their sentiments and articulation of problems they still took it as axiomatic that the renaissance of African cultures lay in the languages of Europe."[27] While I argue the writers at the center of the current discussion did not necessarily tie the cultural revival of Africa to European languages, the practice of writing anticolonial prose in the imperialist idiom did effectively blunt the counterhegemonic potential inherent in their literary production.

Despite those limitations, Francophone West African writers in the 1950s provided an important antidote to the hegemonic image-Africa that informed extra-African consumers' understanding of the continent and its peoples. The novels produced by Mongo Beti, Laye, or Sembène during the late colonial period fall into the category of what Bakhtin calls an "intentional hybrid": "Every type of intentional hybrid is more or less dialogized. This means that the languages that are crossed in it relate to each other as do rejoinders in a dialogue; there is an argument between languages, an argument between styles of language. . . . [I]t is a dialogue between points of view, each with its own concrete language that cannot be translated into the other."[28] The combination of the emblematic form of literary modernity (the novel) with the style of orature constituted the basis of the surreptitious dialogic of the French African novel of the late colonial era. Moreover, the projection of an African identity through the French idiom also formed a dialogic relationship. Thus, the novels written by Sembène, Laye, Birago Diop, and others from French West Africa during the 1950s were doubly surreptitious and represented a significant intervention in the representational field as autochthonous writers sought to claim a voice in the articulation of the image-Africa.

Jean Rouch, a French filmmaker who was influential in the early history of African cinema, lauded this emerging dialogic in "Toward an African Literature," an essay he published in 1949 in *Présence africaine:* "Tragically caught between tradition and progress, the African is still groping his way in search of his own style." Rouch identified what he saw as the essential structure of this distinctly African literary style. He explained that it was forged "on one part by the oral literature created, recounted, and transmitted by the man in the bush, and on the other part, by the literature written in the French language, produced by the educated African in our schools or our universities." However, Rouch cautioned that the pressure to conform to French literary standards might result in the sacrifice of the African element of the narrative. African literature had, he claimed, already "lost almost all of its African character." In fact, he suggested, it wasn't "anything other than French literature." Rouch urged African writers to seek their inspiration "in the bush."[29] Rouch's position was thus not appreciably different from that staked by Delavignette with regard to film at about the same time. Rouch's perspective faithfully reproduced the prevailing colonialist ethos.

The issue of language in its dual senses and what constituted an "authentic" African literary form came to a head in the pages of *Présence africaine* in 1954 with the publication of Camara Laye's *L'enfant noir*, which was, ironically, the very year that the French imperial nation-state passed its most sweeping regulations of the cinema industrial complex in West Africa and founded the federation's censorship committee. The debate played out in the pages of the journal through an analysis comparing three novels published almost simultaneously—Laye's *L'enfant noir*, Eza Boto's (Mongo Beti's) *Ville cruelle*, and Abdoulaye Sadji's *Nini, mulâtresse du Sénégal*. It is not the intention here to provide an analysis of the texts themselves. What is significant for the purposes of the current study is the nature of the discussion over what counted as a legitimate African literature, a question that also bedeviled early West African cineastes with regard to film in the 1960s. Like Rouch earlier, the contributors to *Présence africaine* insisted that real African literature should incorporate the traditional mode of storytelling from orature but convey it in a modern form, prose writing. This would forge the representational basis for a modern image-Africa. However, the content of the narrative should also champion social development. Africa and Africans had to be portrayed as moving into the twentieth century, as having concerns and aspirations that were shared by the rest of humanity. Thus, Boto's and Sadji's books that deal with the difficulties of people from rural areas adjusting to life in the city or women struggling to overcome limitations on their freedom imposed by "traditional" society received praise in the pages of *Présence africaine*. Laye's tale of a child enjoying an idyllic life in primordial rural Africa, on the other hand, came in for scathing criticism, including from Beti himself. Only the poet and future Senegalese president Léopold Senghor came to Laye's defense, claiming his work was a perfect illustration and celebration of the African essence.[30]

What is remarkable in the controversy over the nature of the African novel is that the debates centered either on the content of the stories (Laye being criticized for ignoring or being soft on colonialism) or the narrative structure (the basis of Senghor's defense of *L'enfant noir*). Never do any of the critics engage with the question of the idiom in which the tales were conveyed. In this sense, Thiong'o's claim that anticolonial intellectuals assumed that Africa's cultural regeneration would find its expression in European languages rings correct. Partly this reflected the social position from which the writers and critics spoke, being the elite among the subject population largely on the basis of their facility with the French language. In addition, it indicates the absence of a literary tradition in most of the linguistic communities of West Africa, the very problem the writers of the 1950s sought to redress by creating an indigenous literature, albeit in the vernacular of the colonizer.

Delavignette, Lemaire, and others within the colonial administration had, as we have seen, identified the conundrum of the "disconnect" between orature and literariness and strategically embraced visuality through a politics of film as the best means to connect with the indigenous population and maintain the extant power relations in the federation. In his 1949 report, Lemaire explicitly highlighted the importance of the visual image in imparting knowledge to the colonized: "Having business in many cases with those socially organized on the traditional basis of oral culture and [being] more open to the concrete thing than to the abstract thing, it seems that the image is particularly designed for resolving in part the problem herein posed." Lemaire went on to identify the cinema as the best vehicle for achieving France's objectives following the Second World War.[31] Considering the large and rapidly growing audience for motion pictures in West Africa as well as the colonial government's increasing focus on cinema as a means of control in the federation, it is noteworthy that the circle of activists and intellectuals around *Présence africaine* did not intervene in the field of film until late in the saga of decolonization. Initially, Vieyra's was a lone voice among that group insisting on the importance of the cinema industrial complex in the future development prospects for postcolonial Africa in representational and materialist terms.

Vieyra and the Articulation of an Anticolonial African Film Politics

In fact, while *Présence africaine* debated the nature of an emergent African literary tradition Vieyra and a few intrepid pioneers went further and were already embarking on their own excursions into the cinematic field. In 1954 a group of would-be African filmmakers, including Vieyra, came together to form GAC. In conformity with the ever-tightening legislation that defined the cinema industrial complex, the organization petitioned the high commissioner for French West Africa for permission to make a film in the federation about the social transformations taking place among Africans who were attempting to adjust to urban life after migrating from rural areas. Interestingly, that was also the theme of many of the novels held up as models in the critique of Laye's *L'enfant noir*. GAC's project, then, was to transpose a prominent issue presented in the novelistic discourse onto the silver screen. While government officials did not spend much time discussing the merits or demerits of Africans making a movie in Africa about the daily life of indigenous peoples, they did not grant permission for the film to be made in the region.[32] Consequently, the determined cineastes went around the restrictions in the overseas territories and decided to make their film in France about Africans living in Paris adjusting to life in the metropole, a slight modification of their original idea. The result was *Afrique-sur-Seine,* which, as the first film "directed by a black African," inaugurated the history of independent African cinema.[33]

The backgrounds of the artists who formed GAC were not that different from those of most West African writers who emerged at about the same time. As Diawara notes, in 1955 Vieyra became the first African graduate of the prestigious Institut des hautes études cinématographiques (IDHEC) in Paris, France. His collaborators in GAC were also West African students in Paris during the early 1950s, just as *Présence africaine* was emerging as an organizational center for intellectuals from the federation. In fact, Sembène recalls meeting Vieyra frequently at the offices of *Présence africaine* in the mid-1950s, where they exchanged ideas on film, literature, theater, and any number of cultural and political subjects.[34] The early members of GAC included Robert Carristan, Jacques Milo Kane, and Mamadou Sarr, who hailed from territories throughout French West Africa. Born in Benin in 1925, Vieyra attended boarding schools from an early age and lived mostly in Senegal and France from the mid-1930s on. His biography thus closely approximates that of Léopold Senghor, Alioune Diop, and other central figures in the cultural politics of decolonization. Vieyra and his associates who founded GAC, though, turned to filmmaking rather than literature as a means by which to intervene in the field of representation and shape the image-Africa. Vieyra's decision to shift from studying biology at the University of Paris to filmmaking at IDHEC in the early 1950s came at a time when the colonial administration was touting Georges Régnier's adaptation of Delavignette's *Les paysans noirs* as the template for cinematic practice in West Africa.[35] The imperial nation-state's promotion of "docu-fiction" that positioned "real" Africans at the center of presenting and calling into being an African modernity (with French assistance) based on rural traditions helped to frame the field of engagement for filmmaking in the federation. Thus, the formation of GAC was part of the developing dialectic of the decolonization process within the realm of cultural politics.

From the beginning Vieyra was more than "just" a filmmaker. He was also a film theorist and had a broad and incisive conception of the cinema industrial complex. Vieyra, then, embodied and helped to call into being the prototype for the early African cineaste—theorist/artist/activist—playing the counterpart to Delavignette, who represented the colonizers. Vieyra argued that cinema had certain advantages over literature in the fight to restore African independence and dignity. Encouraging the development of an African cinema was a means of overcoming the colonial legacy in both the materialist and representational realms. Moreover, within the regime of representation film had the added advantage of being able to actually reach the targeted audience and have a wider impact in the general process of (re)constructing the image-Africa for local and global viewers. As Vieyra put it, the cinema, more than written literature, is "among us Africans

... remarkably useful for destroying the 'pious falsehoods' of colonialism and to remake the spirits according to another ethic, another conception of values."[36] This edge was identified early on by officials within the colonial government and was the basis for their articulation of a film politics as a means of preserving the relationship of power in postwar West Africa. When GAC petitioned the federation's government in 1954 to make a film in the region about the adjustment to urban life among migrants from the countryside, it posed a counterpoint to the theme of rural development by African peasants, a distinct African modernity, that was at the center of France's reconceived civilizing mission and portrayed in the film *Paysans noirs*. This was not the kind of future Delavignette and others envisioned for West Africa. The Commission du cinéma d'outre-mer's decision to deny permission for Vieyra's group to realize their vision was not surprising.

The result of the decision to move production to Paris in the face of this denial was, in some ways, a more powerful indictment of colonialism than the original film might have been had approval been granted to make it in West Africa. It is a misstatement to claim, as Mweze Ngangura does, that "African cinema was born in Europe [since] Paulin Soumanou Vieyra . . . and all its pioneers were trained there." While the members of GAC were trained in France, their roots were decidedly West African and their original idea was to situate the film squarely in the federation in order that it might serve as a direct witness to important processes at work in the region that were largely suppressed in the official presentation of developments in the overseas territories. The circumstance surrounding Vieyra's and his colleague's training and the decision to make their movie in France does not indicate an "overweening European influence on African cinema from the outset."[37] Rather, it reflects the conditions of the possible for Africans attempting to make motion pictures in the context of late colonialism. The result was a triumph of the resolve and determination possessed by those intrepid pioneer cineastes in the face of seemingly intractable obstacles.

The film was a docu-fiction that turned the "anthropological gaze" on France. *Afrique-sur-Seine* was, according to Pfaff, "the first time the French capital and its inhabitants were seen through non-Western eyes" in motion pictures.[38] The movie's theme was similar to that explored in much of the literature of the age and later expertly portrayed in Cheikh Hamidou Kane's 1963 novel *Ambiguous Adventure*: "emigration, alienation, and racial discrimination." *Afrique-sur-Seine* centered on the daily activities of African youths who had left West Africa in order to study in France. The camera followed their routine as they strolled along Paris's famous boulevards while reflecting on their condition.[39] In other words, the product was semiautobiographical; it used "real" people playing fictional characters, who were, in the end, themselves and portrayed real-life situations. This motif later became a defining feature of African cinematic practice (a motif to which I return in chapters 4 and 5). The twenty-two-minute short filmed in 1954, released in February

1955, and screened almost exclusively in art houses and campus theaters in Paris transposed the adumbration of an African modernity onto the streets of France's capital but retained the ultimate objective of "returning to the source" and reclaiming sovereignty over the construction of the image-Africa consumed by African and extra-African audiences. Unlike the modernity portrayed in *Paysans noirs*, GAC's African modernity was urban, cosmopolitan, and economically developed. It also eschewed the idyllic portrayal of the future in favor of one that was more ambiguous and that foregrounded the pervasive anxiety Vieyra and his cohort experienced as a result of the multivalent inequality that structured the world system that Africans were determined to change.

Afrique-sur-Seine had one other attribute that paralleled France's colonial film politics: it was shot on 16 mm stock, the size that overseas officials preferred since it was less expensive and more readily available than the standard 35 mm film used in the commercial cinema. The Commission du cinéma d'outre-mer advocated making educational and docu-fiction motion pictures using 16 mm film for precisely these reasons and even encouraged theater owners in West Africa to convert their equipment to facilitate the screening of films made with 16 mm stock. Thus, materially, thematically, and in terms of cinematic language, GAC's foray into filmmaking perfectly intersected with the structural aspects of the cinematic field of engagement in the late colonial era. As Vieyra put it, "We have the technique in the sense of the syntax that forms the cinematographic language."[40] Unlike in the literary realm, West Africa had a large well-educated and experienced film audience that was able to "read" motion pictures, and the region's pioneer cineastes were avid consumers of movies before they became producers of motion pictures. At this early stage, though, the idiom of the film's dialogue still conformed to French expectations that the colonizer's language be the main vehicle of communication (and cultural expression). In that sense, Vieyra's first effort at filmmaking did not radically diverge from the West African literary tradition being forged at that time as well. The added visual cues, however, did open the door to a larger audience than that reached by Beti, Laye, and Sembène through their novels in the 1950s, something French administrators also acknowledged. As Vieyra noted in 1959, "The novel . . . does not sufficiently penetrate among the people. Even in the present, it is necessary that the cinema adapt a work of literature in order to give it a much larger audience."[41] In fact, many of the films made by West African directors in the 1960s were adaptations of literature to the screen.

For Vieyra, though, film's potential in the project of African liberation extended well beyond the regime of representation. GAC, and especially Vieyra, viewed the promotion of an independent African cinema as essential to postcolonial economic development and as a means by which to break free of the dependent relationship France had imposed on West Africa through generations of imperial rule. Thus, the materialist aspect of the cinema industrial complex was inseparable from its representational dimension. Diawara observes that as early as 1958 Vieyra proposed to his colleagues in the circle around *Présence africaine* that West Africa should immediately begin laying the foundations for an independent "African film industry." Diawara writes that Vieyra "argued that the countries of the Communauté Francophone [formed after the 1958 constitutional referendum] should get together to set up an international film center that would have its headquarters in Dakar." Vieyra believed that the new institution should produce "educational, instructional, and feature films" and should be "funded in the beginning by either the governments of the individual countries or by the central government of the Francophone community, or by both."[42] In other words, the financial aspects of the new sovereign African cinema industrial complex would not be that different from what the French imperial nation-state promoted as part of its film politics. It was, on both sides, essential that state resources be put at the disposal of this vital enterprise. Moreover, even the kinds of films envisioned as part of this project were identical to those advocated by the government of French West Africa in its internal discussions of the late 1940s and early 1950s. Vieyra, then, was proposing nothing less than a thoroughgoing challenge to French control of the cinematic field on every conceivable level. As part of that rejoinder, Vieyra pronounced cinema to be the primary vehicle for carrying out a revolution against both the "mores" and economic system inherited from the colonial period, a revolution that would transform the psychological and physical structures that restrained Africa's growth and constrained its cultural regeneration. While he later admitted that cinema was "not decisive" in winning political independence for West Africa, Vieyra still maintained that such an important step "would not have been possible except by the grace of a series of revolts" that the cinema had "all the same in some small way helped to bring about." Once West Africa had achieved political sovereignty, Vieyra claimed film was to play an even larger role in guaranteeing complete decolonization for the region. Specifically, West Africans would "use the cinema in order to develop the economy."[43]

Vieyra also was a major force in framing the questions that became the basis for defining African cinema in the postcolonial period, and his 1958 essay published in *Présence africaine* stands as a significant moment in the early history of West African cinema. In the essay, titled "Remarks on African Cinema," Vieyra launched a discussion on the nature of a "truly African cinema" while also imploring his fellow cultural activists to pick up the camera and begin making films: "We can cite the names of our poets, our novelists, whereas we cannot name any Negro-African cineastes of such renown as Césaire, Sédar Senghor, Rabemananjara, just to cite a few." It was time to forge a cinematic tradition that would equal and complement the body of literary accomplishments of intellectuals from West Africa. Having been determined by the colonial context, Vieyra observed, "the cinema, most often, hasn't done anything but to illustrate this colonialist philosophy."[44] Even the cultural raw material of African societies had been appropriated by imperialists in order to legitimize their ideology and domination. Motion pictures had played an especially important role in that process. As Vieyra explained, Africans' images had been used "to corroborate a racist and colonialist philosophy," which paved the way for the conquest and ongoing subjugation of the continent via outright military action and the more subtle, but no less dangerous, cultural assault from missionaries and intellectuals.

Vieyra then went on to cite the litany of legislation starting with the Laval decree that had greatly restricted the possibility of producing films that gave expression to the real Africa. He even highlighted the shift in colonialist cinema following the Second World War as an insidious effort to perpetuate tropes of the image-Africa that validated continued foreign control and demeaned African societies. Among those "new" films that Vieyra scorned was *Paysans noirs*. He claimed that such motion pictures perpetuated the tradition of a "cinema of exoticism," confirming Stam and Spence's judgment that "'nice' images might at times be as pernicious as overtly degrading ones, providing a bourgeois façade for paternalism, a more pervasive racism."[45] Vieyra also touched on one of the most important advantages that film had over literature and that gave it the ability to be an effective tool in reaching Africans: language. As a fundamentally visual art form that was also based on orature, the problem of communication in the vernaculars could be overcome. As Vieyra put it, "The problem of languages has also been put at the forefront for African films. . . . Cinema, instrument of knowledge, therefore makes it part of the information [network]."[46]

For Vieyra, though, representation was only part of the terrain on which the struggle within the cinematic field had to be fought. As he cautioned, " It does not suffice [just] to produce films; it is still necessary to distribute them." The materialist aspect of the cinema industrial complex was absolutely inseparable from the aesthetic dimension in conceptualizing the role of film in West Africa's process of postcolonial development. Vieyra asserted that an African cinema could not be brought into existence if making movies was not accompanied by the acquisition of the basic technology of filmmaking or the elaboration of a commercial infrastructure controlled by Africans.[47] The aesthetic innovations of African directors would have only a marginal impact if there was not a concomitant elaboration of the materialist infrastructure through which to distribute the new image-Africa and engage with African audiences in the articulation of their own postcolonial identities. Moreover, the film infrastructure would mean little if it was not used to support the work of African cineastes and to promote counterhegemonic tropes of African modernity and culture. Vieyra's notion of the cinema industrial complex was as comprehensive as that imagined by the French imperial nation-state through its film politics. For Vieyra, though, the same field could be transformed through the forceful intervention of Africans, and ultimately cinema, in his view, should be appropriated as a vital part of economic and cultural reconstruction after West Africa's liberation from colonial rule.

Vieyra's essay was part of the preparations for the Second World Congress of Black Writers and Artists scheduled to take place in Rome, Italy, in 1959. The first congress in September 1956 did not touch on film as part of the cultural struggle to end empire. Despite the importance of motion pictures in the entertainment and cultural life of West Africans and the colonial government's acknowledgment of the need to control and direct the cinematic field, the circle around *Présence africaine* remained fixated on debates within the literary terrain.[48] At the conclusion of the first congress, the delegates endorsed a resolution that crucially did not include any mention of economic development or the transformation of the colonial materialist structures that inhibited African growth and modernization. Instead, the declaration called on "black intellectuals and all men who love justice to struggle for the concrete conditions for the rebirth and the full development of Negro cultures."[49] The basic argument advanced by Diop and others at the congress, which also included Delavignette and Rouch as attendees, was that the recovery of African cultures was a necessary precursor to the realization of political independence. Most of the debates at the congress centered on locating the "authentic" nature of "Negro-African civilization," a term invented by French ethnographers early in the colonial era and appropriated by Senghor and others in the *négritude* movement from the 1930s onward.[50]

In anticipation of the next meeting, Vieyra worked to ensure that cinema made it onto the agenda. While the "literature of struggle" continued to dominate the proceedings, film did earn a new respect among the cultural activists at the congress and was publically debated for the first time among the most prominent intellectuals from West Africa. On the program it was placed under part 3, titled "Commission of Arts." Section 3 of that part was "Cinema," one of whose major topics was the "tasks" of African filmmakers.[51] However, the second congress almost did not take place. It was originally scheduled to be held in September 1958, but in the months preceding the meeting the French Fourth Republic imploded under the pressure of the imperialist war it was waging to retain control of Algeria. Thus, the colonial apparatus was even warier than it typically was during the summer and autumn of 1958 about the idea of an assembly that might focus critical attention on France's role in its overseas territories.

As the crisis of the French state reached a crescendo in May and June 1958, the congress's organizers were forced to focus their energies on the rapidly evolving political situation throughout the French union. When Charles de Gaulle, reinstated as president of the republic amid the turmoil, announced that there would be a referendum on his new constitution in October 1958, Diop and his associates at *Présence africaine* had to announce that the congress was postponed until the following year. The main reason they gave was "the gravity of the political circumstances in September" in France and in Africa under French control.⁵²

September 1958 was the month during which de Gaulle and André Malraux, his top lieutenant, went on a tour of the French empire seeking support for their new constitution, which included provisions for transforming the French union into the French community. The vote took place in October, at which time Guinea voted no and promptly attained independence. The rest of French West Africa voted to join the community, but less than eighteen months later all of those territories had become sovereign as well. Therefore, the second congress took place as French rule in West Africa crumbled. The task of postcolonial development was suddenly a matter of the present rather than an aspiration for the future. Vieyra's push to have the cinema industrial complex considered as a central component of those discussions loomed even more significantly than it had when he published his essay the previous year.

The meeting produced a "resolution on cinema" that clarified the African anticolonial film politics that Vieyra had played such an instrumental role in framing. It called attention to the role film had played in sustaining colonialism and stated that "cinema has contributed in the very least manner to unnerve the autochthonous culture of black Africa and was an instrument of propaganda and of indoctrination [that was] often unfavorable to one's self and to the national pride of the African people." Now that the hour of independence had arrived, motion pictures had to be incorporated as part of the project of postcolonial reconstruction. "The constructive utilization of cinema in the interests of African nationalism and of the legitimate cultural, social, and spiritual objectives," it proclaimed, "is a goal of great importance and has to be made a high priority in the efforts of Africans of culture." It concluded that "the cinema is at once an art and an industry, and the realization of a film requires the kind of effort that cannot be supported by any African state by itself, which at the moment cannot produce [more than] one or two complete films a year." Vieyra and his associates at the congress thus urged the delegates to press their countries to "collaborate to make a cinema industry," an industry that would, among other things, establish training facilities and ensure that the market was regulated so as to protect African films. They urged governments to use the revenue from the theaters to contribute to the expansion of West African cinema as well as other aspects of economic and cultural development.⁵³ Later that year Vieyra published another of his seminal essays in *Présence africaine* titled "Responsibilities of Cinema in the Formation of an African National Conscience." In that article, he reiterated the nature of filmmaking as "an industry and an art" while pointing to the historic opportunity before those willing to pick up the camera: "Of all the areas [of activity], film in Africa has an open field, since there does not yet exist an 'African cinema;' I mean by that a cinema imagined, conceived, and realized by Africans."⁵⁴ When Senegal proclaimed its independence in 1960, President Senghor appointed Vieyra as the new government's minister of information and head of the Bureau de cinéma. His primary job was to promote the development of a national cinema industry and to create newsreels for the dissemination of information to the country.

Postcolonial African Film Politics: Cinema and Revolution

After 1960 several West Africans took up Vieyra's challenge and started making movies. That was no easy task, as the French imperial nation-state had not provided the opportunity for many people from the overseas territories to learn the craft of producing motion pictures. One of the first to follow Vieyra in appropriating the cinema industrial complex for the purpose of postcolonial African development was the novelist Ousmane Sembène. Acknowledging the limited reach of his literary production, Sembène turned to making motion pictures, many of which were often adaptations of his written work. Before he could enter the field of filmmaking, though, Sembène needed to acquire the requisite skills. So, in 1961, Sembène journeyed to the Soviet Union, where he spent two years studying at the famous Gorki Studios under Mark Donskoy.[55] His decision to seek training in the Soviet Union resulted from a number of factors. One was certainly Sembène's affiliation with the French Communist Party and his own Marxist views. Another element was the desire to avoid the taint of being associated with the former colonial power. Already in the early postcolonial period some cultural activists raised concerns about the influence that France might exert through the kinds of instruction, funding, and access to equipment which African cineastes would receive from the ex-metropole. Another factor in Sembène's decision to go to the Soviet Union for film training was that country's importance in the history of cinematic theory and technique, both of which appealed to and had resonance among aspiring directors in the recently independent countries of West Africa. This convergence of interests in a specific film style was confirmed in subsequent years as a number of West African filmmakers also made their way to the Soviet Union for instruction in that country's top cinema institutes.[56] For its part, as Josephine Woll notes, the "Soviets recognized a number of parallels, indeed affinities, between the way their own cinema had emerged in the 1920s and later in the studios established in the Central Asian republics, and the cinema of newly independent states in Francophone Africa."[57]

Even in the 1960s the theoretical insights of the great Soviet cinematographer Sergei Eisenstein formed the basis for the kind of knowledge about the role of film in society and cinematic language that Sembène and other West African filmmakers would acquire during their studies. Following the Marxist notion of the dialectic (also evident in Bakhtin's rendering of the dialogic in literature), Eisenstein asserts that "conflict lies at the basis of every art," including motion pictures. The main tension is constituted "between the frame of the shot and the object." The objective in the composition of the shot is the combination of two (or more) "representable objects [that] achieves the representation of something that cannot be graphically represented."[58] This approach to reading film is not far removed from the way in which French colonial officials understood their project. However, in the hands of the agents of the imperial nation-state the camera became a weapon through which foreign rule and the exploitation of the West African communities could be perpetuated by making the indigenous population complicit in their own subjugation. In the hands of revolutionaries, film technology could be used to undermine the structures of inequality that prevented African development. Following Eisenstein's argument, framing was to be the vehicle through which the essential conflicts that structure and move society would be made visible. The revelation of those elements to the audience would then help them to attain a clearer understanding of their own reality (consciousness), which in turn would furnish one of the key tools that would enable them to transcend current conditions and aspire to a future in which the contradictions of the present had been overcome and a new, presumably more just society had been created. Film, according to this approach, had two main goals: to raise consciousness among the viewers by exposing the fundamental order of social relations and to empower the consumer of the images to become an agent for changing those structures.

In addition to having a conceptually innovative cinematography, the Soviets also had a tradition of using motion pictures to reach largely rural and illiterate audiences spread over vast geographic distances. The experience of Soviet filmmakers in the 1920s and 1930s became a lesson in distribution and popular mobilization that West African cineastes in the 1960s found appropriate for their own circumstances. Specifically, the practice of "cinema on wheels" and "open-air" viewings that turned the filmmaker also into a distributor and projector as well not only had application under West African conditions but was also part of the cinematic tradition in the region going back to the interwar period. As early as 1932, local officials complained that enterprising Lebanese and indigenous businessmen were showing films "in open air" to more than one hundred viewers at a time on occasion. Such practices contributed to the calls for greater regulation of the nascent cinema industrial complex that resulted in the promulgation of the Laval decree in 1934.[59] Consequently, the conceptual approach and cinematographic traditions of the Soviet Union presented aspiring West African filmmakers with an attractive and relevant source of training as they moved into the field of movie production.

Beyond the Soviet Union, other international cinematic trends that in their own way built off of earlier Soviet film practices influenced the pioneers of West African cinema. Among the most important were the Italian neorealists and radical Latin American filmmakers.[60] Ultimately, West African directors found much affinity with their counterparts in Latin America during the 1960s, who sought to harness cinema to the project of countering U.S. neocolonial domination of the Western hemisphere. To cineastes like Sembène, Cissé, Hondo, and Vieyra, the role that

France continued to play in West Africa approximated the relationship the United States had with its neighbors in Latin America, and the structural inequalities of the global capitalist system were as much apparent in West Africa as they were in Latin America. Therefore, the historical task of the filmmaker in Cuba, Argentina, or Brazil was similar to the one that Vieyra had identified for West Africa in the 1950s. As Cham notes, "African cinema is part of a worldwide film movement aimed at constructing and promoting an alternative popular cinema, one that corrects the distortions and stereotypes propagated by dominant Western cinemas and that is more in sync with the realities, experiences, priorities, and desires of their respective societies." He adds that some of the most important influences on early West African film praxis included "Third Cinema (Solanas and Getino); Imperfect Cinema (Julio García Espinosa); and Cinema Novo (Glauber Rocha)."[61]

There are some striking similarities between what became Third Cinema and early West African filmmaking. However, it is important to keep in mind that they grew up together, in dialogue. One did not necessarily serve as a model for the other. African cineastes often collaborated and exchanged ideas with Latin American filmmakers; each emergent tradition thus shaped the other. The Third Cinema movement, as articulated by Solanas and Getino blossomed in the late 1960s, by which time West Africans had spent over ten years elaborating their own anticolonial film politics and had begun to establish a unique cinematic tradition tied to local experiences and conditions. Nevertheless, from the late 1960s into the 1970s African cinema and Third Cinema shared much in common in terms of cinematographic language and the conceptualization of the role film was to play in the process of social change and development. Consequently, as the African anticolonial film politics of the late 1950s evolved into a postcolonial West African film politics, the conversation among specific cinematic tendencies became integral to African cineastes' self-definition. African filmmakers ended up influencing international film theory even as global trends shaped African understandings of moving pictures.

In the founding manifesto of the Third Cinema movement, Solanas and Getino describe their approach as "a cinema of subversion" that "prepares the terrain for the revolution to become reality." One of the genres they claim as integral to Third Cinema technique is "witness-bearing films." They particularly endorse the documentary as "perhaps the main basis of revolutionary filmmaking," adding that "every image that documents, bears witness to, refutes or deepens the truth of a situation is something more than a film image or purely artistic fact; it becomes something which the System finds indigestible." Solanas and Getino view films as a "pretext for dialogue, for the seeking and finding of wills. [The film] is a report that we place before you for your consideration, to be debated after the showing.... [I]t is a way of learning."[62] The ideas at the core of the Third Cinema movement certainly resonated among African filmmakers. In the late 1960s Solanas and Getino outlined an aesthetic and political approach to motion pictures that was similar to what Vieyra argued should be the representational basis for an African film politics a decade earlier. Where Vieyra's conception of the cinema industrial complex differed from that of the theorists of Third Cinema was in his equal insistence on the materialist aspects of film production, which I address in chapter 5.

Despite the critical engagement of many African filmmakers with Third Cinema, Anthony Guneratne observes that it has had the "fate of never being treated seriously as a theory." He argues that much of the "marginalization" of Third Cinema within film studies results from "Eurocentric critical perspectives and philosophical impositions."[63] However, part of the difficulty with Third Cinema resides in the ambiguous conflation of "Third World" and "Third Cinema" found in Solanas and Getino's original manifesto, a confusion that has been subsequently reproduced by film theorists aligned with Third Cinema's fundamental revolutionary goals. For example, Solanas and Getino situate the advent of Third Cinema squarely within the "worldwide liberation movement whose moving force is to be found in the third world countries," but later in the essay they broaden its base to include "their equivalents inside the imperialist countries." Finally, they proclaim that in their opinion, Third Cinema is "the cinema that recognizes in that [anti-imperialist] struggle the most gigantic cultural, scientific, and artistic manifestation of our time, the great possibility of constructing a liberated personality with each people as the starting point—in a word, the decolonization of culture."[64] In his seminal study *Third Cinema in the Third World*, Teshome Gabriel argues that "the principal characteristic of third cinema is really not so much where it is made, or even who makes it, but, rather, the ideology it espouses and the consciousness it displays. The third cinema is that cinema of the third world which stands opposed to imperialism and class oppression in all their ramifications and manifestations."[65] In this single passage, then, Third Cinema is variously described as an ideological approach to filmmaking that is capable of being embraced and expressed by cineastes from anywhere making films about any place in the world, in any country *and* as a genre specific to that part of the world identified as the "third world," which is presumed to produce a specific political response to the structural conditions of oppression afflicting those societies.

Guneratne also highlights the tendency found within early proponents of Third Cinema as well as their "First" and "Second" Cinema counterparts to homogenize the Third World.[66] As a result, some film theorists, including Stam, have pushed for a rereading of Third Cinema as constituting "a wide spectrum of alternative practices" that are fundamentally born of the hybrid experiences of a postcolonial and postmodern world.[67] The danger in that approach, however, is that it dissolves the specificity of Third Cinema as both a theoretical system and a cinematic practice. For Third Cinema to have meaning it must be understood according to its internal foundations, as those foundations relate to the explicit analysis of the world system and programmatic objectives contained within Third Cinema's original adumbration and within the context of its origination. As Gabriel notes, "A critical examination of third cinema cannot take place outside of a comprehensive knowledge of the lives and struggles of third world people, in both their past and their present histories."[68] Thus, both the Third Cinema movement and early West African filmmaking have to be understood within the materialist contexts in which they found their voice and which they attempted to alter according to a project of social liberation.

The film that became the standard for Third Cinema practice was Solanas and Getino's *La hora de los hornos* (*The Hour of the Furnaces*), an epic documentary more than four hours in length and divided into three major parts that was released in 1968. The movie is infused with a feeling of urgency that is accentuated by the montage and point-counterpoint style of editing as well as the violent images that pervade the film's sequences. Following Fanon's conception of violence as a cathartic practice in the service of revolution, Solanas and Getino emphasize the violent nature of colonial and neocolonial domination of Argentina from the first arrival of the Europeans in the sixteenth century to the late 1960s. Such a history of domination begets its own violent response as a means of securing the liberation of society and the person in the course of struggle. As noted film critic James Roy MacBean writes, Solanas and Getino "have put together a remarkable film that is *in, of,* and *for* the revolutionary struggle. . . . The making of the film and the making of the revolution became inseparable."[69]

Sembène also embraced the concept of revolutionary filmmaking. In an interview given in 1970 cited by Pfaff, Sembène explained that what interested him was "exposing the problems confronting my people. I consider the cinema to be a means for political action."[70] The cinematic language that Sembène, Vieyra, Hondo, Cissé, and other pioneers of West African film embraced was that of docu-fiction derived from the conventions of orature rooted in local cultures. It approximated what Solanas and Getino call a "witness-bearing film" that raises the social consciousness of the viewer while also suggesting the underlying dialectical process whereby the injustices of the present can be overcome. The Ethiopian/American filmmaker Haile Gerima states that "Third Cinema was to be placed at the advantage of the struggling oppressed peoples; it was to be an activist cinema, and also a cinema of indigenous, dramaturgical origins."[71] It was critical for West African filmmakers to anchor their cinematic language in autochthonous traditions because by so doing their product would be read broadly according to the intentions of the cineaste. Therefore, strategic silences in the narrative, panoramic shots situating the action in geographic context, the dialogic interaction among characters, and the social setting of the drama became characteristic features of early West African film. As Pfaff describes it, Francophone African directors provided "documentary-like depictions of recognizable spaces that they repeatedly include[d] in their works as the primary landmarks of their dialectical argumentation."[72]

Another advantage of the particular cinematographic language West African filmmakers forged was its familiarity to West African audiences, since even the French colonial government had promoted docu-fiction and rooting the style in indigenous traditions as a means of conveying its own message. In other words, West African moviegoers had the requisite experience and skills to accurately read the film presented for their consumption. The task for cineastes from the region was to alter the message conveyed in that narrative structure so that it served the interests of the people rather than those of the imperialist rulers and to present it in the vernaculars of the audience rather than the idiom of the French colonizers. As the Malian filmmaker Souleymane Cissé noted in an interview with Ukadike, "The question of language has been a major concern for African filmmakers, and I have been a strong advocate of the need to respect the languages of various people."[73] Accordingly, the approach advocated by Solanas and Getino of a guerrilla cinema wherein the dialectical structure of the film exposes the contradictions and sources of oppression in society as well as motivates the viewer to take action in order to overcome the repressive system and foster liberation fit with the agenda and circumstances of Sembène and his cohort of early filmmakers in West Africa.

However, representation was only one part of the African film politics Vieyra and others adumbrated in the late colonial and early postcolonial period. While Solanas and Getino confined their notion of Third Cinema largely to the field of image construction, West African cineastes insisted on the materialist dimension of their project as inseparable from the (re)construction of the image-Africa consumed by African and extra-African audiences. Film, they argued, had to be a vital component of an overarching development strategy that would not only elevate the social consciousness of the viewer but also actively transform the institutional and economic structures of their communities in ways that produced economic modernization. As the Mauritanian filmmaker Med Hondo states, "The role of cinema in Africa must be to function as an educational arm for development, for culture and history."[74] With independence, many West African cultural activists hoped that their governments would become partners in appropriating the cinema industrial complex in order to serve their own national interests. On the eve of West Africa's attainment of political sovereignty Vieyra highlighted the role he expected the new states to play in promoting film production and by extension economic expansion. He wrote, "For a State, to organize its industry, whether it will be cinematographic or not, is to affirm its willful independence, it is to pass from the passive stage to the active stage of the producing countries, it is to make itself known to the outside world." With regard to cinema, Vieyra argued that "film is one of the most efficient ambassadors of inter-State understanding since a film always carries with it a piece of its country of origin. The industry, this mechanical side of the cinema, has this role of the responsibility to form technicians, of workers for our march toward progress." Finally, he claimed, "The cinematographic industry is one important part of the activities of modern countries."[75] The French imperial nation-state had long before identified motion pictures as carriers of France's culture to the wider world. Thus, Vieyra's argument rested on solid historical experience and the proven track record of major film exporting countries like the United States and France.

West African filmmakers in the early postcolonial era offered a variety of plans whereby their new governments could use the cinema industrial complex to support economic development as well as their own culture workers. Again Vieyra set the parameters of the discussions that unfolded among cineastes and their appeals to the sovereign states of West Africa. In his presentation to the Second World Congress of Black Writers and Artists in 1959 he argued that the emerging governments should establish "in each village a movie house or houses without delay. But while we are waiting for the implementation of this plan over a five to seven year period—and the cinema can act as a motor element for the rapid electrification of the continent—the cinema on wheels must assure the [distribution] circuits in a regular fashion." He argued for charging villagers to see the entertainment films but for making education and informational movies available gratis. Vieyra also urged the states to establish national distribution companies that would take that element of control out of the hands of the French monopolies, COMACICO and SECMA. The receipts from the theaters could be plowed back into support of the cinema industrial complex—training institutes and higher education programs in the sciences and arts could be built, the work of local filmmakers could be subsidized, and the exportation of the final products could be supported. Vieyra even went so far as to specify that the "maximum length of each viewing should be two hours" in order to prevent the problem of losing the audience's attention. Vieyra implored African governments and cineastes to regard the film director as "a worker like any other"; in Vieyra's view, he or she should be employed like any other laborer contributing to social development. Finally, Vieyra suggested that West Africa's new leaders support the growth of *ciné-clubs,* as the French had done, which would continue to foster the growth of a cinematic culture in the region, and to establish government agencies to compile regular statistics concerning the cinema industrial complex so that the entire field could be better managed and the appropriate needs assessed for further development.[76]

Francophone West African cineastes in the 1960s widely embraced the film politics Vieyra had done so much to formulate in the heat of the decolonization process. As the Burkinabe filmmaker and theorist Joseph Ki-Zerbo, echoing Vieyra, said, "The African cinema must reroot the imagination of the people, by situating its action and its surroundings deliberately in African territory and also utilizing as a matter of principle African languages."[77] This last point was something that the few African films that had been produced by the early 1960s had not yet tackled as a matter of practice. That task was most notably undertaken by Sembène, who became the dominant figure putting into action the African anticolonial film politics articulated in the transition to political sovereignty. His early motion pictures established a framework within which cineastes could forge a distinctive West African cinematographic language and challenge Western control of the regime of representation that heretofore governed the image-Africa presented to and about the continent and its peoples.

However, even Sembène had shoulders on which to stand as he undertook the personal journey from novelist to filmmaker. In the realm of representation and cinematographic discourse films such as *Afrique 50* (1950) and *Les statues meurent aussi* (1953), in addition to *Afrique-sur-Seine* (1955), provided models for the Senegalese filmmaker as he built his oeuvre. They offered examples of the kind of docu-fiction Vieyra advocated as essential to the articulation of an "authentic" African cinema. They were films rooted in identifiable African contexts with "real" Africans engaged in the banality of daily life that aimed at elevating the consciousness of spectators about the circumstances of their oppression so that they could take action to construct a more just society. In other words, they were early harbingers of a cinema in the service of the people that Sembène, Hondo, Djibril Diop Mambety, and others would tenaciously fight to bring into reality during the first decade after independence. The story now turns to this early production of West African motion pictures to examine how these directors forged a distinctive African film aesthetic.

4 The Postcolonial African Regime of Representation

WITH INDEPENDENCE IN 1960 France lost its official control of the cinema industrial complex in West Africa. Technically, the era of the Laval decree and the colonial film politics built on its foundation had come to a close. Consequently, aspiring West African filmmakers had the space to create their own image-Africa for the first time as well as the opportunity to seize the existing materialist structure of the film industry in the region and direct it toward the economic development of the newly sovereign countries. The cultural activists from the region who wanted to make films confronted a long-entrenched heritage as they sought to enter the business of making motion pictures. Sembène summarized the regime of representation against which they had to struggle: "From the birth of the cinema, the African countries have been subjected to the image of the Western cinema and to its rhythmic movement. On the screens of black Africa were often projected nothing but the histories of a dull stupidity, foreign to our existence." Even if Africans had made it into the films, they were often cast "in the role of a servant or of a public entertainer." "For Africa," he concluded, "the *seventh art* was for a long time unilateral in the sense that it did not transport a single portrayal of our universe."[1]

Decolonization presented an unparalleled opening for Africans to retake control of their own image construction. It was time to pick up the camera and present the "real" Africa so that the actual circumstances of life on the ground could be shown to autochthonous audiences in a comprehensible way as a requisite to meaningful and progressive social development.[2] Such representations exported to the rest of the world also would offer a powerful antidote to the extant colonialist tropes of Africanness undergirding the unequal global power structures that perpetuated imperialist-era relationships. What Sembène and his colleagues of the pioneer generation of West African filmmakers proposed was a revolution in cinematographic grammar and syntax, a revolution through the cinematic encounter. As Sembène explained to his fellow cineastes, "We have to be daring and reconquer our cultural and cinematographic space."[3] This chapter tells the story of Francophone West African filmmakers' efforts to found an African cinema aesthetic rooted in their experiences that would also change the global field of motion picture production.

During the 1960s several cultural activists from throughout West Africa took advantage of the end of French rule in the region and turned their cinematic gaze on their own societies. Over the course of the decade Sembène, Hondo, Cissé, Mambety, and others produced the first African full-length feature film along with the first movie in an African language, helped to found the inaugural African film festivals, and finally worked to create an organization of African cineastes charged with promoting the growth of the cinema industrial complex and with using it to spur on the continent's economic and cultural development. Those achievements were remarkable when viewed in the context of the time period. Not only did Vieyra, Sembène, Hondo, and their cohort confront pervasive (even if subtle) negative portrayals of Africa and Africans projected onto movie screens throughout the world, but they also had to articulate a new cinematographic discourse that on one level resonated with local audiences and on another produced a different way of speaking that gave expression to the urgent self-interested aspirations of the same viewing public. In other words, the task of the West African motion picture artists of the 1960s was similar to the one that colonial officials elaborated in the postwar years, except the objectives of each were antithetical. It was Sembène's, Mambety's, Hondo's and others' job to put into practice the anticolonial film politics adumbrated in the late colonial era so that they could transcend the enduring legacies of imperialism in the field of cinematic production.

Along the way differences of aesthetic perspective emerged among the founders of West African cinema. The divergence of opinion among cineastes, though, should not be overstated as representing sharp ideological divisions. Some scholars have exaggerated the differences among the distinct cinematic approaches that West African filmmakers embraced during the 1960s and have implied that they indicate opposed or unrelated tendencies that split the film community and undermined the potential to construct a meaningful African identity in the field of moviemaking. In this regard, Hondo and Sembène often are treated as representatives for two rival film practices. Shaka describes the "Med Hondo school" of filmmaking as locating the source of Western propaganda in both the *content* and *form* of the prevailing "Hollywood" cinematographic discourse. Therefore, the goal of African cineastes was to develop a different and unique "film style" that countered the hegemonic film language in content and form, or in "grammar" and "syntax." On the other hand, Shaka identifies the "Ousmane Sembène school" of filmmaking as arguing for the "destination as the guiding force." On this approach, ensuring that the film was received by the postcolonial African audience in the way the filmmaker intended was the focus. Shaka asserts that Sembène believed the extant cinematic form (usually associated with the West) should be appropriated to serve the interests of West Africa's people. The altered content consumed by the viewers was what mattered; it was the content that gave rise to a distinct African cinematic identity.[4]

The differences between Hondo and Sembène highlight two points of debate among the early West African cineastes. At its heart, a good deal of that conversation concerned the nature of an African film language and the ways in which it differed from the Western tradition from which the autochthonous communities had gained their knowledge about motion pictures. However, it would be a misreading of the actual production of the 1960s as well as the relationship between Hondo and Sembène, not to mention those who could be read as closer to one or the other, to reify those differences as if they represented real ideological or aesthetic conflicts. I argue that Sembène's films were a conscientious engagement and experimentation with cinematic form as well as content. The markers distinguishing Hondo and Sembène, then, are more subtle than scholars have typically made them out to be.

Ukadike points to the common ground shared by the pioneers of West African cinema. He notes that, despite some differences, "they are united in their opposition to what they see as escapist tendencies in Western cinema." However, he subsequently posits an even sharper demarcation between Hondo and Sembène by titling a subsection of one chapter "Med Hondo and Ousmane Sembène: The Schism between Theory and Practice." In this section Ukadike emphasizes the commonalities in objective between two of the most prominent West African cineastes of the 1960s. He even stresses the similarities in their political approaches to cinematography. However, Ukadike sees a clear disjuncture in the film styles of the two directors: "Whereas Hondo's strategy is to montage unrelated sequences (reminiscent of Dziga Vertov of the former Soviet Union), Sembène uses static camerawork and the effects of the long take (reminiscent of André Bazin's notion of psychological identification in the audience-image relationship) to reach the same goal." In the end, though, Ukadike observes that such differences are in fact defining attributes of African cinema as its aesthetic was forged in the first decade after independence. He concludes that "neither Hondo nor Sembène vilifies the other for this. . . . These elements frequently combine to form the integral force shaping the construction of the 'real' picture of social and domestic life that was lacking in the escapist entertainment cinema of the COMACICO-SECMA years."[5]

Diawara strikes an entirely different pose with regard to the early development of West African cinema. Rather than deal with the aesthetic debates among filmmakers from the region, he focuses on the role that France played in jump-starting moviemaking in its former colonies. Ironically, Africans could now make films, but they only could do so through a neocolonial relationship within a cinema industrial complex still controlled by the French: while France's ministry charged with promoting filmmaking "made it possible for Sembène and Cissé to mature as film directors and to replace directors of the colonial era, such as Rouch, it made no effort to decolonize the tools of production in order for Sembène and Cissé to work autonomously in Africa."[6] In my view, Diawara has melded distinct subjects together and created some confusion as to what was at stake in the 1960s for West African cineastes. One issue is the materialist aspect of the cinema industrial complex through which France continued to exercise disproportionate influence and against which Sembène, Cissé, Hondo, and others worked tirelessly. The next chapter explores this aspect of the story in further detail. A separate but related element is the representational dimension of forging a distinct African film aesthetic. While there was certainly controversy about the degree to which French or other foreign financing might shape the end product, Diawara seems to imply that the room for maneuver on this score was very tightly circumscribed. In this chapter I show that Sembène and his cohort in the early history of West African filmmaking found ways to construct an autonomous and locally resonant image-Africa that undermined existing colonialist tropes, setting African filmmaking on a trajectory to discovering its own unique voice. Rather than hinder early cinematic development, their battles with French institutions and individuals helped to clarify exactly what was at stake and the direction that had to be taken to adumbrate an African-controlled cinema industrial complex.

Harrow takes the conversation further and denounces the pioneer generation of West African celluloid artists as having constructed nothing short of a trap for future filmmakers that is responsible for the contemporary attenuation of the film industry in Africa. His evocative study charts "the price of following Sembène's approach to an ideologically driven cinema." That approach, according to Harrow, entails the absorption and reproduction of the European model of moviemaking, which carries with it the discursive baggage of Western imperialism and patriarchy. He asserts that embracing "the model" of the Western narrative presages "an eventual embrace of authoritarianism on the part of those who possess the correct vision or truth."[7] Harrow thus accuses the entire pioneer generation of West African filmmakers as having set African motion pictures on a false and, ultimately, destructive path that more deeply entrenched Western patterns of cinematic practice with its associated ideological values. For Harrow, the major line of demarcation in the history of postcolonial African film practice is generational rather than technical, political, or even stylistic.

Harrow's study is provocative and evocative. However, his approach is overly critical and often treats the pioneers of West African filmmaking as if they operated in a vacuum or should have been able to do so. Harrow's primary criticism is that the early African cineastes claimed to seek a rupture with Western cinematic practice in a space-clearing gesture that was intended to decolonize the field of film production but ended up either intentionally or inadvertently reproducing the very forms with their ideological baggage that they insisted they were trying to transcend. Harrow does distinguish between the Sembène/Hondo cinema of engagement and Mambety's "postmodernism" in order to ground later African filmmaking as a continuation of Mambety's approach, which he sees as a more fruitful line of motion picture aesthetic.[8] However, he asserts that the practices Sembène instantiated for African cinema paved the way for the history of authoritarian rule that plagued much of postcolonial Africa during the first two to three decades after independence. This last claim is ironic considering the difficulty Sembène, Hondo, and others had in having their films screened in their own countries. Most West African cineastes in the 1960s and 1970s ran into restrictive censorship laws and some were even forced to carry out their production in exile because of the harassment they faced from their own governments.

Whatever the limitations of the first generation of West African filmmakers, they collectively produced an impressive body of work. Melissa Thackway observes that "Francophone African directors have clearly appropriated a medium denied to them under colonial rule. . . . [They] tended to situate their work in the socioeducational vein, using their films to reflect upon the key issues of the time, thereby assuming their political responsibility as artists." While acknowledging Mambety's "new and original style of filmmaking," Thackway locates his production firmly within the emergent tradition of West African cinematic practice, its key attributes being found in Sembène's and Hondo's work as well.[9] Certainly Mambety's early work—for example, *Touki-bouki* (Senegal, 1973)—came in for criticism from some of his contemporaries. However, neither the kind of work he was doing nor the debate that ensued interfered with the process of forging a unique African film aesthetic or discourse. On the contrary, I maintain that it was integrally part of the process of founding a Francophone West African cinematographic language designed to refute and transcend the colonialist regime of representation that had held sway to that point. Mambety's films *Contras' City* (Kankourama, 1969,) and *Touki-bouki* belong in any examination of pioneer West African cineastes' articulation of their own representational form and cinematographic language along with movies such as Sembène's *Borom Sarret* (Doomireew, 1963), *La noire de . . .* (Doomireew, 1966), and *Mandabi* (Doomireew, 1968) and Hondo's *Soleil Ô* (Shango, 1967).

In this chapter I chart the construction of an early West African film aesthetic through an analysis of the representational aspects of the cinema industrial complex following independence of the region's countries from French rule. During this period distinctive approaches to filmmaking emerged that built on extant practices in West Africa dating to the period of French colonial film politics. Consequently, there were commonalities to what the French imperial nation-state encouraged and permitted in the cinematic field and the film styles embraced by the region's first filmmakers. The pioneers of West African motion pictures generated movies that like the colonialist archetypal film *Paysans noirs* can be described as "docu-fiction," which features long takes, panoramic shots, and amateur local people as performers. Like the general government of French West Africa after World War II, Sembène and his cohort sought to both present "reality" on the ground in a way that also directed the audience toward an "idealized" future African modernity that would be brought into being by the actions of the viewers after their cinematic education. Even the storytelling structure that Sembène and others embraced replicated the pattern evident in *Paysans noirs*. A crisis sets off the action, tyranny threatens, a moment of clarity emerges, and a solution that will move the community forward arises. Gugler, Pfaff, and others have identified similar distinguishing features of African moviemaking.¹⁰

Therefore, I agree with Harrow in a certain sense that there was an identifiable continuity in cinematic practice in West Africa from the 1950s to the 1960s. Although, as he notes, Sembène took in the colonialist model of filmmaking and "redeployed it for liberationist purposes," that does not mean that Sembène (and others in his cohort) "stayed within its parameters."¹¹ The political goals of the film do matter if one is to meaningfully analyze the representational significance and distinctiveness of postcolonial West African motion pictures. As Murphy and Williams point out, "African cinema exists in a Western-dominated global system and its politics of representation must be understood within the full complexity of this situation."¹² Before I enter into a discussion of the representational aspects of exemplary early West African films, I want to look at two films made by French cineastes during the 1950s that contributed in surprising ways to the articulation of the anticolonial film politics outlined in chapter 3, which provided a foundation for subsequent postcolonial African cinematic production. Those films are René Vautier's *Afrique 50* (1950), produced by the Ligue de l'enseignement, and Chris Marker, Alain Resnais, and Ghislain Cloquet's *Les statues meurent aussi* (1953), which was coproduced by *Présence africaine*.

Anticolonial Filmmaking and Late Colonialism

On 22 August 1951 the appeals court for French West Africa based in Dakar, Senegal, handed down a judgment concerning the work of the French filmmaker René Vautier. The previous year he had been charged with violating the Laval decree by making movies in West Africa without prior authorization from the general government and was sentenced to a year in prison. What made Vautier the target of the colonial administration was not so much his illegally making a film as the particular motion picture he produced. In 1950 he finished work on *Afrique 50* and submitted it for screening in French schools. Made in cooperation with Félix Houphouët-Boigny, the rising star of politics in Côte d'Ivoire and leader of the RDA, the anticolonial political party, *Afrique 50* was banned immediately, and Vautier was accused of making anti-French and unauthorized films. Considering the origins of the project, this was a surprising result, and Vautier was himself an unlikely figure to be charged with anti-French activities.

At the time of the film's completion René Vautier was only twenty-one years old. However, he had already achieved high visibility in French society. In 1943, at the young age of fifteen, he joined the Resistance against Nazi occupation and the Vichy regime. Vautier was a highly decorated hero of the Resistance; he received the War Cross when he was sixteen years old, and in 1944, he was awarded the Order of the Nation by Charles de Gaulle for his activities on behalf of France's liberation. Thus, still in his teens Vautier had demonstrated an unwavering commitment to liberty and to France. After the war he enrolled at the prestigious IDHEC, the same school from which Vieyra would later graduate, and obtained his diploma in 1948 with a specialization in film directing. Upon graduation Vautier was contracted by the Ligue de l'enseignement, a civic arm of the Ministère de l'éducation nationale, whose objectives were the promotion of lay education and the production of pedagogical tools for the classroom, to go to Côte d'Ivoire and make short documentaries on the positive role French education was having in the colonies. This was entirely consistent with the evolving film politics of the time. Armed with a 16 mm camera and authorization from the French imperial nation-state, he set off to make documentary shorts of the "reality" on the ground in the colonies. His project (and his personal background) fit the model of what the colonial administration wanted with regard to the cinema industrial complex and followed immediately on the heels of the production of *Paysans noirs,* shot in a neighboring territory.

That all changed upon Vautier's arrival in Côte d'Ivoire in 1949. Once on the ground the Resistance hero was confronted with the ongoing vicious repression of the RDA, which at the time was aligned with the Parti communiste français (PCF). Founded in 1946, the RDA scored impressive (and surprising) victories in the 1948 general elections in French West Africa. Advocating African nationalism and taking a strident anticolonial stand, the RDA decided to ally itself in the French national assembly with the PCF, a common practice at the time, for by associating themselves with metropolitan groups, African parties were able to enhance their voice in French politics. The RDA, however, was not explicitly communist. Rather, it was a federation of parties based in the individual colonies, some sections of which were more radical than others. Ignoring the nuances of local politics, the colonial administration labeled the RDA "communist" and accused it of fomenting revolution in the region. Its leaders were harassed and imprisoned, members were denied employment, and the security forces used heavy-handed tactics to discourage involvement in it. In 1949, repression of the RDA reached a crescendo. At that moment Vautier arrived in Côte d'Ivoire to shoot his film extolling the virtues of the French education system in the overseas territories.

Still technically following his mandate to film the "reality" of life on the ground, Vautier offered what scholars and critics alike agree is the first French anticolonial film. Shot in Côte d'Ivoire and Burkina Faso (the same region *Paysans noirs* had, ironically, been filmed in the previous year), the seventeen-minute black and white documentary shows the brutality of French rule in its repression of the RDA. The political intolerance, poverty, lack of education, poor health care, and virtually absent infrastructure belied the claims by French officials about the progress the metropole had brought to West Africa since the conquest more than fifty years earlier.[13] The African modernity exemplified by the joyous peasants of Régnier's adaptation of Delavignette's novel seemed as distant as ever. The colonial state got wind of Vautier's shift of focus for his film and attempted to halt production. Through the assistance of Houphouët-Boigny and other RDA sympathizers in the region, Vautier was able to complete filming clandestinely. He attempted to release the picture in 1950.[14] The end result was a "realist" documentary that starred local people engaged in the struggles of daily life while confronting a brutal regime determined to crush liberty at all costs. *Afrique 50* exposed the hypocrisy of a government that claimed to be humanistic and to be "assisting" Africans in their movement toward modernity.

Upon Vautier's completion of *Afrique 50* he was hauled into court and accused of making illegal films in contravention of the Laval decree. He initially defended himself by appealing to the fact that he had been contracted by the Ligue de l'enseignement to make a documentary on conditions in Côte d'Ivoire, which was precisely what he had done. Therefore, the charges that he lacked the proper permits were false. In response, the colonial government argued that *Afrique 50* was not the specific film for which Vautier had been sent to the federation to make. Therefore, he filmed under false pretenses and did not have the requisite permissions to make his documentary. Considering the nature of the finished product and the crackdown at the time on any films that even remotely criticized colonialism or lauded resistance to oppression, the judge's decision was perfunctory. Vautier was found guilty and sentenced to a year in prison in 1951. He was sent first to the military prison Saint-Maixent in the Department of Sarthe, then to Niederlahnstein in the French occupation zone in Germany. The film itself was banned from being shown anywhere, even in France, and remained suppressed for nearly forty years.

Vautier appealed his conviction and obtained a more favorable result. In its judgment on 22 August 1951 the appeals court for French West Africa ruled that Vautier could not be convicted for violating the Laval decree because *Afrique 50* "excluded all possibility of being shown commercially." After all it was banned and could not be seen by anyone, nor was it ever viewed publically. The court cited article 9 in its decision, according to which the decree "establishes the requirement upon which the entrepreneur will fix the days, place, and hours during which it [the film] will be made available for viewing, in order to permit the Head of the Administrative Inspection to verify if the operation realized is exactly conforming to that which was authorized."[15] The court also noted that the Laval decree "provided generous terms to any person so desirous to proceed to make a cinematographic work," but "they must, before anything, obtain the authorization of the governor."[16] The dilemma for the court was that Vautier had received authorization to film but had made a film that did not precisely conform to that for which he had permission. However, that judgment could not be accurately made since the film had not ever been made available for viewing according to the provision of the law. Finally, Vautier claimed his authorization was to make a documentary depicting reality in the colonies, which to his mind he did. Therefore, on technical grounds the appeals court overturned the verdict against Vautier, although the ban on *Afrique 50* remained in effect since the picture itself was a separate matter. The colonial government refused to let up and appealed that decision. It succeeded in getting the original verdict reimposed in the end, and so Vautier did not walk out of prison until June 1952, having completed his sentence.

By then *Afrique 50* had achieved iconic status in the anticolonial movement. Illicit copies of the film circulated in the underground, providing a model of resistance cinematography that informed later work by West African cineastes. In 1958 *Présence africaine* defied the law and held a public screening of Vautier's film. On 18 November, forty-two people gathered at the Maison pour tous at the Place du docteur Roux in Gennevillièrs, a suburb of Paris, as part of a "soirée franco-africaine" organized by the journal. The building was a local cultural center in a neighborhood populated by Africans. The event took place less than two months after De Gaulle's referendum that established the Fifth Republic and replaced the French union with the French community, which Guinea voted against, promptly receiving independence. Consequently, the screening of *Afrique 50* took place at a moment of intensified anticolonial fervor and political upheaval in France.

An internal police report submitted to the high commissioner for French West Africa on 19 November 1958 described *Afrique 50* as "a documentary against colonialism." The anonymous author of the document wrote that the film "shows an African village in celebration and in contrast, the same village deserted except for very young children. The adults disappeared in order to escape the payment of taxes and the forced enlistment in the army. A local chief sees his village destroyed, the inhabitants massacred (one distinguishes only the traces of [bullet] impacts on the walls), the cattle slaughtered and left in place, put out to pasture for the vultures." The report continues, "There then follows the appearance of the buildings of the large African commercial companies which, 'as other vultures,' relentlessly exploit the African people, who work for 50 francs a day. The film finishes with a satire on colonialist methods; 'the Blacks work with primitive tools, even as modern machines could advantageously replace them.'" The author of the report mentioned that Alioune Diop, editor of *Présence africaine,* gave a short speech prior to the film "in the course of which he evoked the gulf traced by colonialism between the peoples of the metropole and those of Africa. He demanded that the representatives of the [African] people come together in equal numbers with those from the metropole to discuss their grievances and decolonize the countries of Black Africa." The report also observed that Jacques Rabemananjara, former deputy in Madagascar, was there and was celebrated for having been imprisoned for his anticolonial activities. He was introduced by Pierre Stibbe, a lawyer who worked on Rabemanajara's release from prison and who in 1958 was a candidate for the Union pour la démocratie française (UDF), a coalition of non-Communist leftists opposed to the return of de Gaulle to the presidency. The author wrote that Stibbe "presented his electoral program, commenting most particularly on the Algerian affair and demanding an immediate cease-fire and negotiations with Ferhat Abbas," leader of the Front de libération nationale (FLN), which at the time was fighting its liberation war against France.[17]

The event is remarkable on many levels. However, for the purposes of the current study its main significance resides in the incredible lengths to which the forces around *Présence africaine* were willing to go in order to incorporate film as part of the anticolonial struggle. The decision to hold a public screening of *Afrique 50* in the midst of such a high level of political turmoil in France and its overseas territories marks an important stage in the articulation of an anticolonial film politics by activists from West Africa. The viewing also occurred after the Second World Congress of Black Writers and Artists had been postponed, the program for which included a section devoted to the cinema as an element of the decolonization process and postcolonial development. Vieyra's essay on the role of the motion picture industry in the reconstruction of African cultures and economies had been published earlier that year in anticipation of the congress. The symbolism of convening around Vautier's documentary also gave a tacit endorsement to the film as a prototype of anticolonial filmmaking, and the film itself followed the outlines sketched by Vierya in his description of what such a genre might look like. Moreover, it validated Vieyra's own initial foray into cinema, *Afrique-sur-Seine*, his documentary on the struggles of African migrants in Paris, that had its own complicated history dealing with the Laval decree. Despite the importance of *Afrique 50* in the prehistory of the articulation of a West African cinematographic language, scholars rarely go further than simply mentioning Vautier's work. Usually they point out that it was banned and cite it as an early example of French anticolonial filmmaking.[18] The internal colonial government's report on the film's screening by *Présence africaine* gives a far more detailed and insightful account that accords the film a more significant place in the liberation struggle than researchers have given it.

Beyond the public screening, though, *Afrique 50* is important for its representational aspects, which presaged later West African film production, including Vieyra's *Afrique-sur-Seine*. The film begins with a general overview of seemingly banal aspects of daily life like children playing in the fields, women weaving cloth, men fishing, and such. This is perhaps what the Ligue de l'enseignement had in mind when it dispatched Vautier to French West Africa. He makes constant comparisons between the activities of Africans and those of French citizens, in one instance comparing the work of rope makers who are preparing fishing nets with the activities of fishermen in Brittany. However, the filmmaker's narration undermines the imagery on the screen, showing such affinities between France and Africa to be false. About one minute into the film the "reality" behind the pictures conveyed on the surface is exposed as being far more sinister. As Vautier narrates, "Without any doubt you will see picturesque things [in West Africa], but little by little you will find out how big the misery behind this picturesque view is." Vautier's camera continues to follow the daily labors of the Africans, but now it becomes clear that the reason the children are so happily playing all day is that there is no school for them to attend. The viewer learns there is no doctor, unless the colonial companies want fit workers for one of their projects. The audience also sees the kinds of work performed by Africans, all of which could be performed by modern machines, except that using colonial labor is cheaper than providing a tractor or even electrical generation.

Vautier makes use of montage and point-counterpoint composition to emphasize the connections between the activities of the colonized population and the exorbitant profits of the European companies based in urban office buildings. He shows the wealth of Africa literally leaving the continent on European ships anchored in harbor. Finally, the spectator is shown blood-spattered walls that bear witness to the murder of Africans, including a pregnant woman, by French colonial troops. Razed villages, executed indigenous people, and pilfered natural resources is the kind of modernity France has bequeathed Africa. However, Vautier shows the audience that Africans are becoming conscious of their plight and the source of their misery. The camera captures scenes of rallies, debates, and marches. He explains that Africans are learning how to fight for their liberty, how "to be free." The smiles return to African faces as they imagine a future liberated from the exactions of colonial administrators and the exploitation by greedy corporations. Again the composition interweaves shots of French citizens marching through crowded streets during the liberation of France from Nazi occupation with those of Africans at political demonstrations. In one scene Africans are pictured among the forces that freed France from the fascist yoke. The two are one, again, but this time it is an honest rendering of "reality."

Vautier's *Afrique 50* established a typology for anticolonial filmmaking of the sort later advocated by Vieyra and the pioneers of West African cinema. Its cinematographic grammar and syntax laid a foundation for that built on by Sembène, Hondo, and Mambety in their early work. Vautier makes use of panoramic shots that clearly situate Africans in their environment. They are grounded in place. The camera lingers on each scene—as, for example, when it is fixated on the back of a man working to free a ship that is stuck in the mud. The shot captures each drop of sweat as it rolls down his back and the contortion of his muscles as he strains to set the ship right. The film shows Africans working collectively, although the audience is also made aware of the individual names of those killed by the French. The penchant of positioning the individual African within the larger social group later became a central trope of West African cinematic practice. Gugler describes some of the key elements of what he identifies as a distinct African film language: proximity to what one would find in "news footage," documentary style, the use of nonprofessionals, lingering shots, deliberate pacing. "Most African films," he concludes, "while establishing distinct individuals, move beyond them to give major play to social, cultural, and political issues. African films tend to focus on groups rather than individuals." These techniques, Gugler notes, are close to those deployed by the Italian neorealists, who were a major force in the cinematic world at precisely the time Vautier made *Afrique 50*.[19]

In the end, though, this is still a "French" film. Vautier was assisted by Africans, including Këita Fodeba, who was an important cultural figure in Guinea, but he was the filmmaker.[20] The documentary is aimed at educating French audiences about conditions in the overseas territories, lifting the blinders from their eyes so that they could engage in real solidarity with their African counterparts. In other important ways *Afrique 50* differs from subsequent West African cinema. It is a documentary, whereas docu-fiction was more typical of Sembène's and others' films. In that manner it also is distinguished from *Paysans noirs*. Vautier's voice assumes a commanding presence, providing the viewer with the "correct" interpretation of the images on the screen and guiding the audience toward the consciousness that will overturn the oppressive system portrayed in the film. Nonetheless, the making of *Afrique 50*, its banning by the colonial administration, and the subsequent screening sponsored by *Présence africaine* indicate that this film was an important element in the articulation of a film aesthetics aimed at challenging the hegemonic regime of representation as it pertained to Africa and Africans in the late colonial and early postcolonial era.

A second French film from this period, *Les statues meurent aussi*, also can be read as contributing to the process of developing an African motion picture aesthetic, especially considering that *Présence africaine* was the producer. The film examines the mystification, degradation, and decontextualization of African culture as the sacred material objects of African societies are excised from their geographic and temporal specificity to be housed in Europe's museums where they are gawked at but not appreciated or understood by Western audiences. The thirty-five-minute documentary by Alain Resnais, Chris Marker, and Ghislain Cloquet is a call for the revival of African cultural worth and the valorization of Africans' past as part of a common human history. At one point the narrator, Jean Négroni, states, "And it is fair that the black feel pride about a civilization which is as old as ours." This gesture is similar to that found in Vautier's film—both ground cultural comprehension in the similarities of aspirations, practices, and histories among Europeans and Africans. Both documentaries appeal to the notion of a "civilization of the universal," which Léopold Senghor popularized through his *négritude* philosophy.

However, in Resnais, Marker, and Cloquet's film the presumed inherent differences between Africans and Europeans occasionally surfaces and are given extensive play midway through the production. For example, about eleven minutes into the film, Négroni, as narrator, claims that every African art object "is sacred because every creation is sacred." The film then goes on to examine the specificity of

African products, pointing to the different ways that Europeans and Africans treat the dead, and the distinct role of sacred objects placed near or with the deceased. Resnais, Marker, and Cloquet sketch two distinct worldviews through the material artifacts each culture manufactures in order to demonstrate the mistreatment of African physical culture by Europeans who have expropriated the continent for their own amusement. In the end, the filmmakers inform the viewer that the pressures of the commercial market to which these sacred and culturally meaningful objects have been subjected transforms them into "indigenous handicraft." African art winds up degraded, fake, and "ugly" by being produced using modern techniques. Resnais, Marker, and Cloquet even turn their camera against the idea of *métissage,* or cultural mixing, treating it as another path leading to the "death of African culture" that also distorts European culture.

Toward the end of the film, the cineastes turn to the contemporary struggle for liberation. The cinematic style shifts to montage, as the "black artist" is shown "returning the blows received by his brother in the street." We see shots of a jazz drummer interspersed with Africans being attacked in the streets by white vigilante forces. Each strike of the baton on the drum emphatically refutes the blasts of the shotgun. Finally, the viewer is brought beyond the confrontations between Europeans and Africans to the possibility of "equality" between the two cultures on the grounds that "there is no rupture between African civilization and ours."

Les statues meurent aussi was a Franco-African production. While the film was directed by French cineastes, its making was sponsored by the main organization of African cultural activists in the late colonial period. Its audience also was mixed. On the one hand, it targeted Europeans with the intention of educating them about their "misinterpretations" and debasement of African sacred objects, the artifacts of everyday life. The goal was to raise awareness among metropolitan viewers so that they would regard Africans and their cultures as part of the common human patrimony that were as valuable as the culture of any other society. The film also was aimed at Africans in that it clearly called for a recovery and renaissance of African culture, a renaissance that would in the process enable Africans to reclaim control over its production and presentation. In a sense, Resnais, Marker, and Cloquet endorsed a counterhegemonic version of the "cooperation" between French and African cultures that was envisioned in colonialist films such as *Paysans noirs. Les statues meurent aussi* pointed to the inequalities and injustices that undergirded the existing relationship between the metropole and its colonies without eschewing the prospect that consciousness of those flaws and the recovery of an African voice in the representation of their own cultures could lead to a more egalitarian, cooperative, and humanist rapport among the different communities. While *Les statues meurent aussi* was more subtle in its anticolonialism than Vautier's earlier film, it nonetheless earned the approbation of censors in West Africa. On 24 March 1954 the movie was banned by the CFCC.[21] The colonial administration seized the prints and refused to release them for ten years and after that only allowed a truncated version of the original to see the light of day. Consequently, it was not until the 1990s (shortly after the ban on Vautier's work was lifted) that audiences were able to see the original in its entirety.

Despite its importance in the history of the origins of Francophone West African cinema, *Les statues meurent aussi* has not received much scholarly attention. Some only mention the picture in passing as an example of the imperial nation-state's deployment of the Laval decree to control celluloid images in the colonies.[22] Lindiwe Dovey and Ukadike provide a more thorough analysis of the film and its significance in the decolonization struggle. Dovey points to the use of montage as a means of visualizing the dialectical confrontation between the colonizers and the colonized as a particularly powerful device in raising consciousness among viewers.[23] Ukadike makes perhaps the most salient point by linking this film with the advent of West African filmmaking. He notes the influence it had on Sembène at a time when he was emerging as a major literary figure. Ukadike quotes the Senegalese filmmaker as declaring *Les statues meurent aussi* to be "the best film ever made on Africa, colonization, and traditional art objects."[24] Moreover, Ukadike demonstrates the thematic similarity between Resnais, Marker, and Cloquet's film and subsequent work by African cineastes from across the continent.[25] As I discuss in the next section, Sembène specifically deploys the symbol of the African mask in one of his most important early films of the 1960s, *La noire de . . . .*

Both *Afrique 50* and *Les statues meurent aussi* helped to set the stage for West African cinematic production by offering powerful models of anticolonial filmmaking in the representational realm. Along with Vieyra and GAC's breakthrough docu-fiction *Afrique-sur-Seine* they contributed to the emergence of a film aesthetic and language that provided a foundation for West African cinema in the early postcolonial period. The end of French rule in the region meant that Africans were freed from the constraints of the Laval decree and that cultural activists could pick up the camera and begin to "shoot back" in their own languages, constructing their own image-Africa for local and international audiences. As Samba Gadjigo writes, "With the magic of cinema, African filmmakers at last had a medium to disseminate alternative, counterhegemonic histories or to reconfigure existing ones differently."[26]

Ousmane Sembène: Pioneer of West African Cinema

To make the transition, though, West Africans needed access to the equipment and technical knowledge that French colonialism had heretofore denied them. Thus, Sembène set off for Moscow's Gorki Studios in 1961 to study with master Soviet cinematographers.[27] In doing so, Sembène paved a pathway followed by other aspiring West African filmmakers who trekked to Moscow or other parts of the Soviet Union to hone their skills and secure financial backing for their early works. Costa Diagne of Senegal trained at the Gosudarstvenyi institut kinematografii (GIK), the Soviet film institute in Moscow, as did Cissé, becoming in 1970, according to Vieyra, the first African to complete the cycle of studies at any "école supérieure de cinéma."[28] Others were either self-taught or, more commonly, the product of French training at IDHEC, such as Vieyra and Blaise Senghor, who hailed from Benin and Senegal and Senegal respectively. By the 1970s West Africa was home to a burgeoning corps of innovative, dedicated, and active filmmakers who played a substantial role in elaborating an image-Africa that challenged the prevailing tropes projected onto movie screens around the world. The first generation of African cineastes included Sembène and Mahama Johnson Traoré, both from Senegal, Oumarou Ganda and Mustapha Alassane from Niger, Désiré Ecaré of Côte d'Ivoire, and Cissé of Mali, among many others.

Above all, though, Sembène emerged as the dominant figure in West African cinema during the 1960s, and his work became iconic in articulating an African cinematographic language and regime of representation that defined postcolonial West African film for years to come. As Harrow writes, Sembène's productions gave rise to a "system of values" that "was widely embraced."[29] An exploration of Sembène's first three films, *Borom Sarret, La noire de . . .* , and *Mandabi*, provides greater insight into the image-Africa and cinematographic discourse that came to characterize West African film in the early postcolonial period.[30] Sembène's work reflects the influences of the training he received in the Soviet Union and at the same time responds to the demands of the anticolonial film politics Vieyra and others had developed in the late imperial era. Moreover, his early motion pictures built on the representational foundations laid by *Afrique 50* and *Les statues meurent aussi* in the 1950s but did so in a way that gave voice to a distinct West African cinematographic discourse.

In 1963 Sembène released *Borom Sarret*, a twenty-minute short hailed by Gugler as "the most important of the early feature films produced by black Africans in Africa."[31] Bakari asserts that "its significance lies in its approach to the representation of African life and society, one that was distinct from the hitherto established empire, colonial and ethnographic films popularised by Hollywood and the cinemas of Britain and France for example." Furthermore, he explains, "Sembène's film was also significant in terms of the alternative narrative conventions which it offered. It suggested a way of storytelling which seemed to indicate the possibility of a distinct identity and aesthetic for a new African cinema."[32] The film follows the banal journeys of a cart driver through the streets of Dakar, Senegal, as a vehicle through which to explore the corruption and injustice directed toward the poor and working people that persisted after independence from French rule. *Borom Sarret* constructs a mediascape that reveals the hopelessness that often confronts individuals as they engage with a global system built on the exploitation of the many to benefit the wealthy few. After a series of misadventures the protagonist remarks, "We all work for nothing" and then follows that observation with the despairing line "I might as well die." Among the vignettes that structure the film are encounters with a policeman who deliberately steps on a military medal and seizes his cart and a run-in with a rich man who uses the cart driver's services but does not pay. In the end, the cart driver is dejected and resigned to his fate. His wife, however, exits the courtyard proclaiming, "We'll eat tonight." We do not know what she intends to do to, but the allusion is to some desperate measure they have been forced to take by a system that resists individual efforts to confront it.

The film shows the misjudgments of a naïve cart driver who is just trying to make ends meet. His decision to drive the rich man into the city when he knows it is forbidden is a risk he takes in full cognizance of the potentially dire consequences. However, he does so because no one has paid him for services all day and this man appears to be a guaranteed paying customer. The cart driver's decision, then, is not simply the free choice of a rational individual in the market place; it is the decision of a person who has been forced into desperate acts in order to survive in a system that does not offer many good options from which to choose. His wife's actions at the end of the film are similarly desperate. Sembène is careful to highlight that it is not the fault of individuals that they are in difficult circumstances or that they are poor; it is the product of a system designed to produce poverty and risky behavior on the part of those who are marginalized in their own societies. As the cart driver suggests toward the end of his misfortunes, "Modern life is a prison."

Sembène's *Borom Sarret* reflects his film education in the Soviet Union and followed in the tradition of revolutionary social realist cinematography pioneered in the USSR between the two world wars. West African cineastes such as Sembène saw in the experience of the Soviet Union after the 1917 revolution a historical proximity to the situation of the newly independent countries of West Africa in the 1960s. As with the USSR in the 1920s, West African societies were largely illiterate and rural. Similarly, West African countries were multilingual. The distribution of Soviet motion pictures via a "cinema on wheels" to the countryside where they were projected on "open air" screens before assembled crowds was a powerful mechanism used by the revolutionary government to bring its message to their people. Moreover, the themes of heroic struggle against oppression and the populace's enactment of the construction of modern Soviet society that Sergei Eisenstein and Dziga Vertov portrayed in film images during the 1920s and 1930s in Soviet Russia were commensurate with the objectives Sembène and other pioneer West African directors embraced in postcolonial West Africa.[33]

A significant difference, though, was that the Soviet Union had not emerged newly sovereign from decades of foreign rule as West Africa did after 1960. Moreover, West Africa had a fully articulated cinema industrial complex replete with its own established cinematic traditions that included a recognizable film language promoted by the French colonial government and partly adapted by anticolonial activists form the region. That meant Sembène and those who followed in his footsteps could borrow certain techniques that proved useful in using film to reach audiences in the interwar Soviet Union, but they also had to articulate a specific cinematographic discourse that responded to and could shape the existing cultural and material conditions of their intended audience in West Africa. Finally, Sembène's project conscientiously sought to avoid the myriad potential pitfalls that Adorno identified as inherent within "realist" film: "The reactionary nature of any realist aesthetic today is inseparable from this commodity character. Tending to reinforce, affirmatively, the phenomenal surface of society, realism dismisses any attempt to penetrate that surface as a romantic endeavor." Adorno concludes by observing that "film today is faced with the dilemma of finding a procedure which neither lapses into arts-and-crafts nor slips into a mere documentary mode. The obvious answer today . . . is that of montage which does not interfere with things but rather arranges them in a constellation akin to that of writing."[34] Sembène set out to make films that avoided Adorno's dilemma and resonated with an audience well versed in reading films.

The film language Sembène produces is "realist" in style but docu-fiction in genre. While *Borom Sarret* does not make extensive use of montage as a technique, Sembène does attempt to convey the reality of the cart driver's experience (as everyman) in a manner that peered below the surface to expose the underlying structures of society that produced the objective situations in which the protagonist found himself. In his first work, Sembène seeks to communicate the routine frustrations of the average person performing his or her normal activities. Honest work is not rewarded, and corruption is not punished. The camera follows the cart driver, but the viewer is not drawn into his consciousness. The cart driver remains an objective symbol that the audience is expected to recognize and from whom the consumer of the film should learn lessons about the "real" relations of power in society. The protagonist is situated within the African landscape, in this case the modern African city, and in identifiable social situations. Through the unfolding of the action the central character reveals for the audience the interrelationship between his poverty and the corrupt practices of the state and the emergent comprador capitalist class. The viewer sees in condensed form the entirety of the system that generates and preserves inequality but that is obfuscated in the daily life of the average person because he or she is unable to transcend his or her subjective position in order to comprehend the objective reality of the world. By the end, the moviegoer knows better and is, presumably, more capable of bringing about social transformation.

However, Harrow overstates the case when he writes, "Sembène opted from the beginning, along with the 'school' he created, to embrace a form of social realism that harmonized with the socialist realism that was dominant in the Russian studios where he . . . first learned . . . filmmaking."[35] *Borom Sarret,* and the subsequent

Sembène cinematographic tradition, is also the product of the specific motion picture experiences extant in West Africa, including the colonialist and anticolonial film politics formulated in the last years of French rule in the region. Government officials and West African cultural activists endorsed the "docu-fiction" as the most effective means for conveying their competing visions of an African modernity to autochthonous audiences. Woll notes that the portrayal of urban spaces in films by early West African filmmakers differs from the portrayal in Soviet films and that their film and editing techniques deviate from standard Soviet practices. The city for Sembène is an ambiguous zone, where the mark of French domination remains pronounced and generates a sense of alienness even among the city's "natives." Moreover, the pacing and editing do not strictly conform to Soviet techniques but rather favor the film practices that became dominant in West Africa after 1945. There is a significant difference between the frenetic pacing and sharp contrast of Sergei Eisenstein's early films like *Strike* (1925) and *Battleship Potemkin* (1925), for instance, and the lingering shots and deliberate tempo of Sembène's earliest work.[36]

Such continuities with filmmaking characteristic of the colonial period do not indicate that Sembène was perpetuating "the incomplete project of colonialism."[37] For a film to have meaning it must be understood; the motion picture has to speak a "language" that is intelligible to its consumers. Even French colonial officials acknowledged as much in their deliberations concerning the elaboration of a film politics for West Africa. Sembène's *Borom Sarret* fit within a recognizable film discourse while also challenging the hegemonic image-Africa inherited from the period of foreign domination. His inaugural production put into practice for the first time in West Africa the anticolonial film politics elaborated by Vieyra and his colleagues during the waning years of French domination. It was an opening salvo, an example of what Thackway eloquently describes as "Africa shoot[ing] back."[38]

A few years later, in 1966, Sembène released *La noire de . . .*, the first full-length African feature film.[39] The movie interrogates a fundamental legacy of colonialism identified by Fanon: skin color as an insuperable barrier to social belonging in the context of imperialist capitalism. As he writes in *Black Skin, White Masks*, "If there is an inferiority complex, it is the outcome of a double process: primarily economic; subsequently, the internalization—or, better, the epidermalization—of this inferiority."[40] *La noire de . . .* follows the struggle of Diouana as she attempts to preserve a sense of dignity and humanity in an alien and hostile environment. Recruited to take care of a French couple's children in Dakar, she is brought to France while they are on vacation and finds herself trapped as a "prisoner" and "slave." Diouana is made to prepare "genuine African food" for a dinner party even though the mistress never wanted African food while they were in Dakar. The dinner guests conjure up pervasive representations of Africa in the postcolonial period as a continent awash in civil wars, a dangerous place that the European finds inhospitable. One guest remarks, "Their independence has made Africans less natural," as if self-government was not a normal state for Africans and as if colonialism, by implication, was the only means for preserving the "authentic" Africa. This comment displaces the fundamental violence of imperialist capitalism onto its targets, effecting a mystification that deflects consciousness from the true nature of the system onto its effects, thereby inhibiting resistance.

From the start, Diouana's journey is one of humiliation and degradation. She is trapped in a world capitalist system that forces those from the periphery to go door to door seeking work or to sit on curbs waiting to be chosen. The arrival of a letter putatively from her mother pushes Diouana temporarily into extreme despair and fury. Diouana then refuses to work after the mistress withholds food. They tussle over a mask Diouana presented to the mistress as a gift in exchange for her initial employment, perhaps an allusion to *Les statues meurent aussi*. Afterward, Diouana recites a litany of "never again[s]" as she tries to break out of the cycle of abuse. She pronounces emphatically, "She wanted to keep me here as her slave.... Never will she scold me again." However, Diouana is trapped. She cannot get back home. She is exiled in France, where she doesn't have friends or any place to turn for assistance. All Diouana has are her memories of Dakar, including a dramatic one in which she and her boyfriend consummate their relationship in a room bedecked with a series of banners supporting Patrice Lumumba and his Mouvement national congolais during the independence election campaign in 1960. Earlier, one of the dinner guests referenced Congo as an example of the incessant violence that is said to characterize the entire African continent. Yet memories cannot save Diouana. She takes her own life in the bathtub of her employer's home.

The final sequence of the film indicates an emergent consciousness among the oppressed. After Diouana's boss attempts to return the mask and the rest of her belongings to her mother in Dakar, the young boy from whom Diouana originally purchased the mask grabs it and follows the boss back to the airport, whereupon the boy lowers the mask and stares directly at the car speeding off into the distance. This scene, I suggest, could constitute the kind of repatriation and recontextualization of cultural artifacts demanded in Resnais, Marker, and Cloquet's *Les statues meurent aussi* that simultaneously transforms the traditional object into a force for a new, modern Africa that is nonetheless rooted in its own history. The young boy's eyes encapsulate the future, characterized by clarity of understanding, defiance, and determination to right this injustice. Sembène does not give a prescription for the change to come, but the audience is assured that there will be a transformation. In fact, the boy, standing for future generations of Africans, has already achieved transcendence in his being.

Running sixty minutes and shot on 35 mm black and white film stock, *La noire de* . . . is a Franco-Senegalese coproduction filmed in both France and Senegal. As in *Borom Sarret*, Sembène uses Africans to enact their experience of life in the modern world. *La noire de* . . . goes further than *Borom Sarret*, however, by portraying the process of gaining consciousness on the screen as it happens to the protagonists themselves. Thus, Sembène's second film is less subtle than his previous work; it fills in some of the blanks for viewers in terms of the message they are expected to get from the picture. In that sense it is more consistent with the tradition of anticolonial filmmaking derived from *Afrique 50* and *Les statues meurent aussi*. However, it is not a documentary. Its film style is more akin to *Paysans noirs* and *Afrique-sur-Seine* in presenting a fictional story as a crystallization of "lived reality" with the objective of highlighting an African modernity in the course of coming into existence.

La noire de . . . , then, represents a synthesis of anticolonial cinema in the paradigmatic film language of West Africa. The dual aspect of Sembène's first feature film is what ultimately marks it as a significant event in the emergence of a West African cinematographic aesthetic. Even more so than in *Borom Sarret*, Sembène plays the role of the griot in the making of *La noire de. . . .* He draws on the experience of his society in order to produce a moral fable that is, nonetheless, anchored in "reality" so as to guide the audience toward a specific understanding of the world and a correct course of action. He does not spell out what must be done, but in the presentation on the screen the narrative structure implies a mutual comprehension of the direction in which the people will move as a result of their becoming cognizant of the "true" nature of the world. This is akin to the way in which griots function in West African societies. Gabriel notes the similarity between the griot and the filmmaker: "The stories that are woven into African cinema are concerned not simply with the retelling of myths and folklore, with the recording of history; they are part of the effort at mythmaking."[41]

Significantly, *La noire de . . .* is also an adaptation of Sembène's short story of the same title that was originally published in 1964, the first of many such transformations of literature to cinematography by the Senegalese director. Vieyra earlier urged writers to adapt their novels and stories to the screen as a means by which to reach a "greater audience" with their literary messages.[42] However, Gabriel suggests that such adaptations in the African context go beyond merely transferring stories from paper to celluloid: "What people sometimes forget when they speak of stories and narratives is that, in Africa at least, stories are also a matter of images. Narrative, in an African context, has always been visual—has always been, one might say, cinematic."[43] Ultimately, by adapting his short story to the screen Sembène has contributed to the articulation of a specific West African cinematographic language. If *La noire de . . .* is not simply the filming of a short story, it is also something more than the shooting of an oral storytelling performance. The cinema as a specific form of narration has its own mode of communicability. As Metz argues, "A given narrative receives a very different semiological treatment in the cinema than it would in a novel, in classical ballet, in a cartoon, and so on."[44] What Sembène has done, then, is to construct a story that is familiar in its literary and oral manifestations but that is uniquely cinematic as conveyed on the screen. Moreover, he has done so within an extant motion picture tradition that he has pushed to a new level. *La noire de* . . . signified a new and important stage in Francophone West Africans' intervention in the reconfiguration of the image-Africa within the regime of representation that dominated the cinematic field.

Two years later Sembène released *Mandabi* (*The Money Order*), another film adaption of one of his literary works. The movie offers a damning portrayal of West Africa's postcolonial leadership, representing it as corrupt, incompetent, and vindictive toward its own people. Unlike Sembène's first two films, *Mandabi* explicitly shows the region's new governing elite to be culpable in the miserable state in which the masses were living at the time. Sembène shows Africa's leaders to be greedy, self-interested, and willing pawns serving outsiders' interests. For his part Sembène explained, the real subject of *Mandabi* is "not only the misfortunes of the heroes. It is the birth of an African bourgeoisie. In reality the problem underlined by the film is political. It is no longer blacks and whites; the problem is posed in terms of class."[45] From the moment of its release, *Mandabi* caused a sensation. It attained almost instant iconographic status in the still-emerging Francophone West African cinematic tradition.

Even the making of *Mandabi* was controversial. The Senegalese filmmaker made two versions of the film, which is based on his 1964 novel *Le mandat*. Working with the Centre national du cinéma et de l'image animée (CNC) within the Ministère des affaires culturelles, Sembène submitted a screenplay originally in Wolof. That version was filmed, but the funding agency insisted on a French version, which was duly produced. However, the quality of the French version was terrible on all counts. Most of the actors Sembène used were not professional, and for them, French was at best a second language. Consequently, the French came across in the dialogue as stilted and incomprehensible. The Wolof version, which even the CNC admitted was "much better," went on to receive critical acclaim at the Venice Film Festival in 1968, where it received the Special International Critics' Jury Prize.[46] Chapter 5 explores the controversy that surrounded the making of *Mandabi* as illustrative of the materialist limitations to the development of a fully independent African cinema industry.

Sembène frequently asserted that his role as a filmmaker was not to foment a revolution but to raise awareness. Gabriel quotes Sembène's reaction to the reception of *Mandabi* in Senegal as follows: "I had no belief that after people saw it they would go out and make a revolution. . . . But people liked the film and talked about it. . . . I participated in their awareness."[47] The dramatic narrative is set in motion with the arrival of news at Ibrahima Dieng's house in Dakar that his nephew Abdou has sent a 250 franc money order from Paris. Dieng and his two wives go into debt, and at every stage in the process of attempting to redeem the money order the protagonist is met by hustlers, beggars, friends and religious leaders in search of money and by corrupt and indifferent government officials. In this motion picture Sembène employs what Frank Ukadike calls a "counterhegemonic strategy." The main thrust of Sembène's work is aimed at "the restructuring of consciousness as a necessary precondition for a genuinely 'new' society."[48] The final sequence of the film, during which the postman confronts Dieng at his greatest moment of despair, demonstrates Sembène's main objective with *Mandabi*: to raise consciousness in order to prepare the ground for finding solutions to the plight of the oppressed postcolonial subject. At the edge of exasperation, Dieng (played by Makhouredia Guèye) proclaims, "Honesty is a sin in our country." He then asserts that to survive he will become like everyone else—a thief, liar, and con man. At that moment the postman (played by Medoune Faye) retorts, "We will change the country." Dieng asks him who will bring about this change. "You, your family, [and] your children, all of us," the postman responds. Sembène then brings the viewer into Dieng's emerging consciousness through a powerful montage sequence that coalesces the misfortunes that have afflicted Dieng ever since the money order arrived into a condensed space. The postman reiterates that "we will change all of this," lifting Dieng out of his reflection, after which he pronounces not despairingly but defiantly, "I say again, honesty is a sin in our house."

As Vieyra, who was *Mandabi's* production director, noted, while the film is "fictional" it constitutes a documentary act; it is a status "report" on postcolonial Africa less than ten years after independence. Consequently, it can be read as what Solanas and Getino, the theorists of Third Cinema, call a "witness-bearing film."[49] Significantly, *Mandabi* is the first full-length fiction film whose dialogue is mostly in an African language."[50] Sembène conceived of his films as "a night school" for the masses, and using Wolof for the dialogue was meant to reach his audience in a language they understood.[51] For the first time, a West African filmmaker had challenged in a feature motion picture one of the salient aspects of France's colonial film politics, namely, the insistence on "French" as the only approved cinematic idiom. Because colonial officials were keen to utilize film as a vehicle for promoting French as the universal language in West Africa and were even reluctant to allow dubbed films for fear that the language spoken on the screen would still be intelligible to movie audiences in the federation, West African filmmakers also took seriously the double meaning of "film language," regarding the product's idiom as equally important to the cinema's grammatical structure. Filming in African languages became for African cineastes a gesture of defiance directed at the former colonial regime and a filmic device by which to authenticate the work as specifically African.[52] The fact that the government insisted that a second version of *Mandabi* be filmed in French indicates how salient the question of language remained nearly ten years after France relinquished control of West Africa.

Sembène's decision to use nonprofessionals as actors in *Mandabi* also contributes to its documentary aura. These are real people representing fictionalized characters that are themselves composites of actual lived realities for the postcolonial African. Sembène seeks to forge an identification of the audience with the "victim" portrayed on the screen, just as First Cinema does. However, unlike First Cinema, he does not intend the viewer to become absorbed in the film and thereby end up divorced from his or her own lived reality, becoming what Solanas and Getino call "a consumer of ideology" instead of "a creator of ideology."[53] Sembène forges a context that is identifiable in its realism and is peopled by characters that are recognizable, but he does not allow the viewers to lose themselves in the plot or lives of the actors. Rather, he keeps Dieng in camera. The action is never portrayed from Dieng's perspective but always with him in the picture. He is part of the reality, not the authorial voice. Moreover, he is never alone in an entire sequence. Dieng's world is peopled by others who are pursuing their self-interests and who intrude on his world. Even the powerful montage sequence at the end of *Mandabi* is shot with Dieng's visage over the scene, the camera still aimed directly at him, not projecting from his position. As Clyde Taylor notes, "While we sympathize with Ibrahima, we do not identify with him in his simplicity and *naïveté*, for Sembène intercepts identification with his characters as an obstacle to the social reflection that is his main focus."[54]

Taken together, *Borom Sarret, La noire de . . .* , and *Mandabi* illustrate the process whereby Sembène helped to forge a distinct West African cinema aesthetic in the early postcolonial period. In crucial ways each picture marked a "first" that established a baseline against which subsequent film production from the region would be assessed. While not foreclosing the possibility for innovation, Sembène's films denoted the parameters within which a dialogue could begin among the region's cineastes about what constituted an African film. Moreover, Sembène's early work put into practice the African anticolonial film politics articulated by Vieyra and others in the late colonial era, appropriating film as a means to reconstruct the image-Africa that defined Africans' place in the modern world. For the first time, a sub-Saharan African had picked up the camera to shoot in West Africa and challenged the hegemonic regime of representation that excluded or demeaned Africa and Africans. As Sembène explains, "Cinema is as vital for us as building hospitals and schools and feeding our own people. . . . [Cinema] enables us to see, feel and understand ourselves through the mirror of film. Ours is a committed cinema, useful and educational. It is useful because it raises . . . awareness in people. It is educational because it teaches people a mode of conduct, a way of looking at the future and their own lives."[55] Sembène's statement is a perfect illustration of the counterhegemonic film politics Vieyra and others envisioned in the late colonial era as a means of overcoming France's own imperialist cinematic strategy.

Revolutionizing Film Aesthetics: Hondo and Mambety

While Sembène can be credited with inaugurating postcolonial West African cinema, his contemporaries Med Hondo, a native of Mauritania, and Djibril Diop

Mambety, a Senegalese, carried aesthetic innovation even further and helped to move the region into the forefront of developing African filmmaking practice. In 1970 Hondo emerged as a cinematic force with *Soleil Ô*, his debut film. While the picture is the product of Hondo's experience of exile in France, where he had lived since 1958, it nonetheless belongs within the pantheon of signature West African films. Its style, substance, and strategy directly correlate to the paradigmatic cinematographic language of West Africa as well as the trajectory of motion picture practice as mapped by cineastes working in the region from at least the late 1940s. Shot over a five-year period beginning in 1965, Hondo's first foray into cinematography remains today one of the most powerful films from the era and has rightly earned praise as a masterpiece.[56] It was copyrighted in 1967, but filming was not completed until 1969; the movie was first screened in 1970 during the international critics' week at Cannes. In an interview nearly ten years after *Soleil Ô's* release, Hondo said, "I make films to show people the problems they face every day and to help them fight those problems."[57] *Soleil Ô* is strident in its tone, innovative in its style, and profoundly disruptive in its cinematographic language. In many ways, Hondo's first major release is a synthesis of the themes evident in *Afrique-sur-Seine* and the political strategy charted in Sembène's earliest works. *Soleil Ô* stands at a watershed moment in the transformation of West African cinema into a fully developed independent cinematic form.

The film's unsettling mood is established from the opening credits during which an African leader, who is seated center screen, is approached by two colonialists in classic imperialist garb, right down to the pith helmets and khaki pants. The African breaks into a haunting laugh as he too dons a pith helmet and is embraced by his European overlords. In the opening scene the narrator (Hondo) tells the viewer that "we had our own civilization" and then catalogues all the achievements of African societies prior to the European conquest. This echoes the message of *Les statues meurent aussi*. After the credits, the action in *Soleil Ô* cuts to Africans in a church who are undergoing initiation into Christianity by asking forgiveness for speaking their own languages and taking European names as they are baptized. Following their cultural transformation, the initiates carry crucifixes in a disorganized procession, during which they invert the crosses and morph into soldiers carrying fake guns. In front of a European officer, the newly colonized Africans are made to fight one another to the point of exhaustion.

Taken together the first scenes establish the context for the remainder of the film. The violent intervention of European imperialists has forestalled the formation of Africa's own form of modernity replete with advanced technology and innovative manufacturing. In order to instantiate colonial rule, the foreign rulers embark on a systematic campaign to erase African culture and the memory of their own achievements. The architecture, clothing styles, mannerisms, and daily life practices that characterized the African experience prior to colonialism are expunged and supplanted by European forms. Imperialism reaches into the African soul, causing the autochthonous people to feel ashamed of their own past and their inadequacies in the face of the "civilization" imparted to them by the foreign invader. The colonized African is made into the plaything of the European ruler, who uses his subjects for self-amusement and the enactment of grotesque fantasies. The result is a dysfunctional society that has been conditioned to look to the West for validation and sustenance.

That relationship is symbolized by the plight of the "visitor," played by Robert Liensol, who has left West Africa for France to find employment as well as his own identity. Variously confronting racism, economic privation, and isolation, the visitor is forced to confront his subaltern place in the modern world. With the camera framing the visitor's face, the narrator states, "We are all crazy," which he follows with a searching question: "Can you tell me where I am from?" Jean's travails and emergent consciousness constitute the narrative that drives the remainder of the ninety-eight-minute film, which ends with the visitor running through a forest to increasingly powerful and discordant drum beats that mimic a pounding heart and recalls the last part of *Les statues meurent aussi*. The final scene has an almost hallucinogenic feel; Jean undergoes something approaching a nervous breakdown that simultaneously clears his mind and brings him to full consciousness of his present situation and shows him to a potential way out of the predicament in which he and other Africans find themselves. Surrounded by portraits of revolutionary heroes such as Che Guevera, Patrice Lumumba, and Malcolm X as well as burning bushes, the visitor imagines himself prone in the bush holding a machine gun aimed at an unknown enemy, fighting as a guerrilla against the imperialist legacy. When the shot returns to the visitor in the forest he bears a knowing smile that indicates confidence and clarity. This contrasts with the almost maniacal laugh at the opening of the film as the African is made unbalanced through European intervention. *Soleil Ô* ends with the words "to be continued" positioned off center on the right of the screen, which informs the audience that this is not a finish but a beginning of cultural and economic recovery for the African.

Hondo's first major work was shot in black and white on 35 mm film and made on a shoestring budget of little more than $125,000, with nonprofessional actors in the starring roles. As Pfaff notes, *Soleil Ô* bears many similarities to Sembène's films *La noire de . . .* and *Mandabi*, including the motif of a migrant from West Africa facing racism in France and the growing significance of migration to France for postcolonial African societies.[58] While Sembène's early films begin in the present and Hondo's first major feature begins in the precolonial era so as to provide viewers with a benchmark for judging the subsequent history of Africa, both center on a process whereby foreign intervention has disrupted the construction of an African modernity, leading to corruption, distortion, and dislocation. Each filmmaker takes us on a journey of cultural (re)discovery that ends with the protagonist gaining cognizance of the larger social forces at work that structures his place in the world. Finally, Sembène and Hondo leave the viewer with the idea that the "end" of the film is merely the beginning of the emergence of consciousness and resistance. Consequently, the two cineastes helped to construct a Francophone West African cinematographic language that put film in the service of the people, offering insight into contemporary realities in a manner that opened vistas that could lead to correcting social injustice and the legacies of imperial domination.

While Sembène learned filmmaking in the Soviet Union, Hondo was self-taught, using his theater background as a launching point for his transition to the screen. Despite their different pathways to making motion pictures, they were both strongly influenced by Soviet cinematic traditions as well as Italian neorealism, itself inspired by Russian revolutionary filmmaking. Ukadike notes that Hondo's style closely resembles that of the great Soviet cinematographer Dziga Vertov.[59] The Mauritanian cineaste's deployment of montage, cut shots, and point/counterpoint editing throughout the film contributes significantly to *Soleil Ô*'s powerfully disruptive feel. The image-Africa the viewer might bring to the theater is consistently destabilized and undermined. Hondo's technique creates fissures through which he is able to insert a new rendering of Africa and Africans, one that projects an African modernity blocked by European intervention and only now able to resume its development.

However, Hondo is fully cognizant that this will be a modernity shaped by the colonial experience and not simply a recovery of an imaginary or idealistic precolonial past. In one scene Hondo situates the visitor among other Africans in a classroom where European mannequins act as diabolical supernatural interlocutors instructing their pupils in how they should see themselves and their place in the world. The teacher claims "it is true that if we don't force them to accept our way of seeing things there's a good chance they'll carry on in their own way. It's all true—that, not having their consent, we have no reason to be interested in their personal tastes. We are there to impose what amounts to our happiness, and which should become theirs." Hondo then cuts to a map of Africa with an arrow projecting "African culture toward the West," which is met by a counter arrow from Europe labeled "Western culture" that intercepts the African cultural line and knocks off the tip, blunting its movement while the trajectory from Europe continues to penetrate Africa. Next the visitor is situated among a pile of burning rubble with the sounds of war emanating from all directions, and then he is covered in money that he furiously peels from his body.

There is little subtlety in *Soleil Ô*'s message. From the narration to the editing and the shot composition, Hondo hammers away at the paradigmatic image-Africa articulated within colonialist film in order to forge the space in which the "new" African can emerge and seize control of his or her own destiny. He does so by means of the genre of the docu-fiction, which by this point in time had become entrenched, that is both realist in its documentary feel and fictional in its projection of an idealized process of emerging consciousness leading to a progressive African modernity. As Ukadike puts it, "*Soleil Ô* is neither a documentary nor a narrative feature film. It does not necessarily tell a story; instead, the film is segmented, and each scene gives Med Hondo the creative opportunity to slam his audience with a political point in a stylistic amalgam accompanied by an intense, imaginative, and eerie musical score."[60] Hondo's first major release erupted onto the cinematic scene with the subtlety of a nuclear blast.

While Sembène established his reputation as a progenitor of West African cinema and Hondo exemplified the revolutionary filmmaker prepared to use the camera as a blunt weapon against imperialism and racism, Djibril Diop Mambety pushed the aesthetic boundaries even further and offered a less certain vision of Africa's future in his breakthrough film *Touki-bouki*. Mambety had made other short films prior to *Touki-bouki*, including *Contras' City (1969)* and *Badou Boy* (1970), that established his reputation as a competent and innovative filmmaker. Both of his earlier films have been favorably compared to Sembène's first major films, and they generally confirm the paradigmatic cinematographic language that defined West African cinema from the late colonial period. *Contras' City* and *Badou Boy* situate African modernity within a perverted urban space indelibly marked by the colonial experience, a space that engenders delusions among young Africans as well as antisocial behavior. Both are studies in the way a colonialist image-Africa has been imbibed by the indigenous population and the dysfunctional society it gives rise to. In many ways, they imitate and reference Sembène's films—they feature a cart and driver, journeys through the streets of Dakar, and the tragicomic misadventures of seemingly naïve protagonists.[61]

Mambety's *Contras' City* constitutes a bridge between Sembène's *Borom Sarret* and Hondo's *Soleil Ô* in that it combines the narrative motif of Sembène's first short with the militant anti-imperialism of Hondo's epic. *Contras' City* is a twenty-one-minute color short that is a montage of street scenes revealing an ironic composite of life in Dakar nearly a decade after independence from France. The opening shot centers on the majestic Hôtel de ville just off the Place de l'indépendance as the narrator declaims to his young girl inquisitor, "Your sweet France apparently can't stand the sun! . . . Her France!" At that moment a horse-drawn cart conveying a camera crew filming a white actress pulls up in front of the building, a not very subtle reference to Sembène's first film. The narrator then states, "He keeps his oil by his side. It is safer there," at which point the camera trains on a Total building, the offices of France's major petroleum company. Next the viewer is taken to a theater-like edifice, replete with posted bills advertising European plays and a jazz quartet. Then the audience learns that the building is none other than the chamber of commerce. Mambety cuts to the presidential palace, where a disembodied voice, presumed to be that of the president, proclaims that the country must "grant

Senegalese women access to culture." The shot abruptly shifts to women at a newsstand perusing the kind of culture to which they have now gained access—all of the magazines being French and portraying the latest fashions of European women. The film continues with the ironic juxtaposition of pronouncements about the "freedom" attained by Africans and the reality of enduring European cultural and economic domination of the postcolony. This is most dramatically portrayed when the "Marseillaise," France's national anthem, breaks out, as Mambety reveals scenes of shantytowns and abject poverty. In his first foray into filmmaking, Mambety updates Sembène's urban mediascape, infusing it with urgency and expressing frustration at the lack of change in Senegal in the ten years since it won its sovereignty from France. In fact, Mambety presents West Africa's postcolonial leaders as buffoons, whose incompetence contrasts with the banality of daily life as people's paths intersect in Dakar's bustling streets.

Unlike either Sembène's or Hondo's films, *Contras' City* does not seem to offer any recognizable remedy to the postcolonial African predicament. Nonetheless, I suggest the film can be read as a consciousness-raising and witness-bearing act. The narration is bitingly ironic and undermines the illusions generated by the architecture and cultural artifacts that pervade Dakar's urban landscape. Mambety is unyielding in his exposé of Senegal's fraudulent "independence" and the role that its postcolonial leaders play in perpetuating the myth of liberty associated with the attainment of sovereignty. Moreover, he is explicit in drawing the connection between economics and the cultural practices that are forced onto the West African population, even mentioning France's deliberate strategy of "exporting its taste" in the form of cultural commodities, which is perhaps a nod toward the use of film by colonial rulers in the region during the 1950s. Consequently, Mambety's first film rests firmly within the emergent West African cinematographic tradition of the late 1960s even as it contributes to its further development.

If *Contras' City* and his later short *Badou Boy* revealed Mambety's talents as a filmmaker, it was *Touki-bouki* that established him as a highly experimental and provocative cineaste. Filmed on location in Senegal using 35 mm color film, *Touki-bouki* follows the misadventures of two disaffected youths, Mory (played by Magaye Niang) and Anta (played by Mareme Niang), who dream of escaping their corrupt and hopeless society and going to France, where they believe opportunities and excitement abound. The theme is not dissimilar to that of Sembène's *La noire de . . .* and Hondo's *Soleil Ô*. *Mandabi* too begins with a migrant in Paris sending money back to relatives in Dakar. What separates Mambety's film from those of his contemporaries is that his protagonists never attain the kind of clarity or consciousness that suggests there are prospects for progressive social change in Senegal. Such possibilities seem foreclosed by postcolonial circumstances that have stifled even the aspiration to transform their condition. In the end, just as the protagonists are about to embark on their long-awaited voyage to France, Mory decides against joining Anta on the ship and remains in Dakar watching as the boat departs for the former metropole. Thus, Mory does not follow in the footsteps of Diouana in *La noire de* . . . or Jean (the visitor) in *Soleil Ô,* and the viewer is left to wonder about Anta's fate upon arrival in her fantasized destination. When considering the experiences of Jean and Diouana upon their arrival in the "real" France, it is hardly surprising that even the particular motif of the journey from former colony to ex-colonial power should now be foreclosed in *Touki-bouki*. Moreover, Mambety's characters seem at times to be as corrupt as the other figures they encounter on their motorcycle tour of Dakar's environs. They often seem as hopeless and in as much need of being resisted as the wealthy businessmen and politicians they try to scam.

The film opens with a disturbing montage composed of shots of a herd of cattle idyllically being moved along the African savanna and of a slaughterhouse where blood covers the floor, walls, and indiscriminately spurts everywhere. Mambety returns to those images of herds being led to the slaughter throughout the film. Early in the picture, a postman begins his stumbling meanderings through slums and wastes, across highways and into downtown Dakar. Mambety appropriates the image of the postman, who was a heroic figure in Sembène's *Mandabi,* and transforms him into a bumbling drifter who has no apparent destination or purpose but is instead lost in the urban maze of the postcolonial hyper-city. The film's structuring narrative is the perverted desire of two delinquent young lovers—Mory and Anta—to escape the boredom and poverty of West Africa for the luxury and prestige of France. As they decide on their mission, the refrains of "Paris, Gateway to Paradise" play in the background. Mambety's ironic style takes over, as Anta feeds Mory's egotism, proclaiming that upon his return from the journey to France the people of Senegal will "make you their president" and "you'll be able to get fat off of the drought." The action follows the couple's escapades as they travel by motorcycle from Dakar's outskirts into the city center. Along the way, they rip off a sorceress, rob a wrestling match—hailed as "a great day for Senegal. . . . Long standing ties bind France and Senegal"—and steal clothes as well as a car from Charlie, a corrupt playboy with a predilection for young men. Mory strips and rides in the back of Charlie's car as if he were the president in a motorcade. Mambety cuts between scenes of eager crowds lining Dakar's streets barely restrained by the police and Mory triumphantly waving to a nonexistent audience as the driver speeds through dusty roads amid a barren landscape. Finally, the car passes the presidential palace, where it pauses and then continues out of Dakar to an awaiting group that cheers Mory and Anta, now dressed in Charlie's finest clothes. The entire sequence highlights the ridiculousness of the young lovers, but even more so of those who cheer them (and who cheer the president). After their long journey, Mory and Anta arrive at the port and prepare to board the Ancerville for France. At the port's entry a man running from his creditor announces, "This city's rough. 'No

Entry' signs to the left, 'No Entry' signs to the right, 'No Entry' signs everywhere. [It's] all because of too many debts." Then he states, "Debt never killed anybody." In the final scene, Mory finds himself unable to board the ship as he recalls the opening montage during which the cattle are led to the slaughter. Anta goes without him, headed to an uncertain and delusional fate. Mory returns to Dakar filled with despair and hopelessness. Mambety presents his situation as a trap with no good way out. Meanwhile, the postman reappears and walks right past Mory, down the steps, and into the street. Mambety, consequently, disarticulates and undermines Sembène's closing scene in *Mandabi*. The postman and Mory do not connect. The cathartic moment when the protagonist achieves consciousness never happens in *Touki-bouki*.

Universally hailed as a "fresh" contribution to Francophone West African cinema, Mambety's *Touki-bouki* has been embraced by some scholars as an iconic moment that suggested an alternative film aesthetic for a region that otherwise suffered under what Harrow calls "the controlling frames of historicism and class-based analysis" erected by Sembène and Hondo.[62] However, there is a much stronger argument to be made that Mambety is an important contributor to the West African cinematographic language forged in the 1950s by both French anticolonial filmmakers and directors from the region. In fact, *Touki-bouki* largely builds on Mambety's earlier work, which clearly belongs within the aesthetic tradition of Francophone West African filmmaking. If the tone in *Touki-bouki* is more despairing than the earlier films, it nonetheless maintains its critical stance toward the colonial legacy and the postcolonial society that is its product. As Murphy and Williams observe, "It is possible to identify within much of Mambety's work a critique of the effects of capitalist modernity upon Senegalese society."[63] However, this does not indicate his rejection of modernity in favor of a deconstructivist and hybrid "postmodernity" of the sort propounded by Homi Bhabha.[64] Rather, Mambety's *Touki-bouki* claims a place for Africa and Africans in the construction of modernity in the wider world.[65]

In terms of cinematic style Mambety's work clearly belongs in the same tradition as Sembène's, Hondo's, and Vieyra's motion pictures. He uses the same editing techniques of point/counterpoint, montage, and short cut to create a disruptive feel that forces viewers to keep their distance from the actors on the screen even though they are able to identify them as "real" characters in postcolonial West African society. Like its predecessors, *Touki-bouki* uses long shots to situate the protagonists in the African geographic space and presents the dialogue in an African language (Wolof in this instance) that authenticates the product as African. Finally, Mambety embraces the archetypal genre of West African filmmaking, the docu-fiction; the stories are rooted in the contemporary world but at the same time are fictionalized so as to present a meaning that transcends the banal reality the viewers experience in their daily lives.

By the time of *Touki-bouki*'s release in 1973 West Africa had been the site of decades of cinematic practice shaped by the efforts of French and local filmmakers, who sought to intervene in and reconfigure the regime of representation as it pertained to Africa and Africans. By the early 1970s the colonialist image-Africa that hailed Franco-African cooperation as necessary for the construction of an African modernity situated in the countryside and based on agricultural and artisanal production had been forcefully challenged by a body of work created by daring and enterprising cineastes. From Vautier's *Afrique 50* to Mambety's *Touki-bouki,* cineastes from or working in West Africa hammered away at a hegemonic representation of Africa and Africans that had negatively structured audiences' perception of the continent and its people around the world since the invention of motion pictures. Those same debilitating stereotypes also had distorted and disabled Africans' own understanding of their cultures and identities. Through the pioneering efforts of Vieyra, Sembène, Hondo, and other West African cineastes, consumers of celluloid entertainment locally and globally finally could be exposed to an alternative image-Africa that demanded its own modernity, which was urban, progressive, and rooted in Africans' own traditions and historical experiences, including colonialism. As Hondo narrates in *Soleil Ô,* "I am bleached by your culture, but I remain a Negro, as at the beginning. I bring you greetings from Africa." But representation was only one aspect of the cinema industrial complex that West Africans needed to appropriate in order to reconstruct their societies after independence. From Vieyra's first adumbration of an African anticolonial film politics in the mid-1950s, motion pictures were viewed as both an art and an industry. Hondo put it succinctly: "Film is an integral arm of development."[66] The story now turns to an investigation of West African filmmakers' struggles on the materialist terrain of the cinema industrial complex in the postcolonial period.

5 The West African Cinema Industrial Complex, 1960s–70s

IN 1968 ROBERT Delavignette, the ex-colonial administrator and author of *Les paysans noirs*, gave his take on the meaning of the end of French rule in West Africa. Commenting on the prospects for the region's future he wrote, "Decolonization, it is independence. But independence is not real unless it is linked with the economic and social development of the decolonized country." And, for that development to be realized, he added, "the cooperation of the [newly independent] country with some other countries," namely, France, was required.[1] Several years earlier as a participant in a roundtable conference sponsored by the Association française de science politique he had discussed at length the continued necessity of cooperation between France and the former overseas territories after they attained political sovereignty in order for them to develop appropriately. At the meeting Delavignette said, "The subaltern cadres rapidly assimilate the rudiments of the matters that we would want them to learn; they recognize that they derive from [those lessons] some material benefits, and they aspire to progress in the apprenticeship [and obtain] some [of the] secrets of the White people's technical prowess."[2] Delavignette's rhetoric was consistent with France's reconfigured civilizing mission in the late colonial period, in the formulation of which he had played a major part.

However, what is striking is that Delavignette, along with his intellectual and political associates, expected that mission to continue after the formal end of empire. Thus, for the former imperial rulers, the modalities of colonial rule were not a function of the exercise of explicit political power but universal attributes of a beneficent culture charged with a historic task of leading benighted populations along the path to the realization of their culturally specific forms of modernity. The lapse of government control did not call into question the fundamental cultural and socioeconomic relationship between France and Africa. The "cooperation" Delavignette envisioned was unidirectional. Africa needed France's continued assistance in order to achieve its natural expression of modern development, but Africans had nothing to offer the French in return except perhaps gratitude for the helping hand. Hondo's image in *Soleil Ô* of the African cultural arrow blunted and overwhelmed by the projection of European values into Africa can be read, then, as a visual rendering of continued French representational aspirations with regard to Africa as well as an expression of the enduring materialist structural relationship between the former colonizer and the ex-colonies. French rulers expected the parameters of the West African cinema industrial complex as elaborated in the last years of imperial domination to persist largely intact despite France's relinquishment of political authority in the region in 1960.

The pioneer generation of West African filmmakers, though, forcefully countered France's control over the regime of representation within the cinematic field through their increasing productivity and aesthetic innovation during the 1960s. Whether they learned their craft in the Soviet Union, as did Sembène and Cissé, or were self-taught like Hondo and Mambety, cineastes from the region forged a counterhegemonic image-Africa that claimed a place for African self-representation within the international field of motion picture production. While racist tropes and colonialist-era images of a primitive, wild, or dangerous Africa continued to circulate on the world's movie screens long after the end of empire, West African filmmakers had broken its monopoly on perceptions of Africa and Africans available to global and local audiences.[3]

The problem remained, however, of finding ways to overcome France's dominance of the materialist structure of the cinema industrial complex. West African cultural activists identified persistent French ownership of the infrastructure of the film industry from the basic equipment to the distribution network as a threat to the progress already made in the representational arena as well as to the prospects for the further economic development of the region. In 1969 *Présence africaine* sponsored the first Pan-African cultural festival in Algiers, Algeria. In the resolution that resulted from the meeting, the delegates reaffirmed the link between cultural and economic development, declaring that the intellectual's "action must inspire that revolution of the mind without which it is impossible for a people to overcome its economic and social underdevelopment." Neocolonialism, according to the resolution, "aware of the still negative aspects of this situation," conceived "a new, well-concerted form of action" that was no longer violent but nonetheless was just as dangerous. According to the cultural activists gathered in Algiers, the cinema was central to the strategy of continuing to combat negative tropes of Africa and Africans as well as to facilitating the kind of economic development that would contribute to a different model of "real independence" than the one Delavignette imagined. The resolution stated, "In this field, Africa should produce its own mode of expression and choose suitable means to make its expression available to the people. The African States should, therefore, organize themselves to produce, release and market their own films and to fight against the limits which are holding up the development of a truly African cinema."[4]

Vieyra, Hondo, Sembène, and the other founders of West African cinema realized that without command of the materialist dimension of the cinema industrial complex, any progress in the representational realm would be fleeting and reversible. Moreover, a fully articulated and truly independent African filmmaking tradition could not be realized absent independent access to those structural elements that made motion picture production and distribution possible. Finally, without the cooperation of their own governments not only would film fail to take off as a viable form of cultural expression for West African societies, but economic reconstruction could never be achieved for the former colonies and they would remain in a dependent relationship with France and the developed Western world. In 1970 Vieyra repeated his call, first made in 1958, for West African countries to support the construction of an independent film industry as a vital component of the region's future cultural and economic development. A decade after independence, Vieyra noted the near total lack of progress in this area, raising the specter of cultural and economic stasis or even decline. He warned that Africa was beginning to lose its intellectual capital to Europe because there were not enough jobs available for those with an advanced education or specialized training or because there was not an educational infrastructure that could foster such skill development in the first place. Once again, Vieyra turned to film as a vehicle that could easily and quickly furnish a means by which to retain those West Africans with advanced skills or aspiring to attain them. He looked at France's success following the Second World War and argued, as he had in the late 1950s, that African states should commit themselves to providing "technical training and audiovisual technology" for those who wanted to contribute to their country's development. Governments must also, according to Vieyra, "create 'houses of culture' or cultural centers" along with ministries, departments, and so forth to provide institutional support for the cultivation of a fully elaborated cinema industrial complex that would serve the interests of the African people in the project of cultural and economic development.[5] This chapter follows the battle waged by Francophone West African filmmakers to seize control of the materialist dimension of the cinema industrial complex and to harness it to the project of economic development for the postcolonies.

In that struggle, though, France sought to preserve its domination of the material aspects of filmmaking, including the capital, equipment, postproduction facilities, marketing, and distribution that undergirded the entire cinematic enterprise. French officials in the Ministère de la coopération, through its Bureau du cinéma, recognized that they could no longer prevent Africans from picking up the camera to make their own films. However, their dominance of the physical accouterments of the filmmaking process enabled French officials to imagine that they could incorporate African cineastes into France's managed system of "Francophone" celluloid production. Their inclusion within the broader framework of French-language film production would transform African directors' work into vehicles for the promotion of the former metropole's enduring mission. That project held African countries in a permanently dependent relationship with France and pushed them toward the actualization of a colonialist notion of an African modernity situated in rural areas and dedicated to agricultural and artisanal activities that would arise in "cooperation" with the ex-metropole.

The agents that staffed the new Ministère de la coopération had ample experience in Franco-African relations, as most were veteran colonial hands. Moreover, the newly created Ministère des affaires culturelles, which often collaborated with the Ministère de la coopération, had its share of former officials from the Ministère de la France d'outre-mer. Herman Lebovics offers an insightful and detailed account of how the personnel of the former colonial ministry came to form the backbone of France's new cultural ministry, headed from its founding by André Malraux: Malraux "shaped French international cultural policy after decolonization to reclaim French influence by cultural means, venturing France's abundant cultural capital when its political capital had run out."[6] While Lebovics is primarily concerned with the use of the instrumentalities of colonial rule in France that were directed against the French population through the projects of the Ministère des affaires culturelles, the Ministère de la coopération acted as a counterpart for carrying out those same objectives in the former colonies. The "cooperation," as it was known, contained from the outset a mandate directed at maintaining cultural *and* material control in the former colonies, specifically West Africa, long the centerpiece of "greater France." To that end, the cooperation created (or reestablished) the Bureau du cinéma in 1963, replicating the agency that the Ministère de la France d'outre-mer had built within its bureaucracy following the Second World War and that had been locally instantiated in the form of a cinema department for French West Africa. The Bureau du cinéma within the new Ministère de la coopération was responsible for managing not only the representational dimension of the cinema industrial complex but also and most importantly the materialist aspects through which the films it financed or helped to realize would be distributed and produced in the first place. Moreover, it liaised with the Ministère des affaires culturelles' CNC, which played a significant role in financing many early African films. Consequently, even as the West African countries achieved political independence, France reconstituted the institutional structures of colonial rule, specifically with regard to motion pictures. It adapted them to the postcolonial world in a manner that would facilitate the perpetuation of the fundamental Franco-African relationship that characterized imperial rule, a relationship that placed the former colonies in an enduring dependent role.

While scholars have noted the prominent role France played in financing early West African film production as well as the political and aesthetic problems that such a relationship posed for cineastes from the region, few have offered a detailed account of the ways in which the former metropole assiduously sought to perpetuate the fundamental structures of the colonial-era cinema industrial complex in their entirety. In fact, Harrow ignores the materialist dimension of the cinematic field in his critique of the artistic choices early filmmakers such as Sembène and

Hondo made as they struggled to found an independent and socially responsive African cinema.⁷ Ukadike does highlight the ambiguous role of the Ministère de la coopération in the founding of West African motion picture production. He notes the important source of financing and access to postproduction facilities made available through the ministry's Bureau du cinéma but also cites the paternalistic restrictions French officials placed on African directors in giving them access to the money and technology they needed to make films. In the end, Ukadike finds the "neocolonialist aspects" of the Bureau du cinéma's functioning objectionable but, he remarks, "without the type of aid made available by the Ministère de la Coopération it would have taken longer to complete some of the well-crafted films of black Africa or, more likely, some of them may not have been made at all."⁸ Thus, in Ukadike's account it is unclear the degree to which the development of an independent African cinema was delayed, obstructed, or aided by the activities of the French Ministère de la coopération. He does not offer any further analysis of its aesthetic mission in West Africa or of the economic importance of the film industry for France in the postcolonial world. By extension, he separates the process of movie production from the product's distribution, merely noting the continued presence of foreign monopolies in control of West African theaters into the 1960s.

Diawara is even less critical of France's intervention in the process of West African filmmaking. He credits the ministry with "help[ing] newly independent African countries in the field of communication." He specifically refers to the role of the Consortium audio-visuel international (CAI), founded within the ministry in 1961, in "helping African governments produce newsreels and documentaries" and to the role of the Bureau du cinéma in providing "independent African filmmakers with the opportunity to create [motion pictures]." Remarkably, Diawara asserts that it was only *after* decolonization that France (and presumably African filmmakers) recognized that film could be an important arm of economic development.⁹ In previous chapters I have shown that the French government had embraced the cinema as crucial for its own and the overseas territories' economic modernization in the immediate postwar period. Moreover, Vieyra and others in GAC had consistently argued throughout the 1950s that film had to be a centerpiece of postcolonial African reconstruction, culturally and economically.

By the 1960s the struggle for control over the materialist aspect of the cinema industrial complex was well under way. Significantly, it was African enthusiasm for films that forced the French colonial state to become interested in the cinema in the first place. Throughout the late colonial period France tightened its control over the production and distribution of movies throughout West Africa, even elaborating its own cinematographic language to direct the formation of a specific African modernity born of French rulers' own imaginations. The infrastructure for cinematic production was already in place in West Africa and France prior to the creation of the Ministère de la coopération at the end of formal imperial control. The new

French government agency merely took over the tasks that were previously under the purview of the Ministère de la France d'outre-mer and the general government for French West Africa and adapted them to a relationship that could no longer be managed through executive decree but had to be conducted via negotiation and a bilateral treaty.

With political decolonization completed in West Africa by 1960 the *terms* of the struggle for control over the materialist dimension of the cinema industrial complex changed, but the underlying pattern of engagement that had structured the colonial-era interaction between France and West Africa endured. The techniques of control had to be altered in order to maintain the same fundamental relationship that functioned during the age of imperialist domination. The ability of Africans to create their own movies and the establishment of independent African states in the region opened the possibility that the extant cinema industrial complex could be appropriated by locals for the purpose of articulating an African modernity that reflected the aspirations and vision of the indigenous population as expressed through its cultural activists. Senegal's appointment of Vieyra to the cabinet with the responsibility of developing newsreels, documentaries, and films suggested that his vision of a "cinema in the service of the people" could very well become a reality in postcolonial West Africa. It was not certain that France would hold all the material cards with regard to the motion picture industry after 1960. Consequently, the fight for dominance of the cinematic field in West Africa greatly intensified in the early postcolonial period. To explore how that battle unfolded, the narrative first turns to how France adapted to the altered circumstances ushered in by decolonization.

"Cooperation": France and Postcolonial African Cinema

Charles de Gaulle, who returned to the French presidency in the wake of a rebellion by European settlers in Algeria in May 1958, signaled that while France was prepared to cede political sovereignty to the West African states it was not ready to relinquish control over the material and cultural life of the region. At the end of 1960 he stated, "France [is changing] from the outdated colonial system to a system of fruitful and friendly co-operation."[10] The shift from direct imperial rule to a certain form of partnership was embodied in the institutional two-step that transformed the Ministère de la France d'outre-mer into the Ministère de la coopération et l'assistance technique between 1959 and 1961. Those personnel who did not join Malraux at the new Ministère des affaires culturelles, also created in 1959, remained in the Ministère de la coopération overseeing many of the same activities that they had throughout the late colonial era. Even the funds FIDES and FERDES, created in the late 1940s to facilitate the modernization of West Africa, were rolled into the budget of the new bureaucracy, thus preserving their mission. They now operated under the acronym Fonds d'aide et de coopération (FAC) with the responsibility of "fostering development" in Francophone sub-Saharan Africa "through investment subsidies."[11] Part of the funding from FIDES was dedicated to the production of films for distribution in West Africa, such as *Paysans noirs*, released in 1949.

The integration of the former Ministère de la France d'outre-mer's funding programs with the new Ministère de la coopération suggested that the idea of film as a tool of modernization would endure into the postcolonial era and become part of France's new foreign policy with regard to West Africa.[12] The money earmarked for motion picture production became the basis for the operating budget of the resurrected Bureau du cinéma after 1963, headed from its inception by Jean-René Debrix.[13] Just in case the purpose of the new ministry—to ensure continuity between the colonial and postcolonial eras—was not entirely clear, Prime Minister Georges Pompidou elaborated on it upon his accession to office in 1964: "The policy of cooperation follows on from the expansionist policies of nineteenth-century Europe, when vast colonial empires were created or extended and Europe made its economic and political influence felt over an enormous area."[14] By then a semiofficial division of labor had emerged within the upper echelons of the French government whereby the Ministère des affaires culturelles took charge of promoting French culture and values around the world (including to Africa) and the Ministère de la coopération handled the areas of technical aid and assistance to the former colonies. Both agencies through their different mandates played central roles in France's attempt to retain its dominance of the materialist dimension of the cinema industrial complex in West Africa. By promoting French culture in the region and seeking to maintain the area as a captive market for French films, the Ministère des affaires culturelles by default became implicated in the marketing and distribution aspects of film in West Africa. Through its control over the assistance funds that France established for West Africa after 1945 and its management of programs concerned with access to technology, the Ministère de la coopération became the agency through which aspiring African filmmakers were expected to seek capital, equipment, and the technicians necessary for making motion pictures. That mechanism also gave France a way to continue to manage the image-Africa that the former Ministère de la France d'outre-mer had created by means of its film politics during the late colonial period.

At the time of independence West Africa was endowed with an extensive motion picture infrastructure, which had expanded rapidly even as the drama of decolonization unfolded.[15] Vieyra lists at least 160 operational movie theaters, enclosed and open air, in the former federation of French West Africa (excluding Togo and Cameroon) after independence, most owned and operated by COMACICO and SECMA. They included cinemas equipped with both 16 mm and the standard commercial 35 mm projectors. Annual receipts indicated that millions of people ventured into the darkened halls or public spaces to watch the latest releases from Hollywood, France, Hong Kong, India, and elsewhere.[16] The end of French rule meant that the censorship laws dating to the 1934 Laval decree were no longer in force. For the first time in decades West Africans could enjoy any offering from any country without French perceptions of what images were appropriate for indigenous audiences dictating the content they could access on the silver screen. Despite the ever-tightening censorship of the late colonial period, Vieyra's data demonstrates that motion pictures continued to enjoy widespread and growing popularity in the region. As a result, the economic impact of film in West Africa expanded, as new countries emerged from decades of foreign rule.

By the end of the 1960s, television became an additional outlet for films, as governments in the region invested in studios and asked filmmakers, including Vieyra, to make movies specifically for broadcast on the small screen. In addition, the CAI within the French Ministère de la coopération was geared toward financing the production of the types of media that would find their primary outlet through televisions in West Africa. However, the viewing experience in the private home as opposed to the public theater was quite different. One of the hallmarks of the experience of motion pictures in West Africa was the collective act of watching the films and engaging in postscreening discussions over the content and presentation. That aspect of audience engagement with the creative work was integral to the process of making films, whether by colonial or anticolonial cineastes. Most of the pictures designed for air on televisions were documentaries or newsreels, distinct genres from the fiction and docu-fiction movies presented on the big screen, and they were made with little expectation that the viewer would play a significant part in the construction of the product's meaning or participate in a collective process of consumption. They were imagined as vehicles for the dissemination of information rather than as inspirational or motivational works of art, the way motion pictures were viewed. Television programming carried an inherent potential for a more authoritarian relationship between the producing agents and the private viewer. In addition, the spatial component of the motion picture consumption experience offered a means for articulating solidarities in a way that was not possible through watching television with its atomizing tendencies. It was the socialization conduced by the cinematic space, after all, that made the cinema industrial complex a vital component of the modalities of colonial rule as well as a potential vehicle for postcolonial economic and cultural reconstruction. In addition, in the 1960s movie theaters were far more accessible than televisions; owing to the lack of electric infrastructure and transmission networks as well as the cost of owning private sets, most West Africans did not have immediate and regular exposure to the new broadcast medium.[17]

The extensive film infrastructure in West Africa made the region an important market for film exports from France, as it had been from the end of the Second World War.[18] Therefore, part of the French government's strategy after 1960 was to maintain the former metropole's dominance of the regional consumption of films while also providing the means for West Africans to make their own films, which could potentially generate an additional source of revenue through control over the distribution rights to the works of local cineastes. French sponsorship of the production of African motion pictures offered financing and facilities to aspiring filmmakers that simply could not be found in West Africa. By making such services available, France could maintain control over the vital materialist dimension of the cinema industrial complex and present a disincentive for local governments to develop those resources on their own, since those new states would be presumably strapped for cash.

The largesse dispensed by France to support the production of West African films also answered the challenge posed by other potential sources of training, equipment, and capital such as the Soviet Union, Italy, and the United States that were already attracting would-be directors from the region. Sembène's decision in 1961 to journey to Gorki Studios in the Soviet Union in order to learn his craft was a striking example of what France hoped to prevent happening by presenting itself as a beneficent provider of sustenance for the burgeoning West African filmmaking industry. Coincidentally, the Ministère de la coopération established its Bureau du cinéma the year that Sembène finished his study in the Soviet Union and released *Borom Sarret*. Moreover, Cissé began his training at the prestigious GIK in Moscow that year, eventually becoming the first African to complete the entire cycle of studies in an elite cinema school in 1970.[19] Clearly, France had to offer the means whereby Africans could be trained, gain access to equipment and facilities, and be furnished capital if the former metropole hoped to maintain influence within the cinema industrial complex in West Africa, especially over the image-Africa likely to be generated through the work of the new filmmakers from the region.

From its inception, the Ministère de la coopération focused on the provision of equipment and postproduction facilities for aspiring West African cineastes. In return for access to those essential material components of film manufacturing the African director was expected to relinquish "noncommercial" distribution rights. The modalities for dispensing aid to the West African filmmaker revealed the inherent strategic objectives of the ministry with regard to the cinema industrial complex in the former colonies. The funds released to an African director did not go directly to the applicant. Instead, they were officially provided to a French producer with whom the African cineaste was expected to work. This approach illustrated the ideal of "cooperation" advocated by Delavignette in the late 1940s and that was embodied in the very name of the ministry founded to furnish technical assistance to the former overseas territories. The French producer and African director were expected to work in tandem: the African filmmaker would propose the script and treatment and the French partner would be granted the prerogative to make suggestions for revision. Once the "partners" had reached agreement on the film scenario, the ministry provided aid for equipment, facilities, and technicians.[20] While the film could be shot anywhere, this system of aid meant that all the technical aspects of making the motion picture had to be undertaken in France. Thus, the mechanisms by which the ministry released its funds to African directors assured that the money stayed in France and did not contribute in any way to the economic development of the former colonies. As Teresa Hoefert de Turégano surmises, "This form of assistance did little to benefit local African infrastructures and thus perpetuated African dependencies on France for film production."[21] That was, I argue, precisely the point.

Moreover, ceding noncommercial distribution rights to France was more significant than it at first appeared. While the African filmmaker could freely distribute his or her product in commercial theaters, as long as those venues remained in the hands of the same monopolies who ruled the cinematic space during the colonial era, the opportunities for emergent West African cineastes to commercially dispense their films in their home countries was severely circumscribed. Thus, the primary means by which aspiring West African directors could expose their work to the public and gain the reputation that was often necessary to attract a paying audience was through the noncommercial and film festival network, both of which France gained the rights to as part of the bargain that allowed the movie to be made in the first place. In fact, one of the main activities of the ministry's Bureau du cinéma during the 1960s was to facilitate African filmmakers' access to the festival circuit by paying for their attendance and entering the motion pictures into the competitions.[22] Hoefert de Turégano notes that French practices in the materialist dimension of the cinema industrial complex during the 1960s contributed to forcing African filmmakers into the trajectory of the "cultural, noncommercial stream" of motion picture production that made "African" identity and values the central subject for treatment through the cinema.[23] That strategy was not new to the postcolonial era, though, as it was an essential component of France's film politics in the region, which predated West African independence by more than a decade. The ministry was established explicitly as an institution with the objective of maintaining continuity in material and cultural practice as West Africa transitioned from overseas territories to sovereign states. It was designed to enact the kind of "cooperation" explicated by Delavignette that would lead to the realization of the specific African modernity he and his associates in the colonial administration had long envisioned for the region.

The methodology for the provision of aid to African filmmakers that the Ministère de la coopération elaborated was certain to place the aspiring cineastes in an ambiguous situation as well as to serve as a potential source of conflict in the creative process. The Bureau du cinéma's insistence that African directors be paired with French producers who handled the money granted for the project was a not very subtle mechanism by which to enable France to continue management of the image-Africa it had sought to cultivate during the late colonial period. In an environment where one of the top priorities of Africans and presumably one of the great prizes of decolonization was to reclaim control over the construction of their own identities and image-Africa, this "partnership" could not be read by them as anything but neocolonial. It was not as unambiguous a relationship as Debrix liked to make it seem. The director of the Bureau du cinéma proclaimed that "any African director who thinks . . . that he 'has a film in his stomach' can find the means to make that film in freedom at the Bureau du Cinéma."[24]

Despite Debrix's magnanimous explication of the Bureau du cinéma's role in nurturing the growth of Francophone West African film, Sembène became one of the first victims of the kind of censorship that France could still exercise as long as the former colonies did not have control over the materialist dimension of the cinema industrial complex in their countries. Debrix's agency rejected Sembène's request for assistance to make *La noire de . . .* strictly on the basis of its subject matter, indicating that the limited charge of the Bureau du cinéma's review committee to only judge projects on the basis of their feasibility could be very loosely interpreted.[25] Ultimately, though, the near total lack of capital, facilities, and technicians in West Africa meant that Sembène, Cissé, and Hondo had to contrive alternative means whereby they could gain access to the basic materials for filmmaking and garner the experience vital to any cineaste's development as an artist. The material reality of the early postcolonial era gave France a powerful hand to play in the larger strategy of promoting its own cultural and economic objectives around the world generally and most pointedly in its West African ex-colonies. The role of the Ministère de la coopération in the formative years of West African cinema makes explicit the imbricated nature of the materialist and representational aspects of the cinema industrial complex.[26]

One of the most notorious instances of France seeking to use funds from the Ministère de la coopération to control the artistic attributes of an African film was in the case of the making of Sembène's *Mandabi*. After producing his first film on a shoestring budget, largely self-financed, and partnering with a French company to realize *La noire de . . .* despite its initial rejection by the Bureau du cinéma, Sembène turned to the Ministère des affaires culturelles to compete for a grant from the CNC to finance the adaptation of his novel *Le mandat* to the screen. This project was to be Sembène's most ambitious work to date; it was to have a larger cast and a longer script and to be shot on 35 mm film. Consequently, it would require more capital, specialized and expensive equipment, and a larger crew than either of his first two films. Sembène sought to make a feature-length film of a quality that would match the elevated standard of the commercial global film industry. For a sub-Saharan West African, this was to be a first and would, therefore, mark the region's forceful entry into the international cinematic field. The stakes could not have been higher when Sembène received special permission from Malraux's ministry to compete for funding from the CNC. Such money, as Shaka notes, was normally reserved for French filmmakers and had done much to promote the works of the New Wave by auteurs such as Jean-Luc Goddard, François Truffaut, and Chris Marker (who was one of the directors of *Les statues meurent aussi*).[27]

Sembène won the grant and was immediately referred to the Ministère de la coopération's Bureau du cinéma, since French law required that such funds be handled through that agency's FAC program. To make the film the Bureau du cinéma and CNC paired Sembène with executive producer Robert de Nesle, the owner of Comptoir français de productions cinématographiques and the distribution company Comptoir français du film. De Nesle appointed Jean Maumy as production manager. It was Maumy who would be working hands on with Sembène in the making of *Mandabi*. A cursory look at the previous credits of both de Nesle and Maumy suggests that they were not likely to share Sembène's artistic vision. For example, Maumy's other productions included the white slavery melodrama *Marchands de filles* (1957) and the James Bond-esque *Agent Secret FX 18* (1964), while de Nesle had financed a long list of "erotic" and violent action films since the early 1950s, many of which ironically would have had difficulty passing the scrutiny of French West Africa's censorship commission.[28]

It was not long before Sembène ran into problems with his French "partners." The Senegalese filmmaker wanted to shoot the film in black and white, as he had done with *Borom Sarret* and *La noire de . . .* Moreover, his treatment remained faithful to the 1964 novel. Sembène envisioned this project as answering Vieyra's call for West African novelists to adapt their literary works to the screen so that the messages contained within the written texts could be made accessible to larger audiences.[29] While Sembène wrote the novel in French, the film treatment called for Wolof as the primary idiom of the dialogue. When he presented the plan to de Nesle and Maumy, they insisted that Sembène shoot the film in color, include "sexual and erotic scenes" to ensure that the film conformed to Western tastes, and use exoticism to expand its potential reach at the box office.[30] In other words, de Nesle and Maumy wanted Sembène to make a film more to their liking, a film that would represent French interests rather than those of West African viewers. Such a film, had it been produced, would also have revisited some of the worst tropes of the image-Africa from the colonial era that even the imperial administration's film politics had worked to counter in the 1950s.

The Senegalese filmmaker acceded to using color film but would not alter the content of the picture to suit Western tastes. Moreover, he retained Wolof as the film's primary idiom and shot almost the entire picture in Dakar; only a few scenes of the nephew Abdou were shot in Paris. Most of the cast was comprised of nonprofessional Senegalese who were recruited to better convey the documentary feel Sembène desired and because they could speak Wolof. Sembène oversaw all of the creative aspects of the film; his crew was made up of both French and

Senegalese. Once shot, the footage was taken back to Paris to be edited; all postproduction work likewise took place in Paris. The representatives of the Ministère de la coopération's Bureau du cinéma and the CNC then had the opportunity to offer final approval or suggestions for further editing.

As noted in chapter 4, the French government's representatives insisted that Sembène redo his film, this time using French as the primary idiom of expression.[31] Making a motion picture in French would certainly fulfill the mandate of the CNC and the Ministère des affaires culturelles to promote France's culture through its language.[32] However, it flew in the face of a primary aspiration of West African filmmakers to use the cinema as a tool for postcolonial cultural (re)construction. Vieyra had seen clearly in 1958 that making films in autochthonous African languages was essential if the product was to resonate among its intended audience. It was also vital to authenticating the motion picture as African rather than the product of an external imagination.

The dispute between Sembène and the agents of the Ministère de la coopération's Bureau du cinéma and the CNC harkened back to the debates within the colonial hierarchy during the 1950s around the permissibility of showing films in West Africa that were in "foreign" languages and exposed the neocolonial objectives that had been a part of the institutional culture of the new government ministries from their inception. Since the funding that enabled the production of the motion picture originated with the CNC, French officials could hold up release of the film until their expectations had been met. Control over the materialist dimension of the cinema industrial complex gave France leverage by which to influence its representational component as well. The result, as we have seen, was that Sembène made a second, French language version of *Mandabi* to satisfy the demands of the Ministère de la coopération and the CNC, who, having come to the conclusion that the original Wolof version was far superior to the French version, reluctantly gave their approval for the film's release in 1968.[33]

Sembène, after much difficulty, won this round and made the film mostly as he had intended (as well as made a film he had not wanted to make). *Mandabi* won the Special Jury Prize at the Venice Film Festival in 1968 and quickly achieved iconic status in the young history of African cinema. One of the main reasons for its unique place in the history of sub-Saharan African filmmaking is precisely its use of an African language as the main idiom of expression.[34] Not only had Sembène appropriated and further articulated an African cinematographic language in terms of syntax, but he had also introduced real Africans speaking in their own voice and language to the motion picture screens of the world. Sembène's adaptation of his French-language novel into a movie using a Wolof-based dialogue symbolically sought to blunt the European cultural arrow directed at Africa and restore the African projection of values to the wider world through the actions of Africans as agents in their own history. As the Ethiopian-American filmmaker Haile Gerima puts it, "In *Mandabi,* Sembène's characters expressed themselves in their African language. This was a revolution!"[35] *Mandabi* as a movie and Sembène's struggle to make the film the way he wanted exemplify the dialectical struggle between French officials and anticolonial West African cultural activists for control of the cinema industrial complex that had been unfolding since at least the late 1940s.

In fact, Sembène's experience in the production of *Mandabi* exposed another flank on which the aspiring West African cineastes had to fight in order to develop the sort of cinematic tradition they insisted was essential to the region's future economic and cultural regeneration. While the film was celebrated at international festivals and screened in theaters across the United States and Europe, the Senegalese government banned it because of its criticism of the postcolonial government.[36] Even if Senghor's administration had not prohibited Sembène from showing his film in Senegal, *Mandabi* likely would have not reached the kind of audience its maker desired. The continued monopolistic control exerted by COMACICO and SECMA over theaters and the distribution networks in West Africa virtually assured that Sembène would have to follow another practice learned from the Soviet experience and use mobile outdoor cinemas to screen his films personally to audiences gathered in public spaces. As chapter 1 details, the French colonial government also deployed the technique of mobile film projection in the 1950s to overcome the lack of cinematic infrastructure in large parts of rural West Africa, and as such it would not have been unusual in the experiences of the region's film audiences.[37] The multiple and multiplying material obstacles West African filmmakers confronted in the 1960s pushed West Africa's pioneer generation of cineastes beyond the anticolonial film politics of the late colonial and early independence years toward a more explicitly "revolutionary film politics" by the end of the first decade after decolonization. Directors from across West Africa began to engage more systematically in film theory and moved toward organizing to pursue their objective of building a cinema in the service of the people.

Cinema and Revolution: Organization of African Filmmakers

In a later interview, Cissé stated, "I said it many times before that making a film in Africa belongs to the realm of a miracle."[38] However, the precarious state of the cinema industrial complex in West Africa that was the source of Cissé's later frustration was not an inevitable outcome of the struggles waged by West African filmmakers during the 1960s. In the early years of African cinematic production, real possibilities emerged that could have made the region a center of movie making and consuming. After many contentious encounters with French officials either at the Ministère des affaires culturelles or the Ministère de la coopération and the failure of their own governments to protect and nurture filmmakers as they struggled to develop their art, the West African cineastes began to take a more independent and proactive stand. In addition, those structural impediments also influenced the aesthetic direction and political activism of the pioneer generation of West African directors. Increasingly, Sembène, Cissé, and others moved toward viewing the screen images they generated as potential agents of social revolution and to understanding the material process of making movies as a revolutionary act. The visitor Jean crouched in the underbrush with his finger on the trigger of a machine gun in Hondo's *Soleil Ô* was becoming a metaphor for West African cineastes wielding a camera that would fire directly back at the agents of global imperialist capitalism.

The shift from regarding films primarily as a means for correcting the image-Africa projected to audiences throughout the world to conceiving of movies as a means of inciting radical social change fit within larger cinematic trends throughout the developing Third World. In fact, Sembène's *Mandabi* was released the same year that the Latin American filmmakers Octavio Getino and Fernando Solanas produced *La hora de los hornos*, regarded by critics as the founding act of the revolutionary filmmaking movement called "Third Cinema." In 1969, the year that Hondo completed the filming of *Soleil Ô*, which is strikingly similar in style to Getino and Solanas' film, the two Latin American cineastes published the manifesto of their movement, "Towards a Third Cinema: Notes and Experiences for the Development of a Cinema of Liberation in the Third World." Many African filmmakers have testified to the powerful influence that the ideas of Third Cinema exerted on their subsequent work.[39] Conversely, the intervention of West African filmmakers in the cinematic field after 1960 certainly had an impact on the trajectory of the new generation of Latin American film artists as they sought to use the medium to effect social change. In fact, Solanas and Getino articulated their revolutionary theory of motion picture production in response to many of the same frustrations and intractable structural obstacles that bedeviled Sembène, Cissé, and others from West Africa. In their call for a new kind of cinematic practice, the Latin American directors highlighted the near monopolistic control that Western companies exerted over "production, distribution, and exhibition" as posing a fundamental dilemma for any socially conscious filmmaker seeking to practice his or her craft. The materialist constraints of the cinema industry directly circumscribed the artistic dimension of film practice, forcing filmmakers to make movies that conformed to the desires of the world capitalist system or "at best . . . succeeded in bearing witness to the decay of bourgeois values and testifying to social injustice."[40] One could situate Sembène's earliest films as well as Vieyra's work in the 1950s within such a tradition.

To escape the "system's" reach, Solanas and Getino pronounced that "one of two requirements" must be met by the aspiring filmmaker. The first was "making films that the System cannot assimilate and which are foreign to its needs" and the second was "making films that directly and explicitly set out to fight the System." They excluded the experimental work of the New Wave encouraged by France's CNC and

Ministère des affaires culturelles, described as "Second Cinema" (Hollywood commercial cinema being labeled "First Cinema"), on the grounds that such auteurist moviemaking perpetuated bourgeois self-indulgence and escapism. Only a "Third Cinema" could meet either of those requirements and produce "a cinema of liberation."[41] Beyond simply countering negative and debilitating tropes of the non-Western "other" with new empowering images, Solanas and Getino argued for a thorough rethinking of the cinematic endeavor from the original idea to its elaboration to the generation of the end product. They envisioned a populist process of making motion pictures that put working people and nonprofessionals in charge of generating their own story and sharing it with audiences around the world who came from similar backgrounds or had related experiences within the global system of imperialist capitalism. The result would empower those who produced the film and inspire those who consumed it. The kind of cinematic process Solanas and Getino advocated fit with Sembène's idea of filmmaking.[42] In engaging with the same global system of power, filmmakers from throughout the Third World were converging in their ideas about the creative and industrial aspects of making movies.

The cinematographic language Solanas and Getino elaborated as the distinguishing feature of Third Cinema also corresponded with well-developed patterns within the traditions of West African film practice. The Latin American cineastes embraced "documentary" as the "main basis of revolutionary filmmaking." However, Solanas and Getino did not intend for revolutionary filmmakers to simply produce classic documentaries. Their vision of a "revolutionary documentary" film practice was more engaged, requiring the explicit intervention of the filmmaker in the production of the final work: "Revolutionary cinema is not fundamentally one which illustrates, or passively establishes a situation: rather, it attempts to intervene in the situation as an element providing thrust or rectification." In other words, Third Cinema documentary style went beyond recording the present in a realist manner; it also sought to construct a forward-looking vision of what must be done based on the historical and contemporary circumstances that framed the contours of the current struggle for liberation. This recalls Vautier's *Afrique 50* and certainly was exemplified in Hondo's *Soleil Ô*. Solanas and Getino offered a theory of "guerrilla" cinema: "The camera [was] our rifle" and "the projector [was] a gun that can shoot 24 frames per second." For the Latin American revolutionary directors, the film is "a report that we place before you for your consideration, to be debated after the showing. . . . [It counters] a cinema of characters with one of themes, that of individuals with that of masses, that of the author with that of the operative group, one of neocolonial misinformation with one of information, one of escape with one that recaptures the truth, that of passivity with that of aggressions." Finally, Solanas and Getino insisted that the audience become active participants in constructing the film's meaning, which was diametrically opposed to the kind of cinematic experience that Delavignette and the French colonialists sought to create through their circumscribed presentations of an African modernity directed through cooperation with France.[43]

Solanas and Getino's ideas largely coincided with the experiences of the pioneers of West African cinema and their conceptualization of the cinema. Vieyra, Sembène, and Hondo were already practitioners of a docu-fiction style of filmmaking that aesthetically implemented the cinematographic language that Solanas and Getino argued was the hallmark of Third Cinema. From *Afrique-sur-Seine* to *Mandabi* and *Soleil Ô*, Francophone West African filmmakers had been experimenting with a form of guerrilla cinema meant to subvert the hegemonic tropes of the image-Africa constructed by the colonialists and that would ultimately undermine the West's dominance of the materialist dimension of the cinema industrial complex.[44] However, West African cineastes went further and posited the making of the film itself as a revolutionary act, not just the product. The end and the means were inseparable aspects of the total project of liberation.

Beginning in the late 1960s and into the early 1970s there was an increasing coalescence of West African and Third Cinema aesthetics. Sembène, Cissé, and others produced more aggressive films in which moving audiences to political action superseded raising their consciousnesses as the primary underlying goal. Sembène's *Emitaï* (CNC, 1971), *Xala* (CNC, 1975), and *Ceddo* (CNC, 1976) along with Cissé's *Cinq jours d'une vie* (Cissé, 1972) and *Den muso* (Cissé, 1974) illustrate the sharpened critical lens and boldness of West African filmmakers as they took on previously taboo subjects such as religion, "tradition," and archaic practices from the precolonial period, in addition to continuing their assault on neocolonial interference in African affairs and the nefarious workings of the global capitalist system. The films of the early to mid-1970s expanded on earlier themes, launching sharper attacks on the recent colonialist past, on corrupt postcolonial governments that acted as caretakers for the interests of the former imperial rulers, and on religion as a source of oppression in the past and present. In each instance the oppressive system is more starkly presented and the solutions offered are more dramatic and posed in increasingly urgent tones.

Perhaps alluding to the frustration Sembène experienced working with French government agencies and producers in making *Mandabi*, *Emitaï*, his next feature film, tells the story of local resistance to France's military as it attempts to requisition rice from a village in the Casamance region of Senegal during the Second World War. In response, the community's women defy the colonial army, precipitating a brutal crackdown on the people. The film is a stinging portrayal of colonial oppression that simultaneously celebrates the heroic actions of West African women in defiance of foreign exploitation and patriarchal ideas about women's roles in traditional society. As such, *Emitaï* is another significant contribution to African cineastes' (re)construction of the image-Africa consumed through motion pictures around the world. Sembène's subsequent films, *Xala* and *Ceddo*, return to themes evident in his earliest work: the corruption of the postcolonial West African bourgeoisie and the nefarious influence of self-interested religious leaders who participate in blunting the potential progressive development of society as well as the local culture. Each furthers Sembène's project of raising the consciousness of the movie-viewing audience, and in the case of *Ceddo* providing a historical background to contemporary expressions of oppression in West Africa.

In that same period, Souleymane Cissé made his first two major films, both of which took on the archaic and regressive role of religion in Malian society. *Cinq jours d'une vie,* a fifty-minute film shot while Cissé served as a cameraman for the Ministère de l'information, chronicles the delinquent acts of a young boy who drops out of Qur'anic school only to wind up becoming a thief living destitute in the streets. The film is reminiscent Mambety's *Badou Boy,* released two years earlier in 1970. Consequently, Cissé's first significant motion picture participated in an established cinematic tradition that highlighted the difficult and ambiguous process of founding a postcolonial urban African modernity. In fact, the motif of following the contorted and morally ambivalent path of an individual as he navigates the urban landscape was common among West African cineastes of the pioneer generation as is evident in *Afrique-sur-Seine, Borom Sarret, Badou Boy,* and *Cinq jours d'une vie.* Cissé's next film, *Den muso,* was shot using Bambara as the dominant idiom of expression, continuing the practice of using African languages to authenticate the work as African and to intervene in the regime of representation in order to reconstruct prevailing tropes of the image-Africa in the cinematic field. Moreover, *Den muso's* story of the rape of a young girl and her subsequent abuse by society when it is learned she is pregnant offers a powerful indictment of tradition, the failings of Mali's postcolonial government, and the forces of patriarchy that inhibit the country's development. Cissé was arrested and the film was banned on the pretext that the filmmaker had accepted French funding to make the movie, but in reality the government's actions were directed at squelching the image of Mali in the mid-1970s projected in *Den muso* and at silencing Cissé's increasingly radical critique of postcolonial society. Despite the Senegalese and Malian government's efforts to suppress the growing radicalism of West African filmmakers in the early 1970s, the pioneer cineastes refused to relent in their project to deploy motion pictures as a tool for postcolonial economic and cultural development. In fact, those oppressive actions may have incited Sembène, Cissé, and their cohort to engage in even more revolutionary forms of filmmaking, encouraging them to become bolder in their challenge to the global capitalist system that conspired to keep Africa underdeveloped and in permanent dependency on the hegemonic West.

The confidence expressed by the Latin American Third Cinema movement and West African filmmakers that they could realize their aspiration to swing "the balance of the power relationship in favor of using cinema in the interests of the masses" partly resulted from critical advances in film production technology.[45]

Solanas and Getino pointed to "the simplification of movie cameras and tape recorders; improvements . . . such as rapid film that can be shot in normal light; automatic light meters; improved audiovisual synchronization; and the spread of knowhow by means of specialized magazines" as seminal developments that "demystified" filmmaking and brought the basic materials of motion-picture making within reach of larger numbers of people. They also held up Chris Marker, one of the directors of *Les statues meurent aussi,* and his experimentation with "groups of workers [for] whom he provided 8mm equipment" as a potential model that could be emulated by other aspiring amateur cineastes.[46] Sembène also noted the improvements in portable 16 mm color cameras; these cameras were less expensive and could be operated using smaller crews, and the film could be easily blown up to 35 mm for showing in standard commercial theaters. Since West Africa was endowed with an extensive theater infrastructure in both 16 mm and 35 mm formats, such advances meant that the dreams of West Africans who aspired to make movies were more in reach than ever before.[47]

Two fundamental problems remained, though, if West African directors were going to gain access to their intended viewers. One was the lack of postproduction facilities in the region and the other was the enduring monopolistic ownership of the theater network in West Africa by COMACICO and SECMA. As long as the facilities necessary to finish creating a film were located only in the West, in particular Paris, and the foreign corporations, based in France, dominated projection facilities available to West African audiences, cheaper cameras and better film would not enable Sembène, Hondo, or Mambety to gain the kind of exposure for their work that was essential to making film into a tool for the cultural and economic (re)construction of their countries. To overcome those barriers, the West African cineastes had to have the cooperation of their governments. To pressure Senghor, Houphouët-Boigny, and the other leaders of postcolonial West Africa, the filmmakers had to get organized as a group to maximize their influence. By 1970 that organization had become a reality with the founding of FEPACI.

The establishment of FEPACI owed much to a growing formal collaboration with Latin American cineastes through international meetings, many of them sponsored by Cuba's revolutionary government.[48] The specific origins of the seed that would become FEPACI can be traced to a 1966 conference on Third World cinema convened by the Socialist Party of Austria in Vienna. The attendees at that meeting included Sembène, Gaston Kaboré and Idrissa Ouédraogo from Upper Volta (which today is Burkina Faso), Timité Bassori from Côte d'Ivoire, Hondo, and Cissé.[49] In fact, most of the delegates to that gathering were from Francophone West Africa, already indicating the degree to which filmmakers from that region were shaping what was to become African cinema. At the meeting the African directors began informal discussions about the need to have their own group that could advocate for an independent and socially responsive cinema for Africa. In

April 1966 Senegal hosted the first festival of black arts at which GAC, still headed by Vieyra, passed a resolution calling on its members' governments to "support the development of the cinema."[50] By then it was obvious to Sembène, Vieyra, and the handful of West Africans already actively engaged in making motion pictures that they needed an organization to clarify their objectives and to serve as a lobbying force with government officials. The meetings in 1966 were followed by Sembène's difficulties with France's CNC in the production of *Mandabi* and the 1968 Havana Cultural Congress, attended by many of the cineastes who had assembled earlier in Austria. Both experiences in their different ways contributed to the sense of urgency among African filmmakers that they needed to institutionalize their relationship and coordinate the activities of directors from the continent. Solanas and Getino's intervention on the theoretical plane in 1969 and the role that Cuba's government had assumed since at least 1966 in supporting Third World cinema provided some of the elements that were necessary to bringing to fruition the goals of African cineastes to form their own group.[51]

Building on the Havana cultural congress, *Présence africaine* convened the first Pan-African cultural festival in Algiers, Algeria, from 21 July to 1 August 1969. At that gathering, filmmakers such as Sembène and Hondo agreed to meet the following year at the third Journées cinématographiques de Carthage (JCC) film festival in Tunis, Tunisia, to launch a group to represent the interests of cineastes from across the continent and agitate for the appropriation of the cinema industrial complex to serve the interests of the African people.[52] The first JCC held in 1966 was itself a product of the festival of black arts that had been held in Dakar earlier in the year; it had inspired the Tunisian government to sponsor the first ever gathering dedicated explicitly to the art of film on the African continent.[53] The creation of the JCC by Tunisia's culture ministry signified what was possible if African governments got behind their own filmmakers and promoted the local cinema industry in a manner that fostered its growth and integrated it with strategies for economic and cultural development. At the third JCC held from 11 to 18 October 1970 filmmakers from sub-Saharan Africa (most of whom were from Francophone West Africa) met and officially launched FEPACI. The decision to found FEPACI in Tunis was not unusual because the JCC had emerged as a convenient meeting point for emerging West African cineastes. In fact, Sembène's *La noire de* ... won the first ever Tanit d'Or, the festival's highest honor, in 1966, giving the JCC a certain amount of credibility with Francophone West African cineastes.[54]

The establishment of FEPACI finally gave African filmmakers an institutional structure that could pressure governments to support their craft and through which they could promote their vision of the cinema being used as a cornerstone of postcolonial economic and cultural development that did not have to rely on outside, especially French, resources. Rather than dealing explicitly with aesthetic questions, the founders of FEPACI turned their immediate attention to the materialist dimension of the cinema industrial complex. They saw the federation's initial mission as working with governments and the Organization of African Unity, today the African Union, to find ways to overcome the problems confronting African filmmakers in the areas of training, production, and distribution. FEPACI institutionalized Vieyra's enunciation of an anticolonial film politics in its straightforward assessment of cinema as critical to the future cultural and economic development of the continent. The group's charter borrowed generously from the "Pan-African Cultural Manifesto" issued the previous year in Algiers, which had urged governments to support the creation of a "Pan-African Institute for the film industry" and stated that "the African States should . . . organize themselves to produce, release and market their own films and to fight against the limits which are holding up the development of a truly African cinema." Film was particularly important because it was a form of "cultural media which [is] most directly accessible to the people." Therefore, the cultural activists gathered in Algiers urged their governments to promote the construction of movie theaters and other outlets for diffusing the products generated by artists like Mambety, Hondo, and Cissé.[55]

Vieyra, a participant in the meeting that produced the agreement to found FEPACI, reported on the decisions of the filmmakers to join together in pursuit of their common objectives. Under the heading of "An African Cultural Summer," Vieyra reiterated many of the points he and other West African filmmakers had been making since the 1950s about the need to promote the cinematic process from the conceptualization of a project to its realization and diffusion if African countries were going to overcome the representational and material limitations bequeathed to them by the colonial legacy.[56] Vieyra followed his reporting on the cultural festival with his own plea in 1970 directed at African leaders for the creation of government institutions specifically geared toward promoting filmmaking and encouraging the creation of public groups to cultivate a "film culture" among the citizenry.[57] FEPACI was subsequently established to serve as the mechanism through which African cineastes could sustain the creative momentum of the first postindependence decade and leverage their growing productivity to bring African governments to their side in the ongoing struggle for control of the materialist aspects of the cinema industrial complex.

In fact, Maria Roof argues that African filmmakers were beginning to take the initiative of organizing Third World and radical filmmakers on a global scale.[58] Following FEPACI's launch, African filmmakers, among them Sembène, Hondo, and Flora Gomes of Guinea Bissau, helped to convene a meeting of Third World filmmakers in Algiers in 1973. Almost all the attendees were African and Latin American, solidifying the convergence of interests and perspectives between the pioneers of African filmmaking and Third Cinema.[59] That meeting was significant because it addressed aesthetic questions in conjunction with the materialist issues that drove FEPACI's formation. In addition to voicing familiar concerns over the dependency on the West for access to technology and distribution networks, the resolution that resulted from the meeting embraced the Third Cinema movement's identification of "cinema as an instrument of class struggle" to combat the false and distorting images that emanated from Hollywood.[60] By 1973 Sembène, Hondo, Cissé, and the other pioneers of Francophone West African cinema had made the theories of Third Cinema their own and had moved beyond the anticolonial film politics of the transition period between imperialist rule and political sovereignty. Those links were evident in the decision by FEPACI at the 1973 meeting to establish a permanent secretariat in Cuba to regularly liaise with Latin American filmmakers.[61] However, international solidarity was only one part of the broader strategy of African filmmakers to forge a cinema in the service of the people. Ultimately, FEPACI's success would rest on its ability to win the support of its members' governments to implement African filmmakers' vision for cinema in the region. On that front, Francophone West African cineastes could point to encouraging signs by the early 1970s as well.

An African Cinema in the Service of the People

One of the first indications that the tide was beginning to shift in their favor came in 1969. That year a small group of cineastes hosted by Upper Volta's minister of information, Alimata Salembere, convened the Semaine du cinéma africain in the country's capital of Ouagadougou to showcase the remarkable productivity of Africans in the motion picture field since decolonization. It was the first ever film festival devoted exclusively to African cinema, since the JCC included the Middle East and broader Mediterranean world in addition to North and sub-Saharan Africa. Only five countries were represented at that celebration and all of them were former French colonies (Senegal, Upper Volta, Côte d'Ivoire, Niger, and Cameroon), further confirming the preponderant influence of Francophone West African cineastes in forging the aesthetic and institutional bases for African filmmaking generally. While the range of participants was limited, this was the first film festival that a West African government formally sponsored, signaling its support for the work of filmmakers from the region.

The assistance of Upper Volta's administration in providing a space where the creativity of local cinematic artists could be screened marked a significant departure in the relationship between West African filmmakers and the postcolonial governments, as it was only in the previous year that Sembène had been subjected to the contorted and tortuous process of trying to produce *Mandabi* with funding from France and that the film had been banned in Senegal. However, Diawara points out that the French cultural attaché in Ouagadougou and the Ministère de la coopération also provided some of the funds used to organize the festival and furnished many of the films viewed during the week.[62] France's intervention in the arena of film festivals was consistent with its general approach to African cinema, which resulted in largely confining access to the work of cineastes from the continent to the festival circuit and noncommercial distribution. Hoefert de Turégano argues that the ministry's channeling of African film into the festival circuit was the product of French conceptions of the specific nature and task of African cinema, namely, that it should be directed toward forming "African cultural identities."[63] More specifically, France's assistance in convening the Semaine du cinéma africain was a case of its enacting the film politics it had developed at the end of the Second World War. Thus, the inaugural African film festival presented an opportunity for France to remain engaged in the representational dimension of the cinema industrial complex even as African filmmakers were beginning to organize with the aim of challenging foreign domination of its materialist aspects.

At the beginning of February 1970 Upper Volta hosted the second Semaine du cinéma africain in which directors from nine African countries participated, six from the former federation of French West Africa, two from French North Africa, and one Anglophone African country, Ghana, the first former British colony to be represented at the festival.[64] The second gathering in Ouagadougou occurred amid a flurry of conflicting activity among African filmmakers, local governments, and France in the cinematic field that illustrated the growing intensity of the struggle for control over the direction of film and its production in West Africa. Before FEPACI had managed to take form, France's Ministère des affaires culturelles in collaboration with Senghor's administration in Senegal and several other governments of former French colonies convened a summit in Niamey, Niger, that established the ACCT.

Today known as the "Charte de la Francophonie," the charter of the ACCT signed on 20 March 1970 globally institutionalized the neocolonial structures of dependency that had been fostered by the Ministère de la coopération and Malraux's Ministère des affaires culturelles from its inception during the decolonization period. In fact, Malraux was France's representative to the Niamey summit and signed the agreement on the former metropole's behalf.[65] The charter declared that the ACCT's mission was "to put in operation a true multilateral cooperation in the cultural and technical domains." That France had not relinquished its aspirations in the representational arena was made clear in the charter's proclamation that "authentic cooperation should not be effectively reduced only to technical assistance, as important as that is. It is primarily the attentive and fervent search for a permanent dialogue among the cultures." Curiously, the basis of such cooperation was claimed to be the "common usage of the French language" among the signatory countries. Moreover, the charter established the ACCT's permanent headquarters in Paris, a decision that was not merely a symbolic gesture pointing to the fact that France's capital was the center of the French cultural universe. While the ACCT insisted it was a multilateral organization in which all members were "equal" and participated in "mutual exchanges" of technology and cultural expression, the reality was that as long as France retained control over the material infrastructure necessary for economic development, that is, capital, technology, education, and manufacturing, there was little that African, Asian, or other former French colonies could supply to France for its own cultural and structural growth.⁶⁶ The ACCT, in essence, globalized and institutionalized Delavignette's colonialist notion of cooperation wherein France (and French culture through its language) would play a mentoring role to developing countries who would eventually achieve their own, culturally specific forms of modernity. During this period, the former colonial administrator intervened on the subject of the growing collaboration between France and its former colonies, even claiming that Senghor's philosophy of *négritude* "was proof of the combined vitality of the French and the black world."⁶⁷

However, the Niamey summit did not take place in a vacuum and in many ways indicated the degree to which France was being forced to adapt its own policies with regard to the former colonies, especially those in West Africa. While Senegal's president Léopold Senghor is credited with coining the term "la Francophonie" in an essay he published in 1962 in the French journal *Esprit*, the impetus for creating an international organization that would bind the ex-colonies with France in both the cultural and technical terrains resulted from the growing independence that African countries had begun to exercise.⁶⁸ Since 1966 West African states and cultural activists had convened numerous festivals and meetings and had founded organizations that increased solidarity among Africans working in the creative fields and provided potential mechanisms for technical exchange among the countries. The bitter experiences of African filmmakers working through the Ministère de la coopération or the CNC combined with Cuba's assertive role in bringing together cineastes from throughout the Third World forced France to pursue alternative means to preserve its dominant position with respect to the representational and materialist aspects of cinematic production. It is not, I argue, coincidental that only *after* the Havana meetings and the call for a meeting of African cultural activists in Algiers in 1969 did France take steps to build a global, multilateral structure that would maintain the links of the former colonial empire with the ex-metropole at the center.

Before *Présence africaine*'s Pan-African cultural festival could take place in Algiers and just days after the first African cinema festival in Ouagadougou, the French government helped to convene a preliminary meeting of leaders from the former colonies in Niamey at which they prepared the groundwork for the summit that founded the ACCT the next year. At the 1969 meeting the ex-colonies secured a pledge from France that "such cooperation had to be exercised [in a manner] that respected the sovereignty of the States . . . and with the objectives of promoting and diffusing the cultures of each country or group of countries represented within the Agency."⁶⁹ France's willingness to agree to such principles as a precondition of establishing the ACCT was consistent with a certain notion of cooperation that had been at the core of its civilizing mission since at least 1945, but more importantly it indicated that France could no longer unilaterally dictate the terms of its relationship with the former colonies. If the ex-metropole hoped to retain a prominent role in directing the cultural and material life of its former overseas possessions, it would have to tread more lightly and at the very least formally accede to a more equal relationship with the sovereign states of West Africa and others from the former empire. In addition, while the creation of the ACCT did not eliminate the managerial control of the Ministère de la coopération or the Ministère des affaires culturelles over the field of film production, it did provide another outlet through which aspiring West African filmmakers could potentially gain access to the technology and facilities that were essential to practicing their craft.

As France, in conjunction with some of its former West African colonies, moved ahead with plans to create the ACCT, Upper Volta's government signaled that the former imperial power might not be able to retain its monopoly over the materialist aspect of the cinema industrial complex in the region. In the intervening months between the preliminary meeting and the ACCT's founding summit Upper Volta took the extraordinary step of nationalizing the country's motion picture theaters and distribution network. West African filmmakers had long advocated such a move as essential to utilizing the motion picture industry in the interests of postcolonial economic and cultural development. The military regime headed by Major General Aboubakar Sangoulé Lamizana had already taken the initiative to convene the first Semaine du cinéma africain, albeit with French assistance. However, the specific circumstances that led to the French-dominated monopoly distribution and theater chains COMACICO and SECMA being nationalized resulted from the arrogance of the foreign companies in the face of a changing political and cultural landscape.

The U.S.–based American Motion Picture Export Company-Africa (AMPECA) already had attempted to penetrate the West African market shortly after the region attained its independence from France. With French political control gone, Hollywood saw the region, which hitherto had been subjected to relentless colonial censorship, as a potentially lucrative new market for its films. In 1961 a statement from AMPECA's parent organization, the Motion Picture Export Association of America (MPEAA) proclaimed, "The time has come to strike a blow in this Africa that is beginning to emerge. A co-ordinated invasion of the continent is on the agenda."[70] The declaration's stridently imperialist language aside, the pronouncement from Hollywood's distribution cartel amounted to a declaration of war on the French-based COMACICO and SECMA monopolies, now shorn of any formal protection from France. Thanks to the bilateral trade deals struck between France and its former colonies in West Africa at the time of independence, the French film industry enjoyed a certain amount of protection as the decolonization process unfolded. However, AMPECA's success in the Anglophone African countries served as an ominous portent for the future of French cinema's interests in France's former overseas territories. Ukadike notes that by the late 1960s the U.S. film companies had "become so powerful [in the ex-British African colonies] that not only did they determine which exhibitor to rent films to and which to deny such a request but they also controlled the number of films allowed in the market."[71] Ironically, that relationship mirrored the system France had elaborated in its West African colonies after 1945. In 1969 AMPECA formed a subsidiary to specifically concentrate on the Francophone African market, Afro-American Films Inc. (AFRAM), with the objective of undermining the COMACICO-SECMA monopoly in the region and replacing it with a U.S.-centered one. Since West Africa had the most developed and extensive film distribution and viewing network, the region was as central to U.S. motion picture companies' market considerations as it had been to the French during their imperial rule. Francophone West Africa's nearly two hundred movie theaters with seating capacities that ranged from two hundred to nearly two thousand each was a very attractive market and one the French were prepared to defend from Hollywood's encroachments.[72]

Before AFRAM could make much of an impact, though, COMACICO and SECMA ran afoul of Upper Volta's government over an issue seemingly unrelated to the source of the films shown on its screens. The dispute centered on tax receipts from the box office. It is somewhat surprising that this tiny, landlocked country should become the main battleground for control over the materialist dimension of the region's cinema industrial complex, since it had, according to Vieyra, only six cinemas in two cities, Ouagadougou and Bobo-Dioulasso. Each company owned three theaters with a combined seating capacity of around six thousand, hardly the hub of motion picture viewing in Francophone West Africa.[73] Emmanuel Sama estimates that in 1969 the two French-based monopolies earned a combined 70 million CFA francs in Upper Volta but paid only 14.5 percent of those revenues in taxes. He also notes that since 1960 "hundreds of billions of francs" had been "stolen from the continent without any substantial compensation." Most of COMACICO's and SECMA's profits were repatriated to Monaco, where each had their corporate headquarters, but ultimately the money wound up in France and sustained the former colonial power's film industry just as it had done during the colonial period.[74] In late 1969 Lamizana's government demanded a greater share of the revenues from COMACICO and SECMA. When the colonial-era cartels balked, Upper Volta's military regime took the dramatic step of nationalizing the entire cinema industrial complex and creating the Société national voltaïque de cinéma (SONAVOCI) to manage the new enterprise. Backed by France, the two former monopolies used their main source of leverage and organized a general boycott, completely shutting down the distribution network in Upper Volta and threatening to do the same in any other country that might follow that government's example.

Consequently, when filmmakers gathered in Ouagadougou in February for the second Semaine du cinéma africain the air was electric. For many cineastes such as Sembène, Hondo, and Vieyra, the Voltaic government's actions were a dream come true. Occurring shortly after they had laid the groundwork to found FEPACI, Hondo and other Francophone West African filmmakers embraced the nationalization as a first step on the road to actualizing a plan envisioned more than ten years before by GAC. However, the victory was only partial, as the stranglehold exercised by the foreign companies over global access to films, including those made by Africans, meant that although SONAVOCI may have had control over the cinematic viewing spaces, it did not have anything that could be shown there. Lamizana's government eventually resolved its dispute with COMACICO and SECMA by signing a rental agreement that restored the companies' exclusive supply rights but lifted the colonial-era screening quotas and did not require Upper Volta to import a specific number of films.[75]

Despite those concessions, the nationalization had real economic and symbolic importance. The government gained a new source of revenue and could keep more of the money generated by its citizens in the country. It also could choose what would be shown in Upper Volta's cinemas, using the selection process to influence the regime of representation by deliberately importing those films it found acceptable and rejecting others it deemed inappropriate or undesirable. Symbolically, the nationalization was a victory for a tiny country against giant global cartels. The Lamizana government's defiance of the companies that had controlled the region's film viewing experience for decades was a blow in the struggle to decolonize the cinema, the first such act. Over the next several years other states in West Africa followed Upper Volta's example. Mali seized its cinemas in 1970, while Senegal and Benin took control of their theaters in 1974. Guinea had already nationalized its theater system by default in 1958 when that country voted "no" to joining De Gaulle's new French community and the European companies pulled out. However, it was not until 1971 that Guinea had been able, with West German assistance, to reconstruct its cinema infrastructure.[76] Thus, by 1975 five of the eight countries that had comprised French West Africa had nationalized their movie theater system. Only Niger, Mauritania, and Côte d'Ivoire left the cinemas in private hands for the moment.

The convulsions of 1970 prevented Upper Volta from convening a third Semaine du cinéma africain in 1971. However, with African filmmakers now organized in FEPACI and the controversies resolved with the former distribution monopolies, the Lamizana government announced by decree on 7 January 1972 that the African film festival would be institutionalized as FESPACO beginning in March of that year. FEPACI was given a leading role in the selection process for films to be screened at the event, the Étalon de Yennenga (for best film) was awarded for the first time (to Oumarou Ganda from Niger for *Le wazzou polygame*), and the organizers incorporated thematic discussions as an integral part of the event.[77] The structure of FESPACO, then, embodied some of the core aspects of Third Cinema, in particular the notion that film viewings should be contexts that sparked discussion and that those conversations should take place among the audience in the theater upon viewing the motion picture.[78] Only in 1979 did Upper Volta and Tunisia agree to stagger their festivals: FESPACO became a biennial festival convened in odd-numbered years, while the JCC continued to be held in even-numbered years. Since then, every two years Ouagadougou has been host to the largest gathering of African filmmakers and screenings of African movies in the world. As a result of its boldness in taking on the distribution monopolies and hosting the first African film festivals, Upper Volta (now Burkina Faso), "had by the end of the 1970s become a major force in African cinema."[79] Subsequently, it also became the headquarters for FEPACI, and in 1989 African cineastes chose Ouagadougou as the site for the location of the African Film Library, one of the most important repositories in the world for materials related to the history of African cinema.[80]

The momentous events of the late 1960s and early 1970s in the development of Francophone West African filmmaking culminated in the historical FEPACI meeting in Algiers, Algeria, in 1975. At the founding conference in 1970, FEPACI had agreed to basic organizational structures and that its immediate mission was to pressure local governments to break the COMACICO and SECMA monopolies. With success mounting in that arena as well as on account of the growing number and quality of African films from across the continent, FEPACI gathered in Algiers to issue a declaration of principles about the nature and role of motion pictures in postcolonial Africa. The "Algiers charter" agreed to at the end of the congress is one of the most important documents and events in the history of African cinema.

Under the heading "For a Responsible, Free and Committed Cinema," the Algiers charter established the basic representational and materialist objectives that led to the formation of the association of African filmmakers and that it pledged to fight for. It updated the anticolonial film politics that Vieyra first articulated in the late 1950s and also signaled a transition to a new stage in the struggle for control of the cinema industrial complex. After acknowledging the continued deleterious influences of the ex-colonial powers on the "political, economic, and cultural" development of postcolonial African societies, FEPACI focused on the cultural question, treating the articulation of a new, progressive image-Africa as an essential ingredient in the ultimate process of economic and political liberation. The Algiers charter endorsed the cinematographic language that the pioneers of African filmmaking had constructed through their early films. FEPACI argued that African film, in order to play a meaningful role in the social life of the continent's people, had to take on the historic task of challenging the colonialist image-Africa that had saturated the world's silver screens for decades and that also imposed "on our peoples models of behavior and systems of values whose essential function is to buttress the ideological and economic ascendancy of the imperialist powers."[81] In fact, the French colonial government intentionally and assiduously constructed a cinematic aesthetic that by modeling behavior and values Delavignette and other imperial officials expected Africans to embrace as their own was intended to preserve France's cultural, economic, and political influence in the region.[82]

However, the filmmakers gathered in Algiers recognized that success in the representational aspect of the cinema industrial complex could not be achieved without commensurate progress in winning control of its materialist dimension. And advances in the industry of motion picture making could only be measured by the control over the means of production that a filmmaker secured, not by a film's financial triumph. FEPACI's declaration summarily dismissed "commercial" cinema as coterminous with escapist Western imperialist entertainment. Following the theoretical approach of Latin American Third Cinema, the Algiers charter asserted that "commercial profit can be no yardstick for African film-makers. The only relevant criterion of profitability is the knowledge of whether the needs and aspirations of the people are expressed, and not those of specific interest groups." To realize those objectives, FEPACI explained, " all the structural problems of their national cinema must be of paramount importance for African film-makers." In fact, the Algiers charter reaffirmed the deepening connections and theoretical convergence between African cineastes and the Latin American Third Cinema movement. FEPACI repeatedly asserted in the document the importance of solidarity between African culture and cultural struggles around the globe and also proclaimed that the continent's directors "must be in solidarity with progressive film-makers who are waging anti-imperialist struggles throughout the world."[83] The call for international unity among revolutionary cineastes echoed Solanas and Getino's assertion that "no internationalist form of struggle can be carried out successfully if there is not a mutual exchange of experiences among the people, if the people do not succeed in breaking out of the Balkanisation on the international, continental, and national planes which imperialism is striving to maintain."[84] By 1975, African cinema had firmly instantiated itself as a vital force in the global field of motion picture production. Despite the ongoing debates about the nature and meaning of African cinema, filmmakers from the continent, led by those from Francophone West Africa, had staked a claim as independent agents in articulating cinematographic languages and had made advances in procuring control over the film industry's materialist dimension.

The second FEPACI congress in many ways marked the synthesis of a thirty-year process that had been inaugurated with France's articulation of a colonial film politics that was a response to the explosive popularity among West Africans and the growing economic importance of the cinema in the region. After three decades of dialectical engagement, by 1975, African directors had secured the upper hand in the struggle for control of the cinematic field. The Algiers charter issued by FEPACI that year reflected the confidence that resulted from those successes and projected what African filmmakers hoped would be the next stage in the fight to ultimately create a cinema in the service of the people that could aid Africa's economic and cultural development. It signaled a convergence of interest among African cineastes and those from other developing regions of the world. The charter solidified the bonds forged through experience and the commonality of objectives among non-Western filmmakers struggling to overcome the legacies of foreign domination as well as the enduring neocolonial structures and practices that preserved their societies in dependent relationships.

While France's Ministère de la coopération remained a significant source of capital and facilities for film production even after several West African governments had nationalized the theater system, it was no longer the only place African filmmakers could turn to in order to finance their projects. With funding and equipment available through the ACCT as well as through the production companies that several cineastes such as Hondo and Sembène formed, the ministry's onerous and paternalistic stranglehold over Africans' ability to make their own films had been curtailed. The inauguration of the JCC and FESPACO gave African directors an independent outlet through which to showcase their work and celebrate their achievements. The links West African filmmakers established with other radical cineastes in Latin America and elsewhere furnished new avenues through which they could dialogue about film theory and collaborate on projects outside of the purview of Western corporate and government control. Finally, by the time of the second FEPACI congress in 1975 African cineastes, particularly those from Francophone West Africa, could celebrate a decade of remarkable productivity in terms of sheer quantity of films as well as the tremendous growth in the quality of their motion pictures. Twenty years removed from Vieyra's production of *Afrique-sur-Seine* the delegates gathered in Algiers could justly express confidence that the vision and aspirations he and others articulated in the late colonial period could be realized. A "cinema in the service of the people" was taking shape that would facilitate the economic and cultural regeneration of African society after decades of colonial rule that had been partly sustained through an imperialist-dominated cinema industrial complex.

Postscript: Francophone West African Cinema to the Present

THIS STUDY HAS argued for the importance of the cinema industrial complex as a site of contestation between French colonial (and postcolonial) officials and West African cultural activists from the late 1940s to the mid-1970s over the shape and nature of African cultural and economic development in the region. In the mid-1970s West African cineastes could point to significant progress in wresting control over the materialist and representational aspects of the cinematic field from France and foreign distribution companies. By the time FEPACI gathered for its second congress in 1975 dozens of filmmakers from the region had picked up the camera and produced remarkable work. From Sembène's 1963 release of *Borom Sarret* to Mambety's *Touki-bouki* a decade later, Francophone West African cinema had undergone profound growth both qualitatively and quantitatively. Cineastes from the region had produced the first full-length feature, the first color feature film, and the first motion picture primarily in an African language. Moreover, Hondo, Cissé, Mambety, and others had contributed to the articulation of an African cinematographic discourse that was multivalent but that still could be described as specifically "African." Despite ongoing debates about aesthetics and commercial vs. political film, by the mid-1970s there was an African cinema that did not exist a decade earlier.

African filmmakers also had carved out an independent place within the global cinematic field, and they assumed prominent roles in both theoretical conversations and institutional developments throughout the world. Moreover, West African governments were beginning to take on the foreign distribution monopolies and realize the potential economic benefit that could be derived from the cinema industrial complex. For cineastes grouped in FEPACI, the nationalization of the theater systems in Upper Volta, Senegal, Mali, and elsewhere opened the prospect that their work could be consumed by audiences in their home countries on the silver screen rather than being confined to the festival circuit. Movie theater patrons in Dakar, Bamako, and Ouagadougou could finally be exposed to a counterhegemonic image-Africa that undermined the negative imperialist tropes propagated by both colonialist and entertainment films throughout the period of foreign domination.

However, Vieyra's project of creating a "cinema in the service of the people" had not yet been realized. In fact, years later he noted that the mid-1970s marked a turning point. Rather than inaugurating a new, vibrant age of motion picture making, it marked the end of an era. Vierya pointed to a dramatic fall in productivity after 1975 even among the most well-established West African cineastes. After the 1976 release of Sembène's *Ceddo* (1976), it was another decade before the "father of African cinema" reemerged with *Camp de Thiaroye* (1988). Mambety practically vanished from the cinematic field after *Touki-bouki*, taking nearly twenty years to release his next major feature film, *Hyènes* (1992). The experiences of those prominent West African cineastes were typical of almost all others who wanted to make movies after the mid-1970s.

The problem for African filmmakers resided in the enduring structural obstacles they confronted in making motion pictures. The materialist aspect of the cinema industrial complex remained largely beyond West Africans' control. Consequently, in 1989 Vieyra could write that "in Africa there are no film industries.... The materials required to make African films are imported from all over the world.... [T]here is virtually no industrial base for African cinema, [and] its commercial organization is in its first and hesitant stages."[1] Upper Volta's nationalization of the theater system in 1970 points to the intractable obstacles faced by Africans as they attempted to develop their economies and reconstruct their cultures. While COMACICO and SECMA lost control over the physical space of the movie theater, they could still use their leverage as distributors of the films to force Upper Volta to sign exclusive commercial treaties to purchase the product from them. Moreover, France's funding for filmmaking through the Ministère de la coopération and even the ACCT required that African directors surrender the rights to noncommercial distribution of the films. The result was that African motion pictures became another export commodity largely consumed in the West, primarily through the festival circuit, and that the revenues generated from their exploitation either went to paying off the debts incurred by the directors in making the movie or wound up in the coffers of Western distribution companies and the French government. As Hondo said in a later interview, "Today my whole life is inundated with debts. It is a situation of misery and poverty."[2] Worse still, African motion pictures were not even manufactured through a local film industry, so the money Sembène, Hondo, and others had to borrow to make their pictures was largely used to purchase equipment and access to postproduction facilities in Paris or other Western cities. Echoing other aspects of the neocolonial relationships that underpin the global capitalist economy, Africans provided the creative raw material for the generation of a finished product that was then distributed through the international market by foreign corporations, usually for the profit of Western companies and governments.

If there was one area in which African cineastes could point to enduring success, it was in the representational aspect of the cinema industrial complex. Through their films Sembène, Vieyra, Hondo, Mambety, and others had constructed a counterhegemonic image-Africa that challenged the deleterious tropes of Africa and Africans that pervaded the world's movie screens almost from the moment of filmmaking's invention. West African directors had picked up the camera and wielded it as a weapon to smash the colonialist representations of Africans as primitive and Africa as a wild, exotic backdrop to Western adventures. Hondo, Mambety, and Cissé contributed to reshaping notions of African reality, presenting the continent and its people as struggling to find their own appropriate forms of modernity that would respond to the needs of Africa's people. That exposition included strong critiques of postcolonial African rulers and archaic customs that limited the prospects for progressive social and cultural development. As film theorist Peter Wollen writes, "The cinema cannot show the truth, or reveal it, because the truth is not out there in the real world, waiting to be photographed. What the cinema can do is produce meanings, and meanings can only be plotted not in relation to some abstract yardstick or criterion for truth but in relation to other meanings."[3] The pioneer generation of West African filmmakers consciously built a cinematic aesthetic in response to the colonialist imagery that they claimed had damaged African societies by convincing Africans of their own backwardness and the need to be dependent on foreign assistance.

The choices Sembène, Hondo, and Vieyra made in terms of cinematographic language and the specific imagery composed on the screen did not occur in a vacuum. As this study has shown, the French colonial state articulated a film politics designed to actualize a certain African modernity predicated on a form of "cooperation" with France that subordinated the overseas territories. Consequently, West African cultural activists understood that meaningful postcolonial cultural and economic reconstruction required the elaboration of countervailing images that exposed the reality and sources of Africans' oppressed condition, the forces structuring that situation, and the mechanisms whereby they could take control of their own destiny. The "burdensome seriousness" that Harrow sees as characterizing "the straightjacket of the African 'aesthetic'" developed by the early generation of West African filmmakers was historically necessary given the conceptual and material limitations that West Africans faced in producing films in the immediate postindependence period.[4] Sembène could have yielded to French demands that he make *Mandabi* according to Western commercial standards and produce a cinema of "surface" as opposed to "depth," but he refused and made a film that became an important "event" in the history of African cinema. *Mandabi*'s production was an act of decolonization in the specific context of the cinematic field and in the broader context of society at large as Africans fought to reclaim control over the creation of their own images.

Despite the progress West African cineastes made in securing influence within the regime of representation, they faced significant obstacles to reaching the intended audience in their home countries. Not only were many of Sembène's films censored by the Senegalese government, but *Ceddo* was banned outright. His experiences were, unfortunately, not atypical among other West African filmmakers, as noted in chapter 5 in connection with Cissé's release of *Den muso* and the Malian state's reaction to that. While some West African countries had nationalized the theater system, they did not necessarily open them to the projection of the works of local filmmakers, and foreign films continued to dominate the big screens across the region. Even the revenue Vieyra and others knew governments were obtaining from the box office receipts was not put in the service of the further elaboration of local production facilities or the financing of the creative activity of African directors. Instead, it was often pilfered through the very forms of corruption Sembène, Mambety, and others denounced in their motion pictures. As a result, African audiences continued to be bombarded with foreign images, along with the surviving colonialist tropes of African primitiveness and exoticism. The exposition of African films was constrained primarily to the festival circuit, including FESPACO, and to Western art-house theaters. This was what the Bureau du cinema at France's Ministère de la coopération sought from the outset while at the time seeking to maintain West Africa as a captive market for the export of French films.[5]

As early as 1958 Vieyra argued that an independent African cinema in the service of the people could not become a reality without the active support of African governments and the control of the local film market.[6] The race by many postindependence African leaders to "cooperate" with France that culminated in the establishment of the ACCT in 1970 further indicated the dangers of collusion between local rulers and the former imperial power that preserved the fundamental relationship extant during the colonial period. Through the arrangements agreed to in Niamey, France endured as the source of technology and capital. African societies, in the meantime, furnished the creative labor used to glorify the universality of French culture. The material relations that Vieyra warned in 1969 were causing a "brain drain" from the continent had become enshrined through international treaty.

Despite those limitations, in a condensed and tumultuous period of time Francophone West African filmmakers of the pioneer generation achieved incredible results. For thirty years cultural activists from the region waged a heroic struggle to wrest control of the cinema industrial complex from France in an attempt to put it in the service of the cultural and economic development of their societies. The idea expounded by Vieyra, Sembène, Hondo, and others from the late colonial through the early independence eras of using the cinema as a vehicle through which African societies could modernize and the people could recover their dignity was entirely feasible. The French colonial government had assisted in the construction of the cinema industrial complex in West Africa to pursue precisely the same goals, albeit for the benefit of France's economy and to sustain French cultural influence in the region. By the 1960s the region was home to a flourishing theater system patronized by millions of moviegoers annually. As Sembène related in recounting his own childhood, West Africans were avid consumers of motion pictures, and Hondo later succinctly noted, "The public exists."[7] Not only was there a vast potential audience for African films; the screening infrastructure was also well developed and the creative ability to make movies had already been demonstrated through GAC's triumphant production of *Afrique-sur-Seine* in the face of rigid censorship, government persecution, and lack of resources.

The fact that the cinema could be an integral arm of economic development had been amply attested to by France's own postwar policies in West Africa and the continued protection it sought to afford its domestic film industry after the colonies gained their sovereignty.[8] Moreover, it had the advantage of being a strategy for modernization that was not dependent on access to raw materials such as fossil fuels or precious metals that invited aggressive foreign interest. The core component that goes into film production is the creative imagination of the cineaste. However, to realize that vision, the director needs access to the tools of the trade and financing. As this study has revealed, the ultimate limitation barring the way to postcolonial economic and cultural reconstruction in West Africa was the West's enduring monopolization of the technology and capital that enabled the manufacture of motion pictures as well as the lack of control local governments had over their own domestic markets. The conditions that France's Ministère de la coopération imposed on aspiring West African filmmakers who sought access to the equipment and money essential to the practice of their art were not materially different from those imposed by the International Monetary Fund through its structural adjustment programs on African governments saddled with unsustainable debt burdens. Those financial problems also were not dissimilar to the private debts that restricted Hondo's, Cissé's, and other filmmakers' ability to make films. Moreover, the International Monetary Fund's conditionalities routinely contain provisions that insist that recipient countries open their markets to the global economy and allow access by multinational corporations. Such debt relief programs are not qualitatively different from French colonial and postcolonial governments' attempts to preserve West Africa as a captive market for their film exports or to preclude the development of local competition.

Today, the state of the cinema industrial complex in West Africa is illustrative of the legacy of decades of neocolonial practices in the global capitalist economy as well as technological changes in the field of filmmaking. As of 2012, the walled compound of the Alliance française is the only facility in Dakar where a patron can view films on the big screen. Of the nearly two hundred operational movie houses in former French West Africa in the 1960s, only a handful remain standing today.

Even Dakar's famous Vox cinema, which had welcomed tens of thousands of movie patrons from the 1930s on, could not withstand the ravages of the global economy's impact on Africa over the last few decades. Since the mid-1970s the entire African continent has been dealt a series of economic shocks, each of which has enabled outside agencies and governments to gain greater control over the continent's material and creative wealth. Even the aid France provided to West African filmmakers, controversial though it was, has been severely cut since the late 1970s.[9]

Beyond neocolonial materialist structures, technological changes in the film industry have generated new challenges to the prospect of using the cinema as a viable means to foster economic and cultural development in the twenty-first century. The late 1970s saw the introduction of video technology, which presented another outlet for viewing movies independent of the public space of the theater. Video films gave more potential to television and the private sphere of the home as a location for the consumption of images and the generation of meaning. However, as I noted in chapter 5, this form of engagement is inherently atomizing and produces a different form of socialization than the movie theater. The subsequent advent of handheld Super-8 cameras and lately cell phone video recorders also signal possible major changes in the way films are made and consumed. While African filmmakers have attempted to make use of the new technologies, questions of cost, financing, and distribution remain as intractable obstacles to the dissemination of the image-Africa they are trying to create. The new tools also raise the issue of audience access to the cinematic images. Videos require VCRs and TV sets. Cell phones with video recording and viewing capabilities are expensive. Computer access remains limited throughout Africa. Therefore, new and cheaper production technology in the West does not necessarily translate into easier access to those tools for Africans. Diminished incomes and declining employment in many parts of Africa along with energy shortages suggest that the continent's people do not have any greater ability to be consumers of motion pictures today than they did during the colonial period. In fact, the erosion of the cinematic infrastructure in West Africa indicates that the capacity for Africans to both produce and consume their own images is perhaps lower now than it was during the early postcolonial period.

Finally, many of the pioneer filmmakers have passed from the scene. This represents a loss of creative energy and historical experience that could aid in the skill development of the younger generation of cineastes. However, it is a testament to the successes of the progenitors of West African cinema in the face of difficult circumstances that the film aesthetics they helped to create persists in some of the most important recent releases from the region's directors, including the Mauritanian/Malian filmmaker Abderrahmane Sissako's *Bamako* (Chinguitty, 2006), and that aspiring cineastes continue to find ways to make motion pictures. In addition, FESPACO draws thousands of film enthusiasts to Ouagadougou every two years, and African movies remain among the most celebrated works that are screened at other international festivals. In fact, Sissako's *Bamako,* a docu-fiction that puts the IMF and World Bank on trial for their complicity in impoverishing Africa even as the banality of daily life transpires through the juridical space, encapsulates the hope and frustration that has characterized the long history of the fight by West Africans to take control of the cinema industrial complex and deploy it for the social and cultural development of their communities. Filmmaking is a young art, and African cinema is even younger. Just like the architectural landscape of downtown Dakar described at the beginning of this study, the history West Africa's cinema industrial complex is a testament to the progress and setbacks of the region's people in their struggle to overcome the legacies of slavery, imperialism, neocolonialism, and neoliberalism. Most importantly, though, this study tells the story of the heroic struggle of West African cultural activists of the late colonial and early postcolonial period to contribute to their societies' liberation from all forms of oppression and forge an African modernity that was progressive, developed, just, and egalitarian. The work of contemporary West African cineastes that carries on the legacy of the pioneer generation of filmmakers bears witness to the unfinished project and durability of Vieyra's aspiration to create a "cinema in the service of the people."

Notes

Introduction

1. FEPACI, "The Algiers Charter on African Cinema."
2. Vieyra, "Responsabilités du cinéma dans la formation d'une conscience nationale africaine," 66. The article was first published in *Présence africaine* in 1959. The 2004 *Présence africaine* issue commemorates fifty years of African cinema and is called "Cinquante ans de cinéma africain: Hommage à Paulin Soumanou Vieyra."
3. Adorno, *The Culture Industry*, 180.
4. Armes, *African Filmmaking North and South of the Sahara*, 8.
5. See, for example, Diawara, *African Cinema*, Ukadike, *Black African Cinema*, Bakari and Cham, eds., *African Experiences of Cinema*, and Murphy and Williams, *Postcolonial African Cinema*.
6. This is an argument I have made elsewhere and that I revisit in more depth in this study. See my "Cinema and the Struggle to (De)Colonize the Mind in French/Francophone West Africa (1950s–1960s)."
7. Wilder, *The French Imperial Nation-State*, 21–22.
8. Said, *Culture and Imperialism*, 5, 7.
9. Thiong'o, *Decolonising the Mind*, 3.
10. Galliéni, *Neuf ans à Madagascar*, 59–60, 71, 103, 270–71.
11. Conklin, *A Mission to Civilize*, 2–3.
12. Cooper, *Decolonization and African Society*; Chafer, *The End of Empire in French West Africa*; Genova, *Colonial Ambivalence, Cultural Authenticity, and the Limitations of Mimicry in French-Ruled West Africa, 1914–1956*; Crowder and Ikime, eds., *West African Chiefs*; Suret-Canale, *L'Afrique noire*.
13. O'Brien, *The Mourides of Senegal*; Clancy-Smith, *Rebel and Saint*; Crummey, ed., *Banditry, Rebellion, and Social Protest in Africa*. On the question of an African modernity and Africa in modernity, see Appiah, *In My Father's House*.
14. Tomlinson, *Cultural Imperialism*, 7.
15. Fanon, *The Wretched of the Earth*, 35–36.
16. Bourdieu, *The Field of Cultural Production*, 42.
17. Gramsci, *Prison Notebooks*, 199; Diawara, *African Cinema*, 153.
18. See Diawara, *African Cinema*, viii, Ukadike, *Black African Cinema*, 16, Armes, *African Filmmaking North and South of the Sahara*, 7, and Cham, introduction, 3–4.
19. Pfaff, "From Africa to the Americas: Interviews with Haile Gerima (1976–2001)," 207.
20. Ukadike, *Questioning African Cinema*, 45. Ukadike conducted the interview with Gubara at the 1995 FESPACO. At the time Gubara was assistant secretary (eastern region) of FEPACI.
21. Vieyra, "Responsabilités du cinéma dans la formation d'une conscience nationale africaine," 68.

22. This idea was formally incorporated into "'The Algiers Charter on African Cinema, 1975,'" agreed to at the Second Congress of FEPACI, but was carried over from the original founding of the organization in 1970.
23. Baudry, "Ideological Effects of the Basic Cinematographic Apparatus," 287.
24. Adorno, *The Culture Industry*, 185.
25. Baudry, "Ideological Effects of the Basic Cinematographic Apparatus," 287, 288.
26. Solanas and Getino, "Towards a Third Cinema," 35, 36, 46.
27. Ukadike, *Black African Cinema*, 1, 7.
28. Ukadike, *Questioning African Cinema*.
29. Barthes, "Diderot, Brecht, Eisenstein," 172–73, emphases in the original.
30. Metz, "Problems of Denotation in the Fiction Film," 59, emphasis in the original.
31. Barthes, "Diderot, Brecht, Eisenstein," 173.
32. Metz, "Problems of Denotation in the Fiction Film," 40, 38, emphases in the original.
33. Thiong'o, *Decolonising the Mind*, 93.
34. Cameron, *Africa on Film*, 11.
35. Slavin, *Colonial Cinema and Imperial France, 1919–1939*, 3.
36. Ukadike, *Black African Cinema*, 31.
37. Ki-Zerbo, "Cinema and Development in Africa," 77. The essay was first published in 1978.
38. Murphy and Williams, *Postcolonial African Cinema*, 27.
39. Slavin, *Colonial Cinema and Imperial France*, 3. See also, for example, Minh-ha, *Cinema Interval*, Chowdhry, *Colonial India and the Making of Empire Cinema*, Sherzer, ed., *Cinema, Colonialism, Postcolonialism*, Landau and Kaspin, eds., *Images and Empires*, and Armes, *Third World Filmmaking and the West*.
40. Althusser, "Ideology and Ideological State Apparatuses."
41. Here I am borrowing the concept of the world system from the work of Immanuel Wallerstein. For a synopsis of this approach to analyzing the world, see his *World-Systems Analysis*.
42. Here I disagree with Kenneth Harrow's general conclusions concerning the negative role the pioneers of African cinema are said to have had on subsequent African filmmaking in *Postcolonial African Cinema*. I engage with Harrow's work more systematically in subsequent chapters.
43. For Benjamin's caution on the role of film in the modern world see Adorno, *The Culture Industry*, 180.
44. Benjamin, "The Work of Art in the Age of Mechanical Reproduction," 740–43.
45. Gramsci, *Prison Notebooks*, 199.
46. My earlier work focused mostly on the writers and intellectuals of this previous generation of anticolonial activists. See my *Colonial Ambivalence*.
47. Cham, introduction, 2.
48. Barry, "Pour la grandeur du cinéma africain, une refonte du FESPACO," 97.
49. Metz, "Problems of Denotation in the Fiction Film," 52, 58–59.
50. Cham, introduction, 1.

1. The Cinema Industrial Complex in French West Africa to the 1950s

1. André Lemaire, "Elements d'un rapport sur les problems d'éducation et d'information audio-visuelles entre l'afrique noire et la métropole," 10 December 1949, CAOM FM 1/AP/2127/9. Lemaire was president of the directorate general of the Société d'applications cinématographiques, a section of the Commission du cinéma d'outre-mer of the Ministère de la France d'outre-mer (formerly the Ministère des colonies).

2. Harris and Ezra, introduction, 2, 3.
3. Genova, *Colonial Ambivalence*, 250–52. See also my "Constructing Identity in Post-War France," 76–77.
4. Cameron, *Africa on Film*; Moore, *Savage Theory*; Slavin, *Colonial Cinema and Imperial France, 1919–1939*; Sherzer, ed., *Cinema, Colonialism, Postcolonialism*.
5. Ukadike, *Black African Cinema*; Bakari and Cham, eds., *African Experiences of Cinema*; Givanni, ed., *Symbolic Narratives/African Cinema* Diawara, *African Cinema*; Gugler, *African Film: Re-Imagining a Continent*; Shaka, *Modernity and the African Cinema*.
6. Diawara, *African Cinema*, 21, 22, 23.
7. Wilder, *The French Imperial Nation-State*, 23. Here Wilder describes the process whereby "reformist administrators and cultural nationalists" engaged one another to structure the imperial relationship.
8. Murphy and Williams, *Postcolonial African Cinema*, 12.
9. Cham, introduction, 1.
10. Ukadike, *Black African Cinema*, 62.
11. Schwartz, *It's So French!*, 8–12. Schwartz provides a compelling case for the importance of reviving the French film industry after the Second World War as part of postwar reconstruction. While her analysis centers on the complex negotiations between French and American officials, it is pertinent to the role of the colonies in that industry as well.
12. Note from Academie des sciences colonial to the Ministère de la France d'outre-mer, 8 February 1950, CAOM FM 1/AP/2127/9.
13. Letter from Ministère des colonies to the governor general, governors, and other officials in French West Africa, 16 March 1932, CAOM FM 1/AP/859.
14. Ukadike, *Black African Cinema*, 31, 30.
15. Daughton, *An Empire Divided*, 3–5.
16. For work on the role of colonial conscripts in the Great War, see Echenberg, *Colonial Conscripts*, Johnson, *The Emergence of Black Politics in Senegal*, Michel, *L'appel à l'Afrique*, and White, *Children of the French Empire*.
17. Browne, "The Spectator-in-the-Text," 110–11.
18. For a discussion of the historic role of Lebanese settlers in the West African economy, see Davidson, *Modern Africa*, Coquery-Vidrovitch, *Africa*, 127, 163, and Nugent, *Africa since Independence*.
19. For a discussion of the ways in which the colonizer marks himself or herself as different from the colonized in the space of the colony, see Memmi, *The Colonizer and the Colonized*, 9.
20. For a discussion of the concept of "desire" as it applies to the colonial context, see Stoler, *Race and the Education of Desire*, 167–69, 176–77, 188–95.
21. Letter from Bureau des affaires politiques to the Ministère des colonies, 11 July 1932, CAOM FM 1/AP/859. The letter was signed by Robert de Guise.
22. Letter from Robert de Guise to the Bureau des affaires politiques, 11 July 1932, CAOM FM 1/AP/859 (1). This letter was also forwarded to the Ministère des colonies.
23. Genova, *Colonial Ambivalence*, 57–63. See also my "Conflicted Missionaries," 52–53.
24. "Décrêt portant du contrôle des films cinématographiques, des disques phonographiques, des prises du vues cinématographiques et des enregistrements sonores en Afrique Occidentale française," 8 March 1934, ARS 21/G/188 [174].
25. Murphy and Williams, *Postcolonial African Cinema*, 12.
26. Ukadike, *Black African Cinema*, 35–48. In this section Ukadike offers an analysis of the kinds of images generally presented about Africa, but he does not make the connection between these images and the coherent film politics that was emerging in French West Africa during the 1930s.

27. "Ayant pour objet de subordonner à un visa la representation et l'exportation des films," ordinance no. 45–1464, 3 July 1945, ARS 21/G/188 [174]. This document, signed by Charles de Gaulle along with Jacques Soustelle, Alain Tixier, Paul Giacobi, Pierre-Henri Teitgen, and René Pleven, acknowledges that the first visas authorizing the projection of films in the colonies were issued on 25 July 1919. However, there was not yet any coherent regulatory system in place that clarified the standard for granting such visas.

28. Letter from Robert de Guise to the minister of colonies, 11 July 1932, CAOM FM 1/AP/859 910.

29. Directive from Louis de Chappedelaine to the governors general, governors, and commissioners of mandated territories, 16 March 1932, CAOM FM 1/AP/859 (1), emphasis in the original.

30. Browne, "The Spectator-in-the-Text," 148, 160.

31. Cinema (1932–40), CAOM FM 1/AP/859 (1). This folder contains a series of requests over those years by filmmakers to make movies in West Africa that would be of an "educational/scientific" nature.

32. "Rapport du directeur de l'enseignement de l'A.E.F. sur l'organisation du cinéma educateur dans les colonies française," 1 October 1938, CAOM FM 1/AP/859. For earlier discussions, see "Note de l'inspecteur general de l'enseignement," subtitled "Le film à l'école," 25 July 1932, CAOM FM 1/AP/859.

33. "Rapport sur l'organisation du cinema educateur aux colonies françaises," March 1938, CAOM FM 1/AP/859.

34. Reports of 1930, 15 January 1935, CAOM FM 1/AP/859. See also the letter from Marcel de Coppet, the governor general of French West Africa, to the Ministère des colonies, 5 October 1938, CAOM FM 1/AP/859.

35. "Cinémas de Dakar," annual report, 1948, ARS 21/G/189 [174].

36. Note on the popularity of the Theater Vox in Dakar, ARS 21/G/14 [1].

37. Withall and Mardy, "Africa: Africa Distribution and Exhibition." Similar information can also be found in "Cinéma et domination étrangère en Afrique noire."

38. Vieyra, *Ousmane Sembène*, 12–13.

39. Jennings, *Vichy in the Tropics*, 77.

40. Letter from COMACICO to the Commission des théâtres et spectacles, 1 October 1941, ARS 21/G/17 [1]; letter from the Commission des théâtres et spectacles to COMACICO, 17 November 1941, ARS 21/G/17 [1].

41. Jennings, *Vichy in the Tropics*, 3.

42. Letter from the Ministère de la France d'outre-mer to the high commissioner for the general government of French West Africa, 8 October 1948, CAOM FM 1/AP/2127/10; "Arrêté 7165 A.P. relative à l'exploitation en Afrique occidentale française des films cinématographiques impressionnés," 5 October 1954, ARS 21/G/192 [174].

43. Browne, "The Spectator-in-the-Text," 116, 117, 118.

44. This edict is outlined in a note dated 19 May 1949 from one Gaston, inspector general of education and youth, to Louis-Paul Aujoulat, secretary of state for overseas France (CAOM FM 1/AP/2149/1).

45. Shaka, *Modernity and the African Cinema*, 158; Cameron, *Africa on Film*, 59.

46. An opinion poll was conducted on 15 April 1946 on the question "What is your opinion [concerning] the indigenous of the colonies having the right to vote?" (CAOM FM 1/AP/2147). The poll drew answers that went beyond electoral politics, though. It revealed a decided shift in the mindset of the French after World War Two: the respondents, especially younger ones, now viewed the colonized on much more equal terms with those from the metropole. I cite this poll in more detail my "Constructing Identity in Post-War France," 59.

47. Thompson, "The Concept of Cinematic Excess," 131.

48. Articles, 27 October 1949 and 29 October 1949, CAOM FM 1/AP/2149/1.
49. Diawara, *African Cinema*, 23.
50. Genova, *Colonial Ambivalence*, 224, 228–30. See also Cooper, *Decolonization and African Society*, 176 (although Cooper does not address FERDES), and Suret-Canale, *L'Afrique noire*, 79, on the Sarraut Plan from 1923.
51. Notes from the meeting of the Commission du cinéma d'outre-mer, 13 October 1949, CAOM FM 1/AP/2127/9.
52. Instructions from the high commission for the general government of French West Africa to the governors of the territories, 16 October 1954, ARS 21/G/192 [174]. These instructions explained the essence of the recent decree regulating the entirety of the cinema industry in the federation.
53. "Renseignements," 27 August 1957, ARS 21/G/192 [174].
54. Note forwarded to the high commissioner for the general government of West Africa, ARS 21/G/14 [1]. The note is unsigned and undated, but it was likely written in 1948.
55. Letter from the governor of Côte d'Ivoire to the general government of French West Africa, 17 October 1956, ARS 21/G/192 [174]. This letter explained the links between Arabic and Islam along with the dangers that both posed to French authority in the region.
56. "Rapport sur la censure du film egyptien 'Aube de l'Islam,'" 6 January 1959, ARS 21/G/199 [174].
57. Schmidt, *Cold War and Decolonization in Guinea, 1946–1958*; Chafer, *The End of Empire in French West Africa*; Genova, *Colonial Ambivalence*.
58. "Objet: Propagande U.S.A. menée par films," 16 November 1947, ARS 21/G/193 [174].
59. Notes of the meeting of the Commission du cinéma d'outre-mer, 13 October 1949, CAOM FM 1/AP/2127/9.
60. Letter from Bernard Cornut-Gentille to M. Josse, 16 April 1955, ARS 21/G/190 [174].
61. Summation of parliamentary "débats," 3 February 1955, ARS 21/G/193 [174]. These debates concerned the question of the impact of western and gangster films on West African youth.
62. Report from the superior commander of land forces of the French West Africa to the high commissioner for the federation, "Objet: Propagande néfaste par le cinéma," 29 November 1949, ARS, 21/G/193 [174]. See also ARS 21/G/193 [174] for complaints forwarded by "citizens" to the CFCC, 16 January 1951.
63. Genova, *Colonial Ambivalence*, 185–86.
64. Note from the territorial government of Niger to the general government of French West Africa, 29 December 1949, ARS 21/G/193 [174]. Odile Georg also notes the impact of *Tête brûlée* in the effort to prohibit all Soviet-made films. See her "The Cinema, a Place of Tension in Colonial Africa," 38.
65. Letter to the high commissioner for the general government of French West Africa, 12 August 1950, ARS, 21/G/193 [174].
66. "Arrêté 7165 A.P. relatif à l'éxploitation en Afrique occidentale française des films cinématographiques impressionnés," 5 October 1954, ARS, 21/G/192 [174]. See also in CAOM FM 1/AP/7165.
67. Reports submitted by SECMA to the CFCC, March 1957, and to COMACICO, November 1958, ARS 21/G/191 [174].
68. Note from SECMA to the CFCC, 1958, ARS 21/G/191 [174]. SECMA emphasized that *Pelerinage Touba* was "une production locale."
69. Decree no. 53–1294, 31 December 1953, ARS 21/G/192 [174].
70. Report of the high commissioner, 13 April 1955, ARS 21/G/190 [174].
71. See ARS 21/G/192 [174]. This file contains numerous notes, letters, and excerpts in reports from 1955 that center on the complaints of COMACICO and SECMA about the fines and the

unrealistic nature of the quota system given the number of films being produced in France at the time.

72. Project to revise the cinema quota system, 1955, ARS 21/G/192 [174].

73. Letter from Bernard Cornut-Gentille to M. Josse, 16 April 1955, ARS 21/G/190 [174].

74. Note from Adolphe Touffait to Bernard Cornut-Gentille, 15 December 1955, ARS 21/G/190 [174].

75. Notes from the meeting of the Commission du cinéma d'outre-mer, 13 October 1949, CAOM FM 1/AP/2127/9. The commission cited what had taken place in Indochina over the previous years as a foretaste of what to expect elsewhere in the coming period. It noted that from 1946 to 1947 roughly 54 imported films made their way into the Indochinese market whereas in 1948 alone an astonishing 529 foreign movies played in that region.

76. "Arrêté ministeriel (F.O.M.) portant création d'une commission du cinéma dans le cadre du comité d'information de la France d'outre-mer," 3 July 1951, ARS 21/G/188 [174]. See also a document entitled "Projet" by the governor of French Soudan (today Mali), 1948, ARS 21/G/188 [174].

77. Law no. 5329/AP 1, 21 July 1954, ARS 21/G/193 [174].

78. Petition from the Union des associations de parents d'élèves des écoles publiques, 3 August 1956, ARS 21/G/193 [174].

79. Letter from the high commissioner for the general government of French West Africa to the territorial governors of the federation, 16 October 1954, ARS, 21/G/192 [174].

80. See ARS 21/G/195 [174] for lists of banned and authorized films released between 1952 and 1955.

81. See ARS, 21/G/193 [174], which contains letters from various Catholic groups to the CFCC from 1955, as well as a letter from the president of the Comité catholique du cinéma au Sénégal to the high commissioner for the general government of French West Africa dated 15 May 1954. That letter seemed to kick off the campaign of Catholic groups' activism in the cinema field.

82. See ARS 21/G/195 [174], which includes a list of banned films in the year-end report for 1954, along with Mauriac's article.

83. ARS, 21/G/195 [174]. These records contain charts for completing assessment of films, including annual lists of banned films, films that were being viewed in the federation at the time, as well as commentary on the process of permitting or proscribing movies in West Africa.

84. "Arrêté ministeriel (F.O.M.) portent creation d'une commission du cinéma dans le cadre du comité d'information de la France d'outre-mer," 3 July 1951, ARS 21/G/188 [174].

85. Notes associated with the report filed by André Lemaire, "Elements d'un rapport sur les problems d'éducation et d'information audio-visuelles entre l'Afrique noire et la métropole," 10 December 1949, CAOM FM 1/AP/2127/9.

86. Notes from the meetings of the CFCC, 13 October 1949 and 15 June 1950, CAOM FM 1/AP/2127/9.

87. Robert Delavignette Papers, CAOM PA 19/18/252. These documents cover the genesis of the project for turning his book *Les paysans noirs* into a film, including the logistics of pulling off the project.

88. See the building code documents spanning the years from 1949 to 26 July 1956, when the new letter classification system was introduced (ARS 21/G/203 [174]).

89. Complaint from COMACICO to the CFCC, 2 December 1955, ARS 21/G/192 [174].

90. For the technical aspects of making a film, see Sharff, *The Elements of Cinema*, and Gannett, *Understanding Movies*.

91. Minutes of the meeting of the Conseil économique de l'Afrique occidentale française, 29 October 1949, 317–18, CAOM FM 1/AP/2149/1.

2. The Colonialist Regime of Representation, 1945–60

1. Robert Delavignette Papers, CAOM 19/PA/18/252.
2. Adorno, *The Culture Industry*, 181.
3. Slavin, *Colonial Cinema and Imperial France, 1919–1939*, 3.
4. Burke, "'Our Mosquitoes Are Not So Big,'" 43.
5. Stam and Spence, "Colonialism, Racism, and Representation," 236.
6. Boulanger, *Le cinéma colonial*, 16.
7. Stam and Spence, "Colonialism, Racism, and Representation," 239.
8. Landau, introduction, 1, 2, 4, 5.
9. Cameron, *Africa on Film*, 13, 14.
10. Slavin, *Colonial Cinema and Imperial France, 1919–1939*, xi, 3, 209.
11. Boulanger, *Le cinéma colonial*, 221–22.
12. Cameron, *Africa on Film*, 56, 59.
13. Cameron, *Africa on Film*, 123.
14. Cameron, *Africa on Film*, 188.
15. Shaka, *Modernity and the African Cinema*, 8, 17, 18, 172–73, 187, 215, 205, 211.
16. Sherzer, introduction, 5.
17. Sherzer, introduction, 9.
18. Jeancolas, "The Reconstruction of French Cinema," 21.
19. "Decrêt portant organization du contrôle des films cinématographiques, des disques phonographiques, des prises de vues cinématographiques et des enregistrements sonores en Afrique Occidentale Française," 8 March 1934, CAOM FM 1/AP/2127/10.
20. Genova, *Colonial Ambivalence*, 97–98.
21. Bazin, "What Is Cinema?," 195–96, 198, emphasis mine.
22. Harris and Ezra, introduction, 2.
23. Wilder, *The French Imperial Nation-State*, 32–33. For additional analysis of the concept of *la plus grande France*, see Lebovics, *True France*.
24. Letter from Marcel de Coppet to the minister of colonies in Paris and the director of political affairs in the federation, 5 October 1938, CAOM FM 1/AP/859.
25. Letter from Films mercure, 6 August 1929, CAOM FM 1/AP/859 (1). The letter requested permission to make propaganda films for the French, which it claimed would extol the "benefits derived from French rule." This is one of many letters from a variety of film companies, including Films Robert Bastardie, that went, as far as can be deduced, without further official action.
26. "Rapport du directeur de l'enseignement de l'A.E.F," 1 October 1938, CAOM FM 1/AP/859. This was report signed by "Davesne."
27. Jennings, *Vichy in the Tropics*, 146.
28. Internet Movie Data Base (IMDb), http://www.imdb.com/title/tt0023379/. My synopsis is a paraphrase of the description from this site.
29. Letter from Georges Poirier to the high commissioner of the general government for French West Africa, 3 May 1947, ARS 21/G/193 [174]. This file also contains other notes and letters that relate to the history of how this particular film was received (in an official sense) in West Africa.
30. List of authorized films for French West Africa, 18 January 1949, amended and expanded 25 January 1949, ARS 21/G/19 [16].
31. Internet Movie Database (IMDb), http://www.imdb.com/title/tt0191993. The plot summary and technical information are drawn from information compiled by this source.

32. Intergovernmental correspondence between officials throughout French West Africa, ARS 21/G/19 (16). This correspondence is undated but was probably written sometime in 1949.

33. Letter from the general government for French West Africa to the Société interfilm, 14 November 1949, ARS 21/G/19 (16). Interfilm was likely the distributor of the film in the federation at the time and, as such, had to get annual approval (the visa or license) to screen films in West Africa.

34. Bazin, "What Is Cinema?" 47.

35. Deren, "Cinematography," 220.

36. Shaka, *Modernity and the African Cinema*, 220–22.

37. Deren, "Cinematography," 224–25, emphasis in the original.

38. Kracauer, "Theory of Film," 293.

39. Kracauer, "Theory of Film," 299.

40. Kracauer, "Theory of Film," 302.

41. Robert Delavignette Papers, CAOM 19/PA/18/252. Delavignette wrote a lengthy report offering his reactions to the film and describing the process of making the film.

42. Robert Delavignette Papers, CAOM 19/PA/18/250.

43. Burke, "'Our Mosquitoes Are Not So Big,'" 53.

44. Stoller, "Regarding Rouch," 74.

45. Robert Delavignette Papers, CAOM 19/PA/18/252. This personal assessment and commentary on the meaning and nature of the film is undated but was likely written in 1948 or 1949, at the time of filming or shortly thereafter, around the time of its release.

46. Genova, *Colonial Ambivalence*, 111–13. See also Sibeud, "Ethnographie africaniste et 'inauthenticité' coloniale," and L'Estoile, "Au nom des 'vrais Africains.'"

47. Stam and Spence, "Colonialism, Racism, and Representation," 238.

48. Stam and Spence, "Colonialism, Racism, and Representation," 242, emphasis in the original.

49. Robert Delavignette Papers, CAOM 19/PA/18/252.

50. Genova, *Colonial Ambivalence*, 55–63.

51. Notes from the meeting of the Commission du cinéma d'outre-mer, 15 June 1950, CAOM FM 1/AP/2127/9.

52. Wilder, *The French Imperial Nation-State*, 76–77. See also Girault, *Principes de colonisation et de législation colonial*.

53. Delavignette, *Les paysans noirs,*.

54. Cohen, "Robert Delavignette," 192.

55. Robert Delavignette Papers, CAOM 19/PA/18/251.

56. Robert Delavignette Papers, CAOM 19/PA/18/249.

57. Here I am borrowing the phrase from John Ellis in his study of the relationship between sound and image in television ("Visible Fictions," 386).

58. Saidou, "Une culture africaine." A transcribed copy of the essay can be found in CAOM, 1/AP/2097/4, among papers from the same period that all deal with general assessments of support for France in the region and any perceived threats to that influence, including from American propaganda. Saidou sought to encourage French officials by assuring them that educated Africans were loyal to the imperial rulers despite these other forces working to undermine French domination.

59. Genova, *Colonial Ambivalence*, 149–51.

60. Shaka, *Modernity and the African Cinema*, 8.

61. Belton, "Technology and Aesthetics of Film Sound," 384.

62. Eisenstein, "Film Form," 40.

63. "Des films pour l'Afrique." A transcription of this article can be found in ARS 21/G/193 [174].

64. Metz, "Film Language," 77, 88, emphasis in the original.

65. Shaka, *Modernity and the African Cinema*, 17.
66. See ARS 21/G/196 [174]. This folder contains favored film treatments with annotations by officials indicating their preference for movies that center on "health, scenery, daily life," as well as those that favor "ethnographic and documentary" formats.
67. Proposal from Studio RIF to the CFCC to make "Civilisation européenne en Afrique," 1957, with the approval of the CFCC, 19 December 1957, ARS 21/G/196 [174].
68. Film treatment proposal from Films Pierre Cellier, Dakar, 2 January 1959, ARS 21/G/196 [174]. This folder also contains another film treatment for "Influsso civilizzatore della civilità europea" suggesting that filmmakers from around Europe and North America got the message about the kinds of films the colonial administration in French West Africa wanted for their audiences on site and abroad.
69. Statement of M. Bouruet-Aubertot, *Bulletin du Conseil économique*, 27 October 1949, 675, CAOM FM 1/AP/2149/1.
70. This is a subject I have explored in greater depth elsewhere; see *Colonial Ambivalence*, 281–82. See also my "Conflicted Missionaries."
71. Statement by the Conseil économique, *Bulletin du Conseil économique*, 29 October 1949, 317–18, CAOM FM 1/AP/2149/1.
72. Belton, "Technology and Aesthetics of Film Sound," 378.
73. Interoffice communication in French West Africa, ARS 21/G/14 [1]. The communication is undated, but it was likely written in 1948, since the rest of the material in this file is stamped for that year. The signature on the memo is illegible. The commentary titled "Egyptian nationalism" is inserted at the end of the text to make the appropriate connection and reveals the primary concern of officials with regard to the problem of the Arab language.
74. Wesseling, *Certain Ideas of France*. In several of the essays included in his volume, Wesseling discusses the particular, even peculiar, French regard for their language and the powers that inhere within it.
75. Bakhtin, "From the Prehistory of Novelistic Discourse," 49.
76. "Relatif à l'autorisation de distribution en version doublée de langue française des films étrangers de long métrage," decree no. 52-838, 18 July 1952, ARS 21/G/188 [174]. The decree was signed by Antoine Pinay, the prime minister of France.

3. West African Anticolonial Film Politics, 1950s–60s

1. Vieyra, "Responsabilités du cinéma dans la formation d'une conscience nationale africaine," 68, 71, 69.
2. Pfaff, introduction, 1.
3. Bernstein, introduction, 2, emphasis in the original.
4. Bernstein, introduction, 2–3.
5. Adorno, *The Culture Industry*, 180.
6. Adorno, *The Culture Industry*, 182, 184.
7. Diawara, *African Cinema*, 23–24.
8. Ukadike, *Black African Cinema*, 7.
9. Cham, introduction, 1.
10. Harrow, *Postcolonial African Cinema*, 22, 37.
11. Diawara, *African Cinema*, 24.
12. "Appel aux ecrivains et artistes noirs," CAOM FM 1/AP/2186. This manifesto was published in *Présence africaine* in 1956.
13. See the articles in *Présence africaine* 1–2 (1955) for an illustration of this point.

14. Diop, "Niam n'goura," 7.
15. Diop, "Niam n'goura," 7–8.
16. For a discussion of the relationship between the novel and national identity formation in the modern world see Bakhtin, "Epic and Novel," 7, 11, and Chaterjee, *Nationalist Thought and the Colonial World*, 39–43.
17. Mudimbe, finale, 435, 436.
18. Genova, "*Africanité* and *Urbanité*," 267–68.
19. Jewsiewicki, "*Présence Africaine* as Historiography," 99.
20. Mortimer, *Journeys through the French African Novel*, 1, 15.
21. Jules-Rosette, "Conjugating Cultural Realities," 14.
22. Bakhtin, "From the Prehistory of Novelistic Discourse," 50.
23. Bakhtin, "From the Prehistory of Novelistic Discourse," 49.
24. Cooper, *Decolonization and African Society*, 241–48; Chafer, *The End of Empire in French West Africa*, 68–70; Sembène, *God's Bits of Wood*, 32–33, 76, 87, 94. See also my "*Africanité* and *Urbanité*," 279–81.
25. Bakhtin, "From the Prehistory of Novelistic Discourse," 77.
26. Ashcroft, Griffiths, and Tiffin, *The Empire Writes Back*, 7.
27. Thiong'o, *Decolonising the Mind*, 5.
28. Bakhtin, "From the Prehistory of Novelistic Discourse," 75, 76. Eleni Condouriotis also identifies this correlation between Bakhtin's notion of the intentional hybrid and the French African novel of the 1950s (*Claiming History*, 4).
29. Rouch, "Vers une literature africaine," 144, 145.
30. See the special issue of *Présence africaine*, "Trois ecrivains noirs," published in 1954. The issue provides excerpts of the three novels as well as reviews of them. The attacks on Laye's style continued into the following year upon publication of his next novel *Le regard du roi*. See *Présence africaine* 1–2 (April–July 1955), in particular the essay by A. B., "Afrique noire, littérature rose," 133–45.
31. André Lemaire, "Elements d'un rapport sur les problems d'éducation et d'information audio-visuelles entre l'Afrique noire et la métropole," 10 December 1949, CAOM FM 1/AP/2127/9–10.
32. Petition from GAC to make a film in West Africa, 1954, ARS 21/G/196 [174].
33. Diawara, *African Cinema*, 23. See also, Armes, *Third World Filmmaking and the West*, 221, Cham, introduction," 1, and Ukadike, *Black African Cinema*, 68. *Afrique-sur-Seine* is often listed alongside Mamadou Touré's *Mouramani*, a film made in Guinea that appeared the same year. However, most scholars generally acknowledge the central importance of GAC's *Afrique-sur-Seine* due to its wider screening, its long-term influence on the direction of African cinema, and the role that Vieyra went on to play in helping to shape postcolonial West African film practice and theory.
34. Sembène, "Moment d'une vie," 21.
35. Armes, *African Filmmaking North and South of the Sahara*, 61.
36. Qtd. in Bassori, "Soumanou Paulin Vieyra," 38.
37. Ngangura, "African Cinema," 62.
38. Pfaff, "Africa from Within," 225.
39. Ukadike, *Black African Cinema*, 68–69.
40. Vieyra, "Responsabilités du cinéma dans la formation d'une conscience nationale africaine," 66.
41. Vieyra, "Responsabilités du cinéma dans la formation d'une conscience nationale africaine," 64.
42. Diawara, *African Cinema*, 36.
43. Vieyra, "Le cinéma et la révolution africaine," 75, 77.

44. Vieyra, "Propos sur le cinéma africain," 106, 107, 108, 109–10, 111.
45. Vieyra, "Propos sur le cinéma africain," 106, 107, 108, 109–10, 111; Stam and Spence, "Colonialism, Racism, and Representation," 36.
46. Vieyra, "Propos sur le cinéma africain," 113, 114.
47. Vieyra, "Propos sur le cinéma africain," 111, 115, 116.
48. Genova, *Colonial Ambivalence*, 278, 281. See also *Présence africaine*, 8–10 (1956), 58–68 (which contain a transcription of a debate between Senghor and Richard Wright about the nature of negro-African civilization and appropriate forms of its cultural expression), and "Ecrivains et artistes noirs sont réunis à la Sorbonne pour leur premier congress," *L'humanité*, 20 September 1956, CAOM FM 1/AP/2186/4.
49. "Resolution of the First World Congress of Black Writers and Artists," 361–64. Jacques Rabenamanjara read the resolution to the assembled delegates, who then voted unanimously in favor of it.
50. Genova, *Colonial Ambivalence*, 278.
51. See *Présence africaine* 24–25 (1959), which published the proceedings of the Second World Congress of Black Writers and Artists. The congress was held in Rome, Italy, from 26 March to 11 April 1959.
52. Diop, "Announcement of the Cancellation of the Second World Congress of Black Writers and Artists," 144.
53. "Résolution de la sous-commission de philosophie," 415–16.
54. Vieyra, "Reponsabilités du cinéma dans la formation d'une conscience nationale africaine," 67, 71.
55. Woll, "The Russian Connection," 225.
56. Woll, "The Russian Connection," 228, 231. Among the other prominent West African filmmakers who spent a considerable amount of time in the Soviet Union and underwent training at their cinema institutes were Souleymane Cissé (Mali) during the 1960s and Abderrahmane Sissako (Mauretania/Mali) in the 1980s.
57. Woll, "The Russian Connection," 224.
58. Eisenstein, "Film Form," 21, 22, 16.
59. Letter from Robert de Guise to the Ministère des colonies, 11 July 1932, CAOM FM 1/AP/859.
60. Woll, "The Russian Connection," 228.
61. Cham, "Film and History in Africa," 49.
62. Solanas and Getino, "Towards a Third Cinema," 35, 36, 46, 55.
63. Guneratne, introduction, 1, 9.
64. Solanas and Getino, "Towards a Third Cinema," 34, 37.
65. Gabriel, *Third Cinema in the Third World*, 2.
66. Guneratne, introduction, 16.
67. Stam, "Beyond Third Cinema," 31–32.
68. Gabriel, *Third Cinema in the Third World*, 95.
69. MacBean, "La hora de los hornos," 31, emphasis in the original.
70. Pfaff, "The Uniqueness of Ousmane Sembène's Cinema," 14. The interview Pfaff cites was printed in *Young Cinema and Theatre* 3 (1970): 27.
71. Ukadike, *Questioning African Cinema*, 269.
72. Pfaff, "African Cities as Cinematic Texts," 100.
73. Ukadike, *Questioning African Cinema*, 24.
74. Ukadike, *Questioning African Cinema*, 67.
75. Vieyra, "Responsabilités du cinéma dans la formation d'une conscience nationale africaine," 67.

76. Vieyra, "Responsabilités du cinéma dans la formation d'une conscience nationale africaine," 69, 70, 72.

77. Ki-Zerbo, "Cinéma africain et développement, l'éthique," 106.

4. The Postcolonial African Regime of Representation

1. Qtd. in Hennebelle, "Afrique noire," 96, emphasis in the original.
2. Kaspin, conclusion, 331.
3. Sembène, "Cinema as Evening School," 13–14.
4. Shaka, *Modernity and the African Cinema*, 37.
5. Ukadike, *Black African Cinema*, 2, 103, 104.
6. Diawara, *African Cinema*, 23, 24–25, 34.
7. Harrow, *Postcolonial African Cinema*, 1, 5.
8. Harrow, *Postcolonial African Cinema*, 19–20.
9. Thackway, *Africa Shoots Back*, 1, 9, 8, 10.
10. Gugler, *African Film*, 8–11; Pfaff, *Focus on African Films*, 6; Murphy and Williams, *Postcolonial African Cinema*, 19; Harrow, *Postcolonial African Cinema*, 1–2, 8–9.
11. Harrow, *Postcolonial African Cinema*, 5.
12. Murphy and Williams, *Postcolonial African Cinema*, 5, 27.
13. Thackway, *Africa Shoots Back*, 7, 32.
14. Ukadike, *Black African Cinema*, 48–49.
15. Rendering of the Dakar court of appeals, 22 August 1951, CAOM FM 1/AP/2127/9.
16. Rendering of the Dakar courts of appeals, 22 August 1951, CAOM FM 1/AP/2127/9.
17. "Objet: Soirée franco-africaine organize par le movement 'Présence africaine,'" 19 November 1958, CAOM FM 1/AP/2188/4. The report is unsigned, as the informant was a spy sent by the colonial intelligence services.
18. Diawara, *African Cinema*, 22; Shaka, *Modernity and the African Cinema*, 301.
19. Gugler, *African Film*, 8–10.
20. See ARS 21/G/203 [174]. This file contains an extensive inventory of documents pertaining to Këita Fodeba specifically concerning the "anticolonial" and "communist" activities of his Théâtre africain in 1951. The general government of French West Africa was concerned that this "singer/poet, communist" was actively using his ballet/musical troupe to support the RDA, subject of the repression portrayed in *Afrique 50*. Këita Fodeba was a major figure in the RDA in Guinea and later worked for Sékou Touré's government until being accused of supporting a coup in 1969. He was subsequently imprisoned, tortured, and executed. Police documents on his activities also turn up in "Diffusion par la RDF des oeuvres de M. Këita Fodeba" (CAOM FM 1/AP/2127/9), wherein the cultural activist is accused of "casting discredit on the work of overseas France."
21. Annual list of banned films as of the end of 1954 produced by the CFCC for the high commissioner of French West Africa, ARS 21/G/95 [174].
22. Thackway, *Africa Shoots Back*, 7, 32; Shaka, *Modernity and the African Cinema*, 301; Diawara, *African Cinema*, 23. Diawara gives 1955 as the date of the film's production, but that is incorrect; it was in fact commissioned by *Présence africaine* in 1952, completed in 1953, and banned by 1954.
23. Dovey, *African Film and Literature*, 177, 189.
24. Ukadike, *Black African Cinema*, 49.
25. Ukadike, *Black African Cinema*, 84, 162.
26. Gadjigo, "Ousmane Sembene and History on the Screen," 38.

27. Vieyra, *Ousmane Sembène*, 21.
28. Vieyra, *Le cinéma Africain des origines à 1973*, 106–107, 123.
29. Harrow, *Postcolonial African Cinema*, 1.
30. Diawara, "The Iconography of West African Cinema," 84.
31. Gugler, *African Film*, 126.
32. Bakari, introduction, 3.
33. For example, see Sergei Eisenstein, *Strike!* (1925), *Battleship Potemkin* (1925), *October* (1928), and *Alexander Nevsky* (1938), and Dziga Vertov, *Kinoglaz* (1924), *One-Sixth of the World* (1926), and *The Man with a Movie Camera* (1929).
34. Adorno, *The Culture Industry*, 182.
35. Harrow, *Postcolonial African Cinema*, 16.
36. Woll, "The Russian Connection," 233.
37. Harrow, *Postcolonial African Cinema*, 37.
38. Thackway, *Africa Shoots Back*.
39. Andrade-Watkins, "France's Bureau of Cinema," 114. *La noire de . . .* has also been extensively commented on for its seminal place in the history of African cinema by Diawara, *African Cinema*, 26, Ukadike, *Black African Cinema*, 7, and Armes, *Third World Filmmaking and the West*, 286, among many others.
40. Fanon, *Black Skin, White Masks*, 10–11.
41. Gabriel, forward, x.
42. Vieyra, "Le cinéma et la révolution africaine," 80.
43. Gabriel, forward, x.
44. Metz, "Problems of Denotation in Fiction Film," 58–59.
45. "Interview with Sembène Ousmane."
46. CNC, press statement.
47. Gabriel, *Third Cinema in the Third World*, 22.
48. Ukadike, *Black African Cinema*, 101.
49. Solanas and Getino, "Towards a Third Cinema," 46.
50. Pfaff, "The Uniqueness of Ousmane Sembène's Cinema," 17. See also Diawara, "Popular Culture and Oral Traditions in African Film," 215.
51. Ukadike, *Black African Cinema*, 87; Lequeret, *Le cinéma africain*, 17.
52. Pfaff, "The Uniqueness of Ousmane Sembène's Cinema," 17–18; Lequeret, *Le cinéma africain*, 11.
53. Solanas and Getino, "Towards a Third Cinema," 42.
54. Taylor, "Searching for the Postmodern in African Cinema," 141.
55. Pfaff, "The Films of Med Hondo," 45.
56. Several scholars have heaped praise on Hondo's *Soleil Ô* and offered extensive analysis of it from the perspective of film studies. See, for example, Ukadike, *Black African Cinema*, 78–83, 101–103, Murphy and Williams, *Postcolonial African Cinema*, 75, 79–80, Cham, "Film and History in Africa," 63, and Thackway, *Africa Shoots Back*, 127–29.
57. Pfaff, "The Films of Med Hondo," 45.
58. Pfaff, "The Films of Med Hondo," 45.
59. Ukadike, *Black African Cinema*, 103.
60. Ukadike, *Black African Cinema*, 83.
61. Murphy and Williams, *Postcolonial African Cinema*, 91–92.
62. Harrow, *Postcolonial African Cinema*, 20.
63. Murphy and Williams, *Postcolonial African Cinema*, 94.

64. For Bhabha's idea of the postmodern hybrid subject, see Bhabha, *The Location of Culture* 38, 86. For Harrow's deployment of Bhabha's insights in understanding Mambety's contribution to African cinema, see *Postcolonial African Cinema*, 39–42.
65. Murphy and Williams, *Postcolonial African Cinema*, 104.
66. Ukadike, *Questioning African Cinema*, 60.

5. The West African Cinema Industrial Complex, 1960s–70s

1. Robert Delavignette, "Cooperation," Robert Delavignette Papers, CAOM, 19PA/25/347. This document is undated, but it was likely written in 1968. It includes notes for *Du bon usage de la decolonization,* his two-volume study published that year.
2. Robert Delavignette Papers, CAOM, 19PA/18/246. The title of the roundtable was "Le recrutement de l'administration: Administration technique et administration generale; Africanisation des cadres." The part in which Delavignette participated was Group A/9/C "L'administration technique."
3. Cameron, *Africa on Film*, 170–78.
4. "Pan-African Cultural Manifesto," 125, 127. This is the resolution of the Symposium of the First Pan-African Cultural Festival, held in Algiers, Algeria, 21 July–1 August 1969.
5. Vieyra, "Centres culturels, et politique de la culture en Afrique," 188, 189.
6. Lebovics, *Mona Lisa's Escort*, 7.
7. Harrow, *Postcolonial African Cinema*, 22–26.
8. Ukadike, *Black African Cinema*, 70, 71.
9. Diawara, *African Cinema*, 24, 25.
10. Qtd. in Bossuat, "French Development Aid and Co-Operation under de Gaulle," 433.
11. Bossuat, "French Development Aid and Co-Operation under de Gaulle," 434. See also the decree of 25 July 1959 and the decree of 10 June 1961, completing the transition to the Ministry of Cooperation (CAC, ver. 19840297).
12. "Cinema: Réforme du contrôle, 1959–1961," CAC, ver. 19840297, art. 6 (F 41 Bis. 03079). The papers originated through the office of the prime minister and detailed the legalities of transforming the Ministère de la France d'outre-mer into the Ministère de la coopération et l'assistance technique, later called the Ministère de la coopération et du développement.
13. Debrix, "French 'Co-operation' . . . and England?," 44. Debrix had previously been the general director of IDHEC, France's most prestigious film school, where Vieyra had been trained in the 1950s and Vautier in the 1940s.
14. Qtd. in Bossuat, "French Development Aid and Co-Operation under de Gaulle," 433.
15. A note dated 18 March 1948 in ARS 21/G/189 [174] to the high commissioner for French West Africa indicates that in 1948 there were no cinemas in Mauritania or Upper Volta and that in Niger only "open air" theaters existed; another note in this file contains a series of petitions from 1947 to open theaters in Bamako.
16. Vieyra, *Le cinéma africain des origines à 1973*, 413–20. In this appendix, Vieyra provides a detailed listing of the theaters operating across West and Central Africa, including the number of seats available in each theater. It presents a remarkable portrait of the extensive cinematic infrastructure inherited by independent Africa.
17. Vieyra, *Le cinéma africain des origines à 1973*, 423. Vieyra contrasts the accessibility of the movie theater with the distribution of television sets (not to mention the limited number of broadcast stations), which shows that television was a very marginal part of the media experience in sub-Saharan Africa at the time.
18. Kuisel, *Seducing the French*, 1–3; Kuisel, *The French Way*, 313–26.

19. Kuisel, *Seducing the French*, 123. See also Ukadike, *Questioning African Cinema*, 19. Ukadike states that Cissé graduated in 1969, whereas Vieyra claims he graduated in 1970.

20. Ministère de la cooperation, "Formation prise en charge par le fonds d'aide et de cooperation: 1960–1967," CAC, ver. 19770316, art. 3–15. These documents detail the procedures for the dispensation of aid to applicants.

21. Hoefert de Turégano, "The New Politics of African Cinema at the French Ministry of Foreign Affairs," 23.

22. Ministère des affaires culturelles/CNC, "Dossiers de participation UFF aux festivals et manifestations cinematographiques internationaux, classés par année: 1965–1974," CAC, ver. 19790254, art. 27–52. See also CNC, "Bureau des festivals," CAC, ver. 19900289, art. 121–38.

23. Hoefert de Turégano, "The New Politics of African Cinema at the French Ministry of Foreign Affairs," 24.

24. Debrix, "Dix ans de coopération franco-africaine ont permis la naissance du jeune cinéma d'Afrique noire," 15.

25. "Cinema: Réforme du contrôle, 1959–1961," CAC, ver. 19840297, art. 6 (F 41 Bis. 03079); Ministry of Cooperation, "Formation prise en charge par le fonds d'aide et de cooperation: 1960–1967," CAC, ver. 19770316, art. 3–15. On the rejection of Sembène's project for filming *La noire de . . .* , see also Diawara, *African Cinema*, 26, and Shaka, *Modernity and the African Cinema*, 306.

26. For a discussion of the role promotion of the culture industry (film in particular), played in French economic considerations, see Lebovics, *Mona Lisa's Escort*, 145.

27. Shaka, *Modernity and the African Cinema*, 310.

28. A list of the credits for both Robert de Nesle and Jean Maumy can be found in both of the two major movie databases, the British Film Institute and the Internet Movie Database. For the BFI, see http://ftvdb.bfi.org.uk; for the IMDb, see: http://www.imdb.com/.

29. Vieyra, "Propos sur le cinéma," 106–108.

30. Shaka, *Modernity and the African Cinema*, 310–11.

31. Pfaff, "The Uniqueness of Ousmane Sembène's Cinema," 17–18; Lequeret, *Le cinéma africain*, 11.

32. Lebovics, *Mona Lisa's Escort*, 186, 193.

33. CNC, press statement.

34. Thackway, *Africa Shoots Back*, 45; Gugler, *African Film*, 134; Diawara, *African Cinema*, 141; Cham, introduction, 6.

35. Pfaff, "From Africa to the Americas," 204.

36. Ukadike, *Black African Cinema*, 86–87.

37. André Lemaire, "Elements d'un rapport sur les problems d'éducation et d'information audiovisuelles entre l'Afrique noire et la métropole," 10 December 1949, CAOM FM 1/AP/2127/9–10.

38. Ukadike, *Questioning African Cinema*, 20, 26.

39. Pfaff, "From Africa to the Americas," 241; Ukadike, "Other Voices of Documentary," 168.

40. Solanas and Getino, "Towards a Third Cinema," 51, 33.

41. Solanas and Getino, "Towards a Third Cinema," 42.

42. Pfaff, "The Films of Med Hondo," 45.

43. Solanas and Getino, "Towards a Third Cinema," 46, 47, 49, 50, 56, 55.

44. Ukadike, "The Other Voices of Documentary," 162. Mbye Cham also notes the connections between African and Latin American filmmaking in the late 1960s and early 1970s. See his "Film and History in Africa," 49.

45. Roof, "African and Latin American Cinemas," 243. Roof cites the resolutions agreed to by the assembled filmmakers at the close of the Third World Filmmakers Meeting held in Algiers, Algeria, 5–14 December 1973, first published in *Cineaste* in 1973; see "Resolutions of the Third World Film-makers Meeting, Algiers, December 5–14, 1973."

46. Solanas and Getino, "Towards a Third Cinema," 44–45.
47. Qtd. in Diawara, *African Cinema*, 49. Diawara, in turn, cites Gabriel, *Third Cinema*, 115. Diawara points out that Sembène continued to use his own 35 mm camera, despite the improvements offered by 16 mm technology.
48. Roof, "African and Latin American Cinemas," 242, 243.
49. Statement of the African Film Summit, held 3–6 April 2006 in Johannesburg, South Africa, 11, http://www.dac.gov.za/events/AFRICAN%20FILM%20SUMMIT%20%20info%20doc%20november%202005.pdf.
50. Clément Tapsoba, "Le grandes dates du cinéma africain," 299.
51. Roof, "African and Latin American Cinemas," 242, 243.
52. See point number 5 on organizing African cinema to overcome structural obstacles confronted by filmmakers, "Pan-African Cultural Manifesto," 127.
53. Bangré, "African Cinema in the Tempest of Minor Festivals," 157.
54. See point number 33 on media, "Pan-African Cultural Manifesto," 127.
55. "Pan-African Cultural Manifesto," 127.
56. Vieyra, "Le cinéma au 1er festival culturel panafricain d'Alger," 190–201.
57. Vieyra, "Centres culturels, et politique de la culture en Afrique," 188, 189.
58. Roof, "African and Latin American Cinemas," 243.
59. Murphy and Williams, *Postcolonial African Cinema*, 5. Murphy and Williams cite Gabriel's *Third Cinema in the Third World*, which locates African cinema "at the cutting edge of a politically and artistically radical 'Third Cinema,' which explicitly rejected the capitalist world order of the West." Murphy and Williams, however, view this as "an excessive generalization."
60. Roof, "African and Latin American Cinemas," 243.
61. "Resolutions of the Third World Film-makers Meeting, Algiers, Algeria, December 5–14, 1973," 472. Roof also comments on this; see "African and Latin American Cinemas," 243.
62. Diawara, *African Cinema*, 129.
63. Hoefert de Turégano, "The New Politics of African Cinema at the French Ministry of Foreign Affairs," 23.
64. Diawara, *African Cinema*, 130.
65. Lebovics, *Mona Lisa's Escort*, 188. While Lebovics does not discuss Malraux's role in founding the ACCT, he does mention the connections between his ministry and West African governments in developing the concept of *francophonie*.
66. Agence de coopération culturelle et technique, *Textes fondamentaux*, 1, 2, 7, 15–16.
67. Delavignette, "Coopération," 1968, Robert Delavignette Papers, CAOM 19PA/25/347.
68. Senghor, "Le français, langue de culture."
69. Agence de coopération culturelle et technique, *Textes fondamentaux*, 2.
70. Qtd. in Sama, "African Films are Foreigners in their Own Countries," 150.
71. Ukadike, *Black African Cinema*, 63.
72. Vieyra, *Le cinéma africain des origines à 1973*, 413–20.
73. Vieyra, *Le cinéma africain des origines à 1973*, 413–20. All of COMACICO's theaters were "open air," while SECMA's were indoor and had both 35 mm and 16 mm projection capabilities.
74. Sama, "African Films are Foreigners in their Own Countries," 149.
75. Sama, "African Films are Foreigners in their Own Countries," 149. See also Diawara, *African Cinema*, 130, and Ukadike, *Black African Cinema*, 63.
76. Vieyra, *Le cinéma africain des origines à 1973*, 104–105.
77. "Les grandes dates du FESPACO," http://www.fespaco-bf.net.
78. Francophone West African filmmakers routinely commented that they expected their films to spark discussions and that such conversations should take place in the environment of the

theater's space. See, for example, Pfaff, "The Uniqueness of Ousmane Sembène's Cinema," 14, 20, and Murphy and Williams, *Postcolonial African Cinema*, 62–63.

79. Murphy and Williams, *Postcolonial African Cinema*, 156.
80. Les grandes dates du FESPACO," http://www.fespaco-bf.net.
81. FEPACI, "The Algiers Charter on African Cinema," 25.
82. Robert Delavignette Papers, CAOM 19/PA/18/252; André Lemaire, "Elements d'un rapport sur les problems d'éducation et d'information audio-visuelles entre l'Afrique noire et la métropole," 10 December 1949, CAOM FM 1/AP/2127/9.
83. Solanas and Getino, "Towards a Third Cinema," 46; FEPACI, "The Algiers Charter on African Cinema," 25, 26.
84. Solanas and Getino, "Towards a Third Cinema," 46.

Postscript: Francophone West African Cinema to the Present

1. Vieyra, "African Cinema: Solidarity and Difference," 195.
2. Ukadike, *Questioning African Cinema*, 62.
3. Wollen, "Godard and Counter-Cinema," 129.
4. Harrow, *Postcolonial African Cinema*, 43.
5. Harris and Ezra, introduction, 1. See also Schwartz, *It's So French!*, 11, 14.
6. Vieyra, "Propos sur le cinéma africain," 114–16.
7. Ukadike, *Questioning African Cinema*, 62.
8. Schwartz, *It's So French!*, 8, 11, 12, 14; Harris and Ezra, introduction, 1, 2.
9. Andrade-Watkins, "France's Bureau of Cinema," 125–26.

Bibliography

Primary

ARS Archives de la République du Sénégal
CAOM
    FM 1/AP   Centre des archives d'outre-mer, Fonds ministériels 1, Affaires politiques
    PA   Papiers d'agents
CAC Centre des Archives Contemporaines

Secondary

Adorno, Theodor. *The Culture Industry: Selected Essays on Mass Culture*. London: Routledge, 1991.
Agence de coopération culturelle et technique. *Textes fondamentaux*. Paris: Agence de coopération culturelle et technique, 1972.
Althusser, Louis. "Ideology and Ideological State Apparatuses." In *Lenin and Philosophy and Other Essays*, 121–76. New York: Monthly Review Press, 1971.
Andrade-Watkins, Claire. "France's Bureau of Cinema—Financial and Technical Assistance 1961–1971: Operations and Implications for African Cinema." In *African Experiences of Cinema*. Edited by Imruh Bakari and Mbye B. Cham, 112–27. London: BFI, 1996.
Appiah, Kwame Anthony. *In My Father's House: Africa in the Philosophy of Culture*. Oxford: Oxford University Press, 1992.
Armes, Roy. *African Filmmaking North and South of the Sahara*. Bloomington: Indiana University Press, 2006.
———. *Third World Filmmaking and the West*. Berkeley: University of California Press, 1987.
Ashcroft, Bill, Gareth Griffiths, and Helen Tiffin. *The Empire Writes Back: Theory and Practice in Postcolonial Literatures*. London: Routledge, 1989.
Bakari, Imruh. "Introduction: African Cinema and the Emergent Africa." In *Symbolic Narratives/African Cinema: Audiences, Theory and the Moving Image*. Edited by June Givanni, 3–24. London: BFI, 2003.
Bakari, Imruh, and Mbye B. Cham, eds. *African Experiences of Cinema*. London: BFI, 1996.
Bakhtin, Mikhail M. "Epic and Novel: Toward a Methodology for the Study of the Novel." In *The Dialogic Imagination: Four Essays by M. M. Bakhtin*. Edited by Michael Holquist. Translated by Caryl Emerson and Michael Holquist, 3–40. Austin: University of Texas Press, 1981.

———. "From the Prehistory of Novelistic Discourse." In *The Dialogic Imagination: Four Essays by M.M. Bakhtin*. Edited by Michael Holquist. Translated by Caryl Emerson and Michael Holquist, 41–83. Austin: University of Texas Press, 1981.

Bangré, Sambolgo. "African Cinema in the Tempest of Minor Festivals." In *African Experiences of Cinema*. Edited by Imruh Bakari and Mbye B. Cham, 157–61. London: BFI, 1996.

Barry, Aminata. "Pour la grandeur du cinéma africain, une refonte du FESPACO." *Présence africaine* 170.2 (2004): 93–97.

Barthes, Roland. "Diderot, Brecht, Eisenstein." In *Narrative, Apparatus, Ideology: A Film Theory Reader*. Edited by Philip Rosen, 172–78. New York: Columbia University Press, 1986.

Bassori, Timité. "Soumanou Paulin Vieyra, un pionnier: Cinéaste et critique." *Présence africaine* 170.2 (2004): 35–40.

Baudry, Jean-Louis. "Ideological Effects of the Basic Cinematographic Apparatus." In *Narrative, Apparatus, Ideology: A Film Theory Reader*. Edited by Philip Rosen, 299–318. New York: Columbia University Press, 1986.

Bazin, André. "What Is Cinema?" In *Film Theory and Criticism: Introductory Readings*. 5th ed. Edited by Leo Braudy and Marshall Cohen, 43–56. New York: Oxford University Press, 1999.

Belton, John. "Technology and Aesthetics of Film Sound." In *Film Theory and Criticism: Introductory Readings*. 5th ed. Edited by Leo Braudy and Marshall Cohen, 376–84. New York: Oxford University Press, 1999.

Benjamin, Walter. "The Work of Art in the Age of Mechanical Reproduction." In *Film Theory and Criticism: Introductory Readings*. 5th ed. Edited by Leo Braudy and Marshall Cohen, 731–51. New York: Oxford University Press, 1999.

Bernstein, J. M. Introduction. In *The Culture Industry: Selected Essays on Mass Culture* by Theodor Adorno, 1–25. London: Routledge, 1991.

Bhabha, Homi. *The Location of Culture*. London: Routledge, 1994.

Bory, Jean-Claude. "Le mandat." In *Les dossiers du cinema*. Vol. 1, 137–39. Paris: Casterman, 1968.

Bossuat, Gérard. "French Development Aid and Co-Operation under de Gaulle." *Contemporary European History*. 12.4 (2003): 431–56.

Boulanger, Pierre. *Le cinéma colonial: De "L'Atlantide" à "Lawrence d'Arabie."* Paris: Editions Seghers, 1975.

Bourdieu, Pierre. *The Field of Cultural Production*. New York: Columbia University Press, 1993.

Braudy, Leo, and Marshall Cohen, eds. *Film Theory and Criticism: Introductory Readings*. 5th ed. New York: Oxford University Press, 1999.

Browne, Nick. "The Spectator-in-the-Text: The Rhetoric of *Stagecoach*." In *Narrative, Apparatus, Ideology: A Film Theory Reader*. Edited by Philip Rosen, 102–19. New York: Columbia University Press, 1986.

Burke, Timothy. "'Our Mosquitoes Are Not So Big': Images and Modernity in Zimbabwe." In *Images and Empires: Visuality in Colonial and Postcolonial Africa*. Edited by Paul S. Landau and Deborah D. Kaspin, 41–55. Berkeley: University of California Press, 2002.

Cameron, Kenneth M. *Africa on Film: Beyond Black and White*. New York: Continuum, 1994.

Centre national de la cinématographie. Press statement. In *La collection Sembène Ousmane*. DVD. Paris: Médiathèque des trois mondes, 2004.
Chafer, Tony. *The End of Empire in French West Africa: France's Successful Decolonization?* New York: Berg, 2002.
Cham, Mbye B. "Film and History in Africa: A Critical Survey of Current Trends and Tendencies." In *Focus on African Films*. Edited by Françoise Pfaff, 48–68. Bloomington: Indiana University Press, 2004.
——. Introduction to *African Experiences of Cinema*. Edited by Imruh Bakari and Mbye B. Cham, 1–14. London: BFI, 1996.
Chaterjee, Partha. *Nationalist Thought and the Colonial World: A Derivative Discourse?* Minneapolis: University of Minnesota Press, 1986.
Chowdhry, Prem. *Colonial India and the Making of Empire Cinema: Image, Ideology, and Identity*. Manchester, U.K.: Manchester University Press, 2000.
"Cinema et domination étrangère en Afrique noire." *Pueples noirs pueples africains*. 13 (1980): 141–44.
Clancy-Smith, Julia A. *Rebel and Saint: Muslim Notables, Populist Protest, Colonial Encounters (Algeria and Tunisia, 1800–1904)*. Berkeley: University of California Press, 1997.
Cohen, William B. "Robert Delavignette: The Gentle Ruler (1897–1976)." In *African Proconsuls: European Governors in Africa*. Edited by L. H. Gann and Peter Duigan, 185–205. New York: Free Press, 1978.
Condouriotis, Eleni. *Claiming History: Colonialism, Ethnography, and the Novel*. New York: Columbia University Press, 1999.
Conklin, Alice L. *A Mission to Civilize: The Republican Idea of Empire in France and West Africa, 1895–1930*. Stanford, Calif.: Stanford University Press, 1997.
Cooper, Frederick. *Decolonization and African Society: The Labor Question in French and British Africa*. Cambridge: Cambridge University Press, 1996.
Coquery-Vidrovitch, Catherine. *Africa: Endurance and Change South of the Sahara*. Berkeley: University of California Press, 1988.
Crowder, Michael, and Obaro Ikime, eds. *West African Chiefs: Their Changing Status under Colonial Rule and Independence*. New York: Africana Publishing Corporation, 1970.
Crummey, Donald, ed. *Banditry, Rebellion, and Social Protest in Africa*. Portsmouth, N.H.: Heinemann, 1986.
Daughton, J. P. *An Empire Divided: Religion, Republicanism, and the Making of French Colonialism, 1880–1914*. Oxford: Oxford University Press, 2006.
Davidson, Basil. *Modern Africa: A Political and Social History*. New York: Longman, 1995.
Debrix, Jean-René. "Dix ans de coopération franco-africaine ont permis la naissance du jeune cinéma d'Afrique noire." *Sentiers* 1 (1970): 15.
——. "French 'Co-operation' . . . and England?" In *African Films: The Context of Production*. Edited by Angela Martin, 43–46. London: BFI, 1982.
Delavignette, Robert. *Les paysans noirs*. Paris: Stode, 1947.
De L'Estoile, Benoît. "Au nom des 'vrais Africains': Les élites scolarisées de l'Afrique colonial face à l'anthropologie (1930–1950)." *Terrain*, 28 (March 1997): 87–102.
Deren, Maya. "Cinematography: The Creative Use of Reality." In *Film Theory and Criticism: Introductory Readings*. 5th ed. Edited by Leo Braudy and Marshall Cohen, 216–27. New York: Oxford University Press, 1999.

Diawara, Manthia. *African Cinema: Politics and Culture.* Bloomington: Indiana University Press, 1992.

———. "The Iconography of West African Cinema." In *Symbolic Narratives/African Cinema: Audiences, Theory and the Moving Image.* Edited by June Givanni, 81–89. London: BFI, 2003.

———. "Popular Culture and Oral Traditions in African Film." In *African Experiences of Cinema.* Edited by Imruh Bakari and Mbye B. Cham, 209–18. London: BFI, 1996.

Diop, Alioune. "Announcement of the Cancellation of the Second World Congress of Black Writers and Artists." *Présence africaine* 20 (June–July 1958): 144.

———. "Niam n'goura; ou, Les raisons d'être de *Présence africaine.*" *Présence africaine* 1 (November–December 1947): 7–14.

Dovey, Lindiwe. *African Film and Literature: Adapting Violence to the Screen.* New York: Columbia University Press, 2009.

Echenberg, Myron. *Colonial Conscripts: The Tirailleurs Senegalais in French West Africa, 1857–1960.* Portsmouth, N.H.: Heinemann, 1990.

Eisenstein, Sergei. "Film Form: Beyond the Shot (The Cinematographic Principle and the Ideogram)." In *Film Theory and Criticism: Introductory Readings.* 5th ed. Edited by Leo Braudy and Marshall Cohen, 15–42. New York: Oxford University Press, 1999.

Ellis, John. "Visible Fictions: Broadcast TV As Sound and Image." In *Film Theory and Criticism: Introductory Readings.* 5th ed. Edited by Leo Braudy and Marshall Cohen, 385–94. New York: Oxford University Press, 1999.

Fanon, Frantz. *Black Skin, White Masks.* New York: Grove Press, 1967.

———. *The Wretched of the Earth.* New York: Grove Press, 1963.

FEPACI. "The Algiers Charter on African Cinema." Translated by Liz Heron. In *African Experiences of Cinema.* Edited by Imruh Bakari and Mbye B. Cham, 25–26. London: BFI, 1996.

Gabriel, Teshome. Forward. In *Questioning African Cinema: Conversations with Filmmakers.* By Nwachukwu Frank Ukadike, ix–xii. Minneapolis: University of Minnesota Press, 2002.

———. *Third Cinema in the Third World: The Aesthetics of Liberation.* Ann Arbor, MI: UMI Research Press, 1982.

Gadjigo, Samba. "Ousmane Sembene and History on the Screen: A Look Back to the Future." In *Focus on African Films.* Edited by Françoise Pfaff, 33–47. Bloomington: Indiana University Press, 2004.

Gadjigo, Samba, Ralph H. Faulkingham, Thomas Cassirer, and Reinhard Sander, eds. *Ousmane Sembène: Dialogues with Critics and Writers.* Amherst: University of Massachusetts Press, 1993.

Galliéni, Joseph-Simon. *Neuf ans à Madagascar.* Paris: Hachette, 1908.

Genova, James E. "*Africanité* and *Urbanité:* The Place of the Urban in Imaginings of African Identity during the Late Colonial Period in French West Africa." In *African Urban Spaces in Historical Perspective.* Edited by Steven J. Salm and Toyin Falola, 266–85. Rochester: University of Rochester Press, 2005.

———. "Cinema and the Struggle to (De)Colonize the Mind in French/Francophone West Africa (1950s–1960s)." *Journal of the Midwest Modern Language Association,* 39.1 (Spring 2006): 50–62.

———. *Colonial Ambivalence, Cultural Authenticity, and the Limitations of Mimicry in French-Ruled West Africa, 1914–1956.* New York: Peter Lang, 2004.

———. "Conflicted Missionaries: Power and Identity in French West Africa during the 1930s." *The Historian* 66.1 (2004): 45–66.
———. "Constructing Identity in Post-War France: Citizenship, Nationality, and the Lamine Guèye Law, 1946–1953." *International History Review* 26.1 (2004): 56–79.
Georg, Odile. "The Cinema, a Place of Tension in Colonial Africa: Film Censorship in French West Africa." *Afrika Zamani* 15–16 (2007–8): 27–43.
Giannetti, Louis D. *Understanding Movies*. Englewood Cliffs, N.J.: Prentice Hall, 1972.
Girault, Arthur. *Principes de colonisation et de législation colonial*. 5th ed. Paris: Sirey, 1927.
Givanni, June, ed. *Symbolic Narratives/African Cinema: Audiences, Theory and the Moving Image*. London: BFI, 2003.
Gramsci, Antonio. *Prison Notebooks*. Vol. 2. Edited and Translated by Joseph A. Buttigieg. New York: Columbia University Press, 1996.
Gugler, Joseph. *African Film: Re-Imagining a Continent*. Bloomington: Indiana University Press, 2003.
Guneratne, Anthony R. "Introduction: Rethinking Third Cinema." In *Rethinking Third Cinema*. Edited by Anthony R. Guneratne and Wimal Dissanayake, 1–28. New York: Routledge, 2003.
Guneratne, Anthony R., and Wimal Dissanayake, eds. *Rethinking Third Cinema*. New: Routledge, 2003.
Harris, Sue, and Elizabeth Ezra, eds. *France in Focus: Film and National Identity*. Oxford: Berg, 2000.
———. "Introduction: The French Exception." In *France in Focus: Film and National Identity*. Edited by Sue Harris and Elizabeth Ezra, 1–9. Oxford, U.K.: Berg, 2000.
Harrow, Kenneth W. *Postcolonial African Cinema: From Political Engagement to Postmodernism*. Bloomington: Indiana University Press, 2007.
Hennebelle, Guy. "Afrique noire: Les plus jeunes cinemas du monde." In *Afriques 50: Singularités d'un cinéma pluriel*. Edited by Catherine Ruelle, 17–19. Paris L'Harmattan, 2005.
Hoefert de Turégano, Teresa. "The New Politics of Cinema at the French Ministry of Foreign Affairs." *French Politics, Culture and Society*. 20.3 (Fall 2002): 22–32.
Jeancolas, Jean-Pierre. "The Reconstruction of French Cinema." In *France in Focus: Film and National Identity*. Edited by Sue Harris and Elizabeth Ezra, 13–22. Oxford, U.K.: Berg, 2000.
Jennings, Eric T. *Vichy in the Tropics: Pétain's National Revolution in Madagascar, Guadeloupe, and Indochina, 1940–1944*. Stanford, Calif.: Stanford University Press, 2001.
Jewsiewicki, Bogumil. "*Présence Africaine* as Historiography: Historicity of Societies and Specificity of Black African Culture." In *The Surreptitious Speech: "Présence Africaine" and the Politics of Otherness 1947–1987*. Edited by V. Y. Mudimbe, 95–117. Chicago: University of Chicago Press, 1992.
Johnson, G. Wesley, Jr. *The Emergence of Black Politics in Senegal: The Struggle for Power in the Four Communes, 1900–1920*. Stanford, Calif.: Stanford University Press, 1971.
Jules-Rosette, Bennetta. "Conjugating Cultural Realities: *Présence Africaine*." In *The Surreptitious Speech: "Présence Africaine" and the Politics of Otherness 1947–1987*. Edited by V. Y. Mudimbe, 14–44. Chicago: University of Chicago Press, 1992.

Kaspin, Deborah D. "Conclusion: Signifying Power in Africa." In *Images and Empire: Visuality in Colonial and Postcolonial Africa*. Edited by Paul S. Landau and Deborah D. Kaspin, 320–36. Berkeley: University of California Press, 2002.

Ki-Zerbo, Joseph. "Cinema and Development in Africa." In *African Experiences of Cinema*. Edited by Imruh Bakari and Mbye B. Cham, 72–79. London: BFI, 1996.

———. "Cinéma africain et développement, l'éthique." In *Afriques 50: Singularités d'un cinéma pluriel*. Edited by Catherine Ruelle. Paris: L'Harmattan, 2005.

Kracauer, Siegfried. "Theory of Film: The Establishment of Physical Existence." In *Film Theory and Criticism: Introductory Readings*. 5th ed. Edited by Leo Braudy and Marshall Cohen, 293–303. New York: Oxford University Press, 1999.

Kuisel, Richard F. *The French Way: How France Embraced and Rejected American Values and Power*. Princeton, N.J.: Princeton University Press, 2011.

———. *Seducing the French: The Dilemma of Americanization*. Berkeley: University of California Press, 1997.

Landau, Paul S. "Introduction: An Amazing Distance: Pictures and People in Africa." In *Images and Empires: Visuality in Colonial and Postcolonial Africa*. Edited by Paul S. Landau and Deborah D. Kaspin, 1–40. Berkeley: University of California Press, 2002.

Landau, Paul S., and Deborah D. Kaspin, eds. *Images and Empires: Visuality in Colonial and Postcolonial Africa*. Berkeley: University of California Press, 2002.

Lebovics, Herman. *Mona Lisa's Escort: André Malraux and the Reinvention of French Culture*. Ithaca, N.Y.: Cornell University Press, 1999.

———. *True France: The Wars over Cultural Identity, 1900–1945*. Ithaca, N.Y.: Cornell University Press, 1992.

Lequeret, Elisabeth. *Le cinéma africain: Un continent à la recherché de son proper regard*. Paris: Cahiers du cinéma, 2003.

MacBean, James Roy. "La hora de los hornos." *Film Quarterly* 24.1 (1970): 31–37.

Martin, Angela, ed. *African Films: The Context of Production*. London: BFI, 1982.

Martin, Michael T., ed. *Cinemas of the Black Diaspora: Diversity, Dependence and Oppositionality*. Detroit, Mich.: Wayne State University, 1995.

———, ed. *New Latin American Cinema: Theory, Practices, and Transcontinental Articulations*. Detroit, Mich.: Wayne State University Press, 1997.

Memmi, Albert. *The Colonizer and the Colonized*. Boston: Beacon Press, 1991.

Metz, Christian. "Film Language: Some Problems of Denotation in the Fiction Film." In *Film Theory and Criticism: Introductory Readings*. 5th ed. Edited by Leo Braudy and Marshall Cohen, 68–89. New York: Oxford University Press, 1999.

———. "Problems of Denotation in the Fiction Film." In *Narrative, Apparatus, Ideology: A Film Theory Reader*. Edited by Philip Rosen, 35–65. New York: Columbia University Press, 1986.

Michel, Marc. *L'appel à l'Afrique: Contributions et réactions à l'effort de guerre en A.O.F., 1914–1919*. Paris: Publications de la Sorbonne, 1982.

Minh-ha, Trinh T. *Cinema Interval*. New York: Routledge, 1999.

Moore, Rachel O. *Savage Theory: Cinema as Modern Magic*. Durham, N.C.: Duke University Press, 2000.

Mortimer, Mildred. *Journeys through the French African Novel*. Portsmouth, N.H.: Heinemann, 1990.

Mudimbe, V. Y. Finale. In *The Surreptitious Speech: "Présence Africaine" and the Politics of Otherness 1947–1987.* Edited by V. Y. Mudimbe, 435–45. Chicago: University of Chicago Press, 1992.

———, ed. *The Surreptitious Speech: "Présence Africaine" and the Politics of Otherness 1947–1987.* Chicago: University of Chicago Press, 1992.

Murphy, David, and Patrick Williams. *Postcolonial African Cinema: Ten Directors.* Manchester, U.K.: Manchester University Press, 2007.

Ngangura, Mweze. "African Cinema—Militancy or Entertainment?" In *African Experiences of Cinema.* Edited by Imruh Bakari and Mbye B. Cham, 60–64. London: BFI, 1996.

Nugent, Paul. *Africa since Independence: A Comparative History.* New York: Palgrave Macmillan, 2004.

O'Brien, Donal B. Cruise. *The Mourides of Senegal: The Political and Economic Organization of an Islamic Brotherhood.* Oxford, U.K.: Clarendon Press, 1971.

"Pan-African Cultural Manifesto." *Présence africaine* 71.3 (1969): 115–32.

Pfaff, Françoise. "African Cities as Cinematic Texts." In *Focus on African Films.* Edited by Françoise Pfaff, 89–106. Bloomington: Indiana University Press, 2004.

———. "Africa from Within: The Films of Gaston Kaboré and Idrissa Ouédraogo as Anthropological Sources." In *African Experiences of Cinema.* Edited by Imruh Bakari and Mbye B. Cham, 223–38. London: BFI, 1996.

———. "The Films of Med Hondo: An African Filmmaker in Paris." *Jump Cut.* 31 (March 1986): 44–46.

———. "From Africa to the Americas: Interviews with Haile Gerima (1976–2001)." In *Focus on African Films.* Edited by Françoise Pfaff, 203–20. Bloomington: Indiana University Press, 2004.

———, ed. *Focus on African Films.* Bloomington: Indiana University Press, 2004.

———. Introduction to *Focus on African Films.* Edited by Françoise Pfaff, 1–11. Bloomington: Indiana University Press, 2004.

———. "Hollywood's Image of Africa." *Commonwealth.* 5 (1981–82): 97–116.

———. "The Uniqueness of Ousmane Sembène's Cinema." In *Ousmane Sembène: Dialogues with Critics and Writers.* Edited by Samba Gadjigo, Ralph H. Faulkingham, Thomas Cassirer, and Reinhard Sander, 14–21. Amherst: University of Massachusetts Press, 1993.

Pines, Jim, and Paul Willemen, eds. *Questions of Third Cinema.* London: BFI Publishing, 1989.

"Resolutions of the Third World Film-makers Meeting, Algiers, December 5–14, 1973." *Cinemas of the Black Diaspora: Diversity, Dependence and Oppositionality.* Edited by Michael T. Martin, 463–72. Detroit, Mich.: Wayne State University, 1995.

"Résolution de la sous-commission de philosophie." *Présence africaine* 24–25 (1959): 403–18.

"Resolution séance de cloture." *Présence africaine,* 8–10 (1956): 361–65.

Roof, Maria. "African and Latin American Cinemas: Contexts and Contacts." In *Focus on African Films.* Edited by Françoise Pfaff, 241–73. Bloomington: Indiana University Press, 2004.

Rosen, Philip, ed. *Narrative, Apparatus, Ideology: A Film Theory Reader.* New York: Columbia University Press, 1986.

Rouch, Jean. "Vers une literature africaine." *Présence africaine* 6.2 (1949): 144–46.
Ruelle, Catherine, ed. *Afriques 50: Singularités d'un cinéma pluriel*. Paris: L'Harmattan, 2005.
Said, Edward W. *Culture and Imperialism*. New York: Vintage, 1994.
Sama, Emmanuel. "African Films are Foreigners in their Own Countries." In *African Experiences of Cinema*. Edited by Imruh Bakari and Mbye B. Cham, 148–56. London: BFI, 1996.
Schmidt, Elizabeth. *Cold War and Decolonization in Guinea, 1946–1958*. Athens: Ohio University Press, 2007.
Schwartz, Vanessa R. *It's So French! Hollywood, Paris, and the Making of Cosmopolitan Film Culture*. Chicago: University of Chicago Press, 2007.
Sembène, Ousmane. "Cinema as Evening School." In *L'Afrique et le centenaire du cinema*. Paris: Présence africaine, 1995.
———. *God's Bits of Wood*. Portsmouth, N.H.: Heinemann, 1995.
———. "Interview with Sembène Ousmane." In *La collection Sembène Ousmane*. DVD. Paris: Médiathèque des trois mondes, 2004.
———. "Moment d'une vie: Paulin Soumanou Vieyra." *Présence africaine* 170.2 (2004): 21–22.
Senghor, Léopold Sédar. "Le français, langue de culture." *Esprit* 11 (November 1962): 837–44.
Shaka, Femi Okiremuete. *Modernity and the African Cinema: A Study in Colonialist Discourse, Postcoloniality, and Modern African Identities*. Trenton, N.J.: Africa World Press, 2004.
Sharff, Stefan. *The Elements of Cinema: Toward a Theory of Cinesthetic Impact*. New York: Columbia University Press, 1982.
Sherzer, Dina, ed. *Cinema, Colonialism, and Postcolonialism: Perspectives from the French and Francophone Worlds*. Austin: University of Texas Press, 1996.
———. Introduction. In *Cinema, Colonialism, and Postcolonialism: Perspectives from the French and Francophone Worlds*. Edited by Dina Sherzer, 1–19. Austin: University of Texas Press, 1996.
Sibeud, Emmanuelle. "Ethnographie africaniste et 'inauthenticité' colonial." *French Politics, Culture, and Society*. 20.2 (2002): 11–28.
Slavin, Henry David. *Colonial Cinema and Imperial France, 1919–1939: White Blind Spots, Male Fantasies, Settler Myths*. Baltimore, Md.: Johns Hopkins University Press, 2001.
Solanas, Fernando, and Octavio Getino. "Towards a Third Cinema: Notes and Experiences for the Development of a Cinema for the Liberation of the Third World." Translated by Julianne Burton. In *New Latin American Cinema: Theory Practices, and Transcontinental Articulations*. Edited by Michael T. Martin, 33–58. Detroit, Mich.: Wayne State University, 1997.
Stam, Robert. "Beyond Third Cinema: The Aesthetics of Hybridity." In *Rethinking Third Cinema*. Edited by Anthony R. Guneratne and Wimal Dissanayake, 31–48. New York: Routledge, 2003.
Stam, Robert, and Louise Spence. "Colonialism, Racism, and Representation: An Introduction." In *Film Theory and Criticism: Introductory Readings*. 5th ed. Edited by Leo Braudy and Marshall Cohen, 235–50. New York: Oxford University Press, 1999.
Stoler, Ann Laura. *Race and the Education of Desire: Foucault's "History of Sexuality" and the Colonial Order of Things*. Durham, N.C.: Duke University Press, 1995.

Stoller, Paul. "Regarding Rouch: The Recasting of West African Colonial Culture." In *Cinema, Colonialism, and Postcolonialism: Perspectives from the French and Francophone Worlds*. Edited by Dina Sherzer, 65–79. Austin: University of Texas Press, 1996.
Suret-Canale, Jean. *L'afrique noire: L'ère colonial 1900–1945*. Paris: Editions sociales, 1962.
Tapsoba, Clément. "Le grandes dates du cinéma africain." In *Afriques 50: Singularités d'un cinéma pluriel*. Edited by Catherine Ruelle, 299. Paris L'Harmattan, 2005.
Taylor, Clyde. "Searching for the Postmodern in African Cinema." In *Symbolic Narratives/African Cinema: Audiences, Theory and the Moving Image*. Edited by June Givanni, 136–44. London: BFI Publishing, 2003.
Thackway, Melissa. *Africa Shoots Back: Alternative Perspectives in Sub-Saharan Francophone African Film*. Bloomington: Indiana University Press, 2003.
Thiong'o, Ngũgĩ wa. *Decolonising the Mind: The Politics of Language in African Literature*. Portsmouth, N.H.: Heinemann, 1997.
Thompson, Kristin. "The Concept of Cinematic Excess." In *Narrative, Apparatus, Ideology: A Film Theory Reader*. Edited by Philip Rosen, 130–42. New York: Columbia University Press, 1986.
Tomlinson, John. *Cultural Imperialism: A Critical Introduction*. New York: Continuum, 1991.
Ukadike, Nwachukwu Frank. *Black African Cinema*. Berkeley: University of California Press, 1994.
———. "Other Voices of Documentary: *Allah Tantou* and *Afrique, je te plumerai*." In *Focus on African Films*. Edited by Françoise Pfaff, 159–72. Bloomington: Indiana University Press, 2004.
———. *Questioning African Cinema: Conversations with Filmmakers*. Minneapolis: University of Minnesota Press, 2002.
Vieyra, Paulin Soumanou. "African Cinema: Solidarity and Difference." In *Questions of Third Cinema*. Edited by Jim Pines and Paul Willemen, 195–98. London: BFI Publishing, 1989.
———. "Centres culturels, et politique de la culture en Afrique." *Présence africaine*. 74.2 (1970): 185–90.
———. *Le cinéma africain des origines à 1973*. Vol. 1 Paris: Présence africaine, 1975.
———. "Le cinéma au 1er festival culturel panafricain d'Alger." *Présence africaine* 72.4 (1969): 190–201.
———. "Le cinéma et la révolution Africaine." *Présence africaine*, 170.2 (2004): 73–81.
———. *Ousmane Sembène: Cinéaste; première période, 1962–1971*. Paris: Présence africaine, 1972.
———. "Propos sur le cinéma africain." *Présence africaine* 22 (1958): 106–17.
———. "Responsabilités du cinéma dans la formation d'une conscience nationale africaine."*Présence africaine* 170.2 (2004): 63–72.
Wallerstein, Immanuel. *World-Systems Analysis: An Introduction*. Durham, NC: Duke University Press, 2004.
Wesseling, H. L. *Certain Ideas of France: Essays on French History and Civilization*. Westport, Conn.: Greenwood Press, 2002.
White, Owen. *Children of the French Empire: Miscegenation and Colonial Society in French West Africa, 1895–1960*. Oxford, U.K.: Clarendon Press, 1999.

Wilder, Gary. *The French Imperial Nation-State: Negritude and Colonial Humanism between the Two World Wars.* Chicago: University of Chicago Press, 2005.

Withall, Keith, and Steve Mardy. "Africa: Africa Distribution and Exhibition." *Third World/Third Cinema.* http://cinetext.org.uk/twtc/africa/#africa_dist.

Woll, Josephine. "The Russian Connection: Soviet Cinema and the Cinema of Francophone Africa." In *Focus on African Films.* Edited by Françoise Pfaff, 223–41. Bloomington: Indiana University Press, 2004.

Wollen, Peter. "Godard and Counter-Cinema: *Vent d'Est.*" In *Narrative, Apparatus, Ideology: A Film Theory Reader.* Edited by Philip Rosen, 120–29. New York: Columbia University Press, 1986.

Index

Abbas, Ferhat, 106
Academie des sciences d'outre-mer, 24
ACCT. *See* Agence de coopération culturelle et technique (ACCT)
activists, 11–12; cultural, 9, 16, 18, 21–22, 70–71, 78, 81, 94, 97, 141, 164; political, 142
actors: of color, 29, 53; real people as, 82, 83, 104, 115–16, 118–19, 121, 140–41
Adorno, Theodor, 11, 45, 71–72, 113
aesthetic, film: anticolonial, 102–10; colonial, 71; emerging, 3, 6, 8–9, 11, 12–13, 96, 116; materialist, 10, 72, 148–49; postcolonial, 97–127; realist, 111–13; revolutionary, 119–23, 144; technology and, 67; West African filmmakers' development of, 86, 142, 148–49, 160, 163–64. *See also* cinema; cinema, West African; filmmakers; filmmakers, early West African; films; films, West African
AFRAM. *See* Afro-American Films Inc. (AFRAM)
Africa and Africans, 2–4, 5, 56, 132, 168n46; cinema industrial complex's service to, 19, 70, 96, 147–57, 159, 161, 164; negro-African civilization, 87, 175n48; rural, 78, 82; sub-Saharan, 2, 7. *See also* audiences, African; autochthonous populations; culture, African; Madagascar; Tunisia; West Africa; Zimbabwe
Africa and Africans, representations of, 99, 103–104, 106–107, 111–13, 115–16, 118–19; colonialist, 3, 11, 97; daily life, 97, 124, 164; filmic, 19, 41, 45–46, 56, 63, 160; hegemonic, 50–51, 127; literary, 75; racist, 45–48, 86, 98; Western, 15, 17. *See also* actors: real people as; image-Africa; regime of representation, West African; representation, in film
Afrique-sur-Seine (film, Vieyra and Sarr), 1, 82, 157, 174n33; as docu-fiction, 83, 96, 106–107, 116; GAC as producer of, 110, 162, 174n33; as guerrilla cinema, 144, 145; political themes, 84, 120
Afro-American Films Inc. (AFRAM), 153
Agence de coopération culturelle et technique (ACCT), 7, 19, 150–52, 157, 159, 161, 180n65
Alassane, Mustapha, 111
Algeria: film festivals in, 147; resistance movement in, 34, 35, 87–88, 133
"Algiers Charter on African Cinema, 1975, The," 2–3, 155–57, 166n22
Althusser, Louis, 15
American Motion Picture Export Company-Africa (AMPECA), 152–53
anticolonialism, 31, 73, 93; cinema industrial complex and, 74–89, 107–108. *See also* film politics, West African: anticolonial
Armes, Roy, 3
art, cinema as, 4, 7–10, 12, 19, 71–72, 88, 127
Ashcroft, Bill, 78–79
Aube de l'Islam (film, *Egypt*), 35
audiences: cultural perceptions brought by, 45–46, 127; effects of film on, 11, 18; engagement with creative work, 76, 135, 143–44, 163; filmmakers' interaction with, 28, 49, 55–62, 72; French, 50, 108; post-film discussions, 155, 180n78; process of watching films, 25, 28–29, 32; raising consciousness of, 144–45; Soviet, 90, 113
audiences, African, 42, 52, 94; French filmmaking targeted at, 32–33; images of Africa seen by, 22, 56, 57–59, 114, 119, 129; increasing numbers, 24, 26–27,

193

31, 81, 84; postcolonial identities of, 86, 98; reception of colonial films, 48–49; restrictions on, 25–26, 27, 30, 37–38, 161. *See also* autochthonous populations; youth
audiences, images of Africa seen by extra-African: documentaries on, 56; French sensitivities to, 17, 27, 33, 78, 129; racist, 45–48, 59
auteurs, 11, 12, 139, 143. *See also* filmmakers, early West African
autochthonous populations: adapting films to, 22, 35, 63; images of Africa shown to, 46–47, 81, 97, 99, 123; imperial degradation of, 88, 121; participation in film productions, 67, 69, 75; traditions of, 93, 94; writers among, 79. *See also* Africa and Africans; audiences, African

Bakari, Imruh, 21, 111
Bakhtin, Mikhail M., 68, 78, 79, 89
Barry, Aminata, 17
Barthes, Roland, 13
Bassori, Timité, and establishment of FEPACI, 146–47
Baudry, Jean-Louis, 10–11, 12
Bazin, André, 51, 55, 78, 99
Belton, John, 62, 67
Benin: film industry in, 111, 154
Benjamin, Walter, 16, 71
Bernstein, J. M., 71
Beti, Mongo (Eza Boto), novels by, 79, 80, 84
Bhabha, Homi, 126
Blé en herbe, Le (film), banning of, 40
Bons pères (Catholic organization), 40
Boto, Eza (Mongo Beti). *See* Beti, Mongo (Eza Boto), novels by
Boulanger, Pierre, 46, 48, 49
Bourdieu, Pierre, 6
Bourgi, Abdou Karim, 30
Bouruet-Aubertot, M., 66, 67
Brecht, Berthold, 16
Britain. *See* Great Britain, film industry
Browne, Nick, study of *Stagecoach*, 25, 28–29, 32

Bureau du cinéma: control over West African cinema, 130, 132, 140, 161; funding from, 136–38, 139; reestablishment of, 131, 134. *See also* Ministère de la coopération et l'assistance technique
Burke, Timothy, 46, 58
Burkina Faso. *See* Upper Volta
CAI, 132, 135
Cameron, Kenneth M., 14, 21, 47–48, 49
capitalism, 11, 71, 180n59; domination of Africa by, 2, 15; global, 91, 142, 143, 145, 159, 162–63, 163–64; imperialist, 23, 114, 115
Carristan, Robert, 82
Catholics, activism in cinema field, 40, 170n81
censorship: cinema industrial complex, 27, 68, 80; colonial, 49, 173n68; of dialogue, 63, 66–68; postcolonial, 100–101, 135, 138; Vichy government's, 53–55. *See also* films, West African: banned; Laval decree of 1934
Centre national du cinéma et de l'image animée (CNC), 117, 131, 138–39, 140, 147, 151. *See also* Ministère des affaires culturelles
CFCC, 39–41, 55, 65–66, 67, 109–10
Cham, Mbye B., 16, 19, 21, 73, 91
Chappedelaine, Louis de, 27–28, 29
"Charte de la Francophonie" (ACCT), 150. *See also* Agence de coopération culturelle et technique (ACCT)
China, financial aid from, 1, 2
cineastes. *See* filmmakers, early West African
ciné-clubs, 95
cinema: guerilla, 94, 143, 144; revolutionary role of, 15, 89–96; role in France's postwar reconstruction, 4, 31; Western, 97, 98, 99. *See also* films; postcolonialism: cinema's role in; Third Cinema movement
cinema, West African, 40, 154; anticolonial, 18, 91, 116; colonial, 14–15, 26, 45–55, 59, 61, 64, 66–69, 86, 102, 158;

Index | 195

commercial, 33, 156; dialogic, 62–63, 66–68; firsts in, 7, 82, 98, 103, 114, 120, 158; foundations of, 21, 71, 74; French management of, 24–31; independent, 2–4, 7, 10, 73, 82, 84–87, 99; literature turned into, 82–83, 116–17; postcolonial, 2–4, 20–21, 49, 50–51, 132; as propaganda instrument, 28, 33–34; realism in, 113–14; in service to the people, 19, 70, 96, 147–57, 159, 161, 164. *See also* aesthetic, film; films, West African; languages, cinematographic

cinema industrial complex, French, 4, 31, 37, 81, 167n11

cinema industrial complex, West African, 7–10, 92, 158; anticolonialism and, 74–89; censorship of films by, 39–41; colonial, 48, 60, 70, 71, 103, 162; contemporary, 162–63; development of, 20, 24, 41–44, 46, 55–62, 98; economic development and, 3, 17, 70, 163; French control of, 3, 46, 55, 66–67, 69, 99–100, 150, 152–53, 157; funding for, 19, 85, 95; independent, 85, 127; postwar, 38–44; pre-1945, 24–31; promotion of, 41–42; regime of representation and, 45, 62–69; regulation of, 32, 33, 80, 81, 90; as site of decolonization, 20–44; Upper Volta's nationalization of, 10, 152, 153–54, 155, 158, 159. *See also* distribution, control of; funding; production

cinema novo, 11, 15, 91

cinema on wheels, 24, 41, 90, 95, 112, 141. *See also* home movie showings

Cinémathèque de l'agence des colonies, 41

cinematography, 51, 105, 112. *See also* languages, cinematographic

Cissé, Souleymane, 19, 94, 111; constraints on, 138, 162; and establishment of FEPACI, 146–47; on making films in Africa, 141, 158; on revolutionary filmmaking, 90, 142, 149; Soviet film training, 15, 111, 129, 136, 175n56, 179n19

Cissé, Souleymane, works by, 93, 98, 148; *Cinq jours d'une vie*, 144, 145; *Den muso*, 144, 145, 161

civilizing mission, French, 5, 36, 45, 68, 69, 108, 121; African modernity and, 60, 83; cinema's role in, 64–65, 130–31; goals of, 27, 51. *See also* cooperation, Franco-African

class, cinema and, 48, 92, 117, 126, 149

Cloquet, Ghislain. *See Statues meurent aussi, Les* (film, Cloquet/Marker/Resnais)

CNC. *See* Centre national du cinéma et de l'image animée (CNC)

codes, cinematic, 13, 14, 15, 16, 18, 63

Cohen, William B., 61

Cold War, 36, 54

colonialism, French, 34, 73, 162; cinema as organ of, 24–31, 33, 43, 47, 50, 56–57, 86, 88, 95, 143–44; cinema industrial complex's relationship to, 48, 103, 131; late period, 102–10; legacies of, 5, 127, 148, 157; legitimating, 14–15, 36; as modernizing force, 59, 60; postwar reestablishment of, 31–38, 58; representations of, 45–48, 77; resistance to, 9–10, 15, 74–78, 83, 105. *See also* anticolonialism; postcolonialism

colonies. *See* West Africa

COMACICO. *See* Compagnie africaine cinématographique industrielle et commercial (COMACICO)

Commission du cinéma à l'assemblée de l'union française, 41

Commission du cinéma d'outre-mer, 32–33, 34, 41, 55, 60, 84

Commission fédérale de contrôle des films cinématographiques (CFCC), 39–41, 55, 65–66, 67, 109–10

Communauté Francophone, 85

Compagnie africaine cinématographique industrielle et commercial (COMACICO), 22–23; breaking monopoly of, 95, 152–54, 155, 159; censorship and, 53, 54; expanding market share of, 30, 31; and movie

theater quota system, 37–38, 43, 134, 141, 146, 169n71
consciousness, emerging nationalist, 31, 110, 115–16, 118, 122–24, 126, 144–45
Conseil économique de l'Afrique occidentale française, 33–34
Consortium audio-visuel international (CAI), 132, 135
cooperation, Franco-African, 58, 61, 63, 109, 127, 128–41. *See also* civilizing mission, French
Coppet, Marcel de, 52
Cornut-Gentille, Bernard, 35
Côte d'Ivoire: film industry, 111, 154
Cuba, support for Third World cinema, 146, 147, 151
cultural development, cinema's role in West African, 9, 43, 70, 87, 98, 121, 163; postcolonial, 2–4, 85, 87, 130, 140–41, 145–48, 152, 160, 162. *See also* cinema, West African: in service to the people; economic development, West African; social development, West African
culture: industry of, 8–9, 11, 71; role in decolonization process, 72, 92
culture, African: artifacts of, 108–10, 115; cinema's role in, 2–4, 6–7, 28–29, 32, 71, 148; French synthesized with, 62, 66, 68, 95, 128–29, 131, 150–51; imperialist attempts to erase, 120–21; modern, 4–5, 60, 86; racist stereotypes of, 45, 46; revivification of, 12, 72; traditional, 20, 60, 61. *See also* Africa and Africans; Africa and Africans, representations of

Dakar, Senegal: descriptions of, 1–2, 123, 164; movie theaters in, 25–26, 30, 31, 162–63. *See also* Senegal
Dakar-Niger rail strike of 1947–48, 1, 78
De Gaulle, Charles, 52, 53–54, 87–88, 105, 133
De Guise, Robert, 26, 27
De Nesle, Robert, 139
Debrix, Jean-René, 134, 138, 178n13

decolonization, 14, 35; African identities and, 97, 138; cinema industrial complex as site of, 20–44; cinema's role in, 4, 18, 81, 85, 99, 106, 149–50, 154; culture's role in, 72, 92; elements of, 6, 128; film politics and, 23, 82, 95–96, 152; struggle for, 5, 78, 110, 160. *See also* colonialism, French; postcolonialism; West Africa: independence for
decrees, French government, 4; of 1949, 41; of 1954, 31–32, 37–38, 39, 80. *See also* Laval decree of 1934
Delavignette, Robert: on African cultural recovery, 75, 87; cinematic goals of, 49, 143–44; on economic development, 128, 129; film politics of, 68, 70, 80, 81; on Franco-African cooperation, 128, 136–37, 151; on meaning of film, 45, 54, 72, 76, 172n45; as prototype filmmaker, 82, 83. See also *Paysans noirs, Les* (film and novel, Delavignette)
Der Rebell (film, Germany), 53–54
Deren, Maya, 56–57
development, 32, 34; postcolonial, 87–88, 134; role of cinema industrial complex in, 81, 94–95. *See also* cultural development, cinema's role in West African; economic development, West African; social development, West African
Dia, Mamadou, 62
Diagne, Costa, 111
dialectics, 15, 82, 89; of African modernity, 62, 82; of cinema, 50, 93–94, 156; colonizers *vs.* colonized, 110, 141
dialogue: African-language, 118–19, 126, 139–40; cultural, 150; filmic, 4, 61–63, 66–69, 84, 91, 157; in novels, 61, 79; of tradition *vs.* modernity, 78. *See also* languages, cinematographic
Diawara, Manthia, 21–22, 176n22; on French film politics, 34, 72, 99–100, 132, 149; on Sembène, 177n39, 180n47; on Vieyra, 82, 85

Diop, Alioune, 74, 75, 76, 82, 87, 105
Diop, Birago, novels by, 79
discourse: cinematic, 13, 28–29, 96, 98, 101, 113, 158; novelistic, 78
distribution, control of, 42; by filmmakers, 11, 90; French, 9, 19, 27, 37, 55, 65, 129, 132, 136–37, 148; independent, 24, 86, 130, 159; local, 10, 19, 42, 95; Soviet, 112; Upper Volta's nationalization of, 10, 152, 153–54, 155, 158, 159; Western, 142–43, 149. See also Compagnie africaine cinématographique industrielle et commercial (COMACICO); Société d'éxploitation cinématographique africaine (SECMA)
docu-fiction films, 122–23, 135; France's promotion of, 22, 82, 83–84; West African, 93–94, 96, 113–14, 126, 144, 164. See also *Mandabi* (*Money Order*, film, Sembène, 1968); *Paysans noirs, Les* (film and novel, Delavignette)
documentaries, 42, 43, 56, 135; anticolonial, 18, 105; British, 22, 27; colonial, 37, 63–64, 103–104; revolutionary uses of, 24, 91, 93, 143–44
Donskoy, Mark, 89
Dovey, Lindiwe, 110
dubbing, 63, 67–68, 118

Ecaré, Désiré, 111
economic development, French, 128–33; cinema's role in, 21, 23, 37, 38–39, 43–44, 162
economic development, West African, 12, 34, 62, 121, 151; cinema's role in, 10, 70, 97–98, 129, 135, 141, 146, 156–57, 162–63; culture's role in, 8–9, 75; postcolonial, 2–4, 17, 84–87, 97, 132, 145, 147–48, 152, 160. See also cultural development, cinema's role in West African; social development, West African
editing, 13, 93, 114, 122, 126, 140. See also framing, cinematic; montage technique

education: French, 60, 61–62, 103, 172n58; using images for, 10, 20, 29, 43, 81, 84, 90
educational films, 22, 32–33, 52, 63–64, 84, 95
Egypt, 34–35, 39, 173n73
Eisenstein, Sergei, 62–63, 89–90, 112, 114
elite, African, 20, 21, 117; French-educated, 60, 61–62, 172n58. See also intellectuals: West African
England. See Great Britain, film industry
entertainment films, 25–26, 29–30, 51, 52–53, 95, 158. See also feature films; fiction films
equipment: access to, 9, 42, 110, 157, 159; French ownership of, 129, 136–37
Europe, 48, 124, 128–29. See also France; Great Britain, film industry
Ezra, Elizabeth, 20, 52

FAC, 133–34, 139
Fanon, Frantz, 6, 15, 93, 114
feature films, 64, 98, 111, 114–17, 158. See also entertainment films
Fédération panafricaine des cinéastes (FEPACI): establishment of, 7, 10, 19, 146–49, 150, 154–55; second congress of, 2–3, 10, 156–57, 158, 166n22
FERDES. See Fonds d'équipement rural et de développement économique et social (FERDES)
Festival panafricain du cinéma et de la télévision de Ouagadougou (FESPACO), 7, 10, 154–55, 157, 161, 163
fiction films, 63, 135. See also docu-fiction films; entertainment films
FIDES. See Fonds pour l'investissement en développement économique et social (FIDES)
film festivals, 19, 98, 137, 161, 163–64; Pan-African, 7, 129, 147, 151; Semaine du cinéma africain, 149–50, 152, 153–54
film industry, West African: nationalizing, 10, 152, 153–54, 155, 158, 159; regulation of, 129, 168n27, 169n52, 172n33. See also cinema industrial complex, West

African; distribution, control of; funding; production
film politics, French imperial, 6, 77, 84–86, 131, 134, 137; development of, 6, 26, 55–56; government decrees, 4, 17, 28
film politics, West African, 46, 47; anticolonial, 18, 70–96, 98, 102, 106, 111, 127, 141, 148, 149, 155; colonial, 20–44, 55, 63, 72–73, 97, 101, 103, 114, 156, 160; counterhegemonic, 18, 70–71, 119; early African filmmakers', 3, 7–10, 81–89, 91, 95–96, 99, 114, 141–42, 167n26; materialist dimension of, 23, 94–95; postcolonial, 89–96; postwar, 31–38, 41, 43–44, 45–46, 55–56, 62, 83; pre-1945, 24–31; representational dimension of, 45, 51, 58–59, 92–94; revolutionary, 141–49. *See also* Laval decree of 1934
filmmakers: audiences' interaction with, 28, 49, 55–62, 72; European, 24; French, 50–51; Latin American, 142, 149; Third World, 148–49, 151, 179n45
filmmakers, early West African, 6–19; aesthetics developed by, 149, 160, 163–64; anticolonial filmmaking by, 102–10; docu-fiction made by, 93–94, 108; documentary, 56; on film language, 84, 94, 98–99; film politics of, 3, 7–10, 81–89, 91, 95–96, 99, 114, 141, 167n26; firsts among, 7, 82, 98, 103, 114, 120, 158; images generated by, 15, 71, 100, 144; independent, 72, 129–30; intentions of, 55–62; legacies of, 158, 163–64, 166n42; obstacles encountered by, 2–4, 7, 9, 83, 129, 162; organization of, 19, 98, 141–49; origins of, 23, 73, 110, 132; partnering with French producers, 136–39; postcolonial, 17, 95, 100–101, 159; regime of representation influenced by, 73–74, 161; revolutionary work by, 91–94, 97, 145; Soviet training of, 15, 90, 111, 122, 129, 136, 175n56; as storytellers, 11, 63–64, 80, 101–102, 116–17; Third Cinema's influences on, 11–12, 15, 74, 156, 157. *See also* film politics, West African; *and individual filmmakers*

films: French, 32, 135–36, 161; imported, 32, 161, 170n75; Kracauer's theory of, 57; reading, 25, 28–29, 32, 54, 90; Soviet, 36–37, 114, 169n64; witness-bearing, 55–56, 91, 93, 118, 124. *See also* aesthetic, film
films, West African, 3, 14–15, 28, 50, 64, 94, 111, 140; banned, 34–41, 52–55, 102–10, 145, 149, 161, 170n83, 176n20; as commodities, 16–17, 33; literature transformed into, 74–81, 84, 86, 116, 117, 138–39; popularity of, 24, 135, 138; size and length requirements, 43, 84, 95. *See also* cinema, West African; cinema industrial complex, West African; *and individual titles and types of films*
Films Pierre Cellier Dakar (production company), 66
Films Robert Bastardie (production company), 171n25
First Cinema, 119, 143. *See also* Hollywood film industry
FLN. *See* Front de libération nationale (FLN)
Fodeba, Këita, 108, 176n20
Fonds d'aide et de coopération (FAC), 133–34, 139
Fonds d'équipement rural et de développement économique et social (FERDES), 34, 133
Fonds pour l'investissement en développement économique et social (FIDES), 34, 41–42, 133–34
framing, cinematic, 89–90, 121
France: African migrants adjusting to life in, 82, 106, 121, 124; cinematic strategies in, 12, 119; collapse of Fourth Republic, 87–88; colonial resistance to, 5–6, 69; funding of African filmmaking, 19, 99–100; liberation from Nazis, 30, 31, 107; postcolonial domination of Africa, 8, 124, 128–29, 162; postwar reconstruction, 4, 21–22, 31,

37, 38, 43, 45, 167n11. *See also* cinema industrial complex, French; civilizing mission, French; colonialism, French; cooperation, Franco-African; nation-state, French imperial; West Africa: relationship with France
"Francophonie, la": origin of term, 151, 180n65; Organisation international de la Francophonie, 7
Frankfurt school, 3, 71
Front de libération nationale (FLN), 106
funding: access to, 9, 100, 138, 157, 159, 161–62; mixed, 41–42, 60; sources of, 19, 131, 132, 133–34, 136

Gabriel, Teshome, 92, 93, 116, 117
GAC. *See* Groupe africain du cinéma (GAC)
Gadjigo, Samba, 110
Galliéni, Joseph-Simon, 5
Ganda, Oumarou, 111; *Le wazzou polygame*, 154
gangster films, 35–36, 52, 169n61
Georg, Odile, 169n64
Gerima, Haile, 8, 93, 140–41
Getino, Octavio, 119, 146; revolutionary vision of filmmaking, 12, 91–94, 142–44, 156; on Third Cinema, 118, 147
GIK. *See* Gosudarstvenyi institut kinematografii (GIK)
Givanni, June, 21
Goddard, Jean-Luc, 139
Gomes, Flora, 148
Gorki Studios, 89, 110, 136
Gosudarstvenyi institut kinematografii (GIK), 110–11, 136
Gramsci, Antonio, 6
Great Britain, film industry, 22, 27, 33
Griffiths, Gareth, 78–79
griots, 6, 16, 76, 116. *See also* storytellers and storytelling
Groupe africain du cinéma (GAC), 84, 132, 147, 154; founding members of, 81, 82, 83; production of *Afrique-sur-Seine*, 110, 162, 174n33
Gubara, Gadalla, 8

Gugler, Joseph, 21, 102, 107–108, 111
Guinea: film industry in, 154, 174n33; independence for, 88, 105
Guneratne, Anthony R., 92

Harris, Sue, 20, 52
Harrow, Kenneth W.: on early filmmakers, 73, 100, 126, 131, 160, 166n42; on Sembène, 102, 111, 113–14
Haute comité Méditerranéan artinisat-cinéma, 29
Havana Cultural Congress (1968), 147
hegemony: countering, 118, 122; cultural, 14, 48; in film language, 98. *See also* imperialism; oppression; power relations
Hoefert de Turégano, Teresa, 137, 150
Hollywood film industry, 12, 35, 98, 119, 143, 152–53
home movie showings, 26, 42, 163. *See also* cinema on wheels
Hondo, Med, 119–23, 148, 157; censorship of, 12, 100–101; constructing African identity, 14, 19, 50, 160; docu-fiction films, 93, 144; and establishment of FEPACI, 146–47; filmmaking techniques, 98, 99, 107, 123; on role of cinema, 3, 94, 146, 158; securing funding, 159, 162; struggle for independence in filmmaking, 12, 73–74, 90, 129–32, 138, 149, 154; themes of, 126, 127. See also *Soleil Ô* (film, Hondo, 1967)
Houphouët-Boigny, Félix, 102, 104, 146
humanism, colonial, 52, 60

identities, African: cinema's role in modern, 50, 98, 137–38; construction of, 9–10, 14; France's efforts to control, 52, 79, 138; representations of, 59–60, 111; revivification of, 12, 71, 72, 75. *See also* Africa and Africans, representations of; image-Africa; modernity, African
IDHEC. *See* Institut des hautes études cinématographiques (IDHEC)

image-Africa: audiences' consumption of, 19, 22, 56, 57–59, 71, 78, 114, 119, 129; cinematic, 10, 45–46, 75, 97, 100, 110, 116–17; colonialist, 17, 86, 123, 127, 129, 155–56, 167n26; counterhegemonic, 11, 15, 73, 79, 111, 129, 158, 160; flattening of, 47–48, 48–49; French control of, 32, 33, 38–39, 41, 44, 134, 136, 138; hegemonic, 14, 47–48, 96, 114, 144; prose, 77, 80; racist, 69, 86; reconstructing, 59, 82–84, 94, 119, 122, 142, 144–45, 163. *See also* Africa and Africans, representations of; identities, African

images, cinematic: filmmakers' use of, 55–63, 69; French, 44, 45–46; language of, 13, 68; national, 20–21, 52. *See also* education: using images for; representation, in film

imperialism, 15, 78–79, 97, 143, 145, 167n7; cinema's role in, 20, 39, 46–47, 49, 50–52, 59, 67, 119, 157; negative images of Africa, 59, 158; postwar reestablishment of, 31–38, 68–69; promotion of, 32–33, 37, 56, 57; resistance to, 5–6, 21, 34, 44, 60, 92, 123, 142, 155–56; violence associated with, 120–21; Western, 4–5, 14, 15, 47, 100, 156. *See also* film politics, French imperial; hegemony; oppression; power relations

independence, West African. *See* West Africa: independence for

indigénat, (native law code), 26

indigenous populations. *See* Africa and Africans, representations of; autochthonous populations

Indochina, imported films in, 170n75

industry, cinema as, 4, 7–10, 12, 19, 71–72, 88, 127. *See also* film industry, West African

informational films, 33, 41, 89, 95, 135

Institut des hautes études cinématographiques (IDHEC), 82, 103, 111, 178n13

instructional films, 7–10, 50, 51, 64

intellectuals: French, 86; West African, 5, 6, 16, 77, 81, 82, 85. *See also* elite, African

International Monetary Fund, 162, 164

Islam, 35, 55, 169n55; Muslims, 5, 49, 145

JCC. *See* Journées cinématographiques de Carthage (JCC)

Jeancolas, Jean-Pierre, 50

Jennings, Eric T., 30, 31

Jewsiewicki, Bogumil, 76

Journées cinématographiques de Carthage (JCC), 147, 149, 155, 157

Jules-Rosette, Bennetta, 77

Kaboré, Gaston, and establishment of FEPACI, 146–47

Kane, Cheikh Hamidou, *Ambigous Adventure*, 83

Kane, Jacques Milo, 82

Ki-Zerbo, Joseph, 14, 95

Kracauer, Siegfried, theory of film, 57

Lamizana, Aboubakar Sangoulé, 152, 154

Landau, Paul S., 47

languages: colonialist, 84, 86, 123; dialogic, 68, 118, 126; hegemonic, 78–79, 98; literary, 80, 89; vernacular, 67, 77, 78, 81, 86, 94

languages, cinematographic, 13, 18, 62–65, 72, 93; African, 95–96, 98–99, 107–108, 111, 116–18, 120, 139, 140–41, 145, 158; Arabic, 34, 35, 39, 67–68, 169n55, 173n73; filmmakers' use of, 84, 89, 96, 110, 160; Francophone West African, 122, 156; French, 66–69, 78, 94, 112–13, 117–18, 132, 140, 150, 173n74; Sembène's, 113–14; of Third Cinema, 91, 144; West African, 106, 116. *See also* dialogue; dubbing

Latin America: filmmakers in, 142, 149; neocolonialism in, 90–91, 93. *See also* Third Cinema movement

Laval decree of 1934, 17, 42, 52, 72, 86, 90, 106; deployment of, 22, 110; end of, 97, 135; film politics and, 27, 29–30, 33,

51, 55; violations of, 102, 104. *See also* decrees, French government
Laye, Camara: novels by, 79, 80, 81, 84; style of, 77, 174n30
Lebanese immigrants, movie theater ownership, 25–26, 30
Lebovics, Herman, 131, 180n65
Lemaire, André, 1949 report, 20, 24, 41–42, 81
Les films mercure (production company), 29
liberation, 92, 106, 124; cinema of, 16, 143, 144. *See also* France: liberation from Nazis; revolution, cinema's role in
liberation, West African: cinema's role in, 2, 3–4, 11–12, 14, 18, 84–87, 164; struggle for, 72, 74, 109
Ligue de l'enseignement, 102, 103, 106
literacy, orality and, 60, 76–77, 78, 81
literature: cinema compared to, 82–83, 86; film adaptations of, 74–78, 84, 86, 116, 117, 138–39; language of, 80, 89; of struggle, 87; West African tradition of, 78–81, 84. *See also* novels, West African

MacBean, James Roy, 93
Madagascar: movie theater protests in, 30–31
Mali, 111, 145, 154, 158, 161
Malraux, André, 7, 88, 131, 133, 180n65. *See also* Ministère des affaires culturelles
Mambety, Djibril Diop, 96, 100, 119–20, 123–27, 129, 161; filmmaking approach, 98, 107, 146, 158
Mambety, Djibril Diop, works by, 148; *Badou Boy*, 123, 124, 145; *Contras' City*, 101, 123–24; *Hyènes*, 159; *Touki-bouki*, 101, 123, 124–27, 158, 159
Mandabi (*Money Order*, film, Sembène, 1968), 7, 101, 111, 117–19, 149, 160; comparisons to, 121, 125, 126, 142; making of, 138–41, 144, 147, 149
Marker, Chris, 139, 146. See also *Statues meurent aussi, Les* (film, Cloquet/Marker/Resnais)

Marxism, 3, 11, 89
materialism, as dimension of cinema industrial complex, 39, 69, 84–87; breaking monopoly on, 152–53, 156, 158, 159; colonialism and, 60–61, 71, 131; struggles for control, 99–100, 132–33, 134, 136–37, 138, 151; West African filmmakers and, 142, 144, 147–48
materialism, in film, 13, 15–17, 33, 46, 70, 73–74, 75; achieving African independence in, 22, 46; African film aesthetic and, 70, 72, 73–74, 75; film politics and, 23, 94–95; French control of, 21, 27, 33, 82, 128–33, 134, 148; imperial discourse of, 11, 35; neocolonialist, 163
Maumy, Jean, 139
Mauriac, François, 40
Mauritania: film industry in, 7, 154
meaning, construction of, 13, 32, 45–46, 56–57, 143–44, 163
Mensah, Albert John, 26
metropole. *See* France
Metz, Christian, 13, 18, 63, 116
migrants and migration, African: to France, 106, 121, 124; intracolonial, 25, 81–82, 83. *See also* Lebanese immigrants, movie theater ownership
Ministère de la coopération et l'assistance technique, 130–41, 178n12; funding from, 149, 157, 159; maintaining control over West African cinema, 151, 161, 162; neocolonialist structures of, 44, 150
Ministère de la France d'outre-mer, 32, 34, 131, 133–34, 178n12
Ministère de l'éducation nationale, 103
Ministère des affaires culturelles, 44, 133, 141, 150. *See also* Centre national du cinéma et de l'image animée (CNC)
missionaries, Christian, 24, 86
Mitterrand, François, 41, 68
mobile cinemas, 24, 41, 90, 95, 112, 141. *See also* home movie showings
modernity: capitalist, 71, 126; colonial, 4; French, 52; literary, 79; tradition *vs.*, 75–76, 78

modernity, African: cinema as tool of, 60, 69, 70, 75–76, 132, 134, 161–62; colonialist notion of, 49, 67, 130–31; European direction of, 64, 65, 121–22; filmic representations of, 50, 56, 62, 86, 101, 127; formation of, 74, 120–21, 128; France's role in, 58, 59, 61, 83, 107, 137, 144, 151, 160; in *Les Paysans noirs*, 84, 103; literary tradition of, 76, 78; postcolonial, 18, 115–16, 119, 133–34, 145, 160; progressive, 5, 164; urbanization and, 114, 123. *See also* image-Africa

montage technique, 93, 110, 113; Hondo's use of, 99, 122; Mambety's use of, 123, 125, 126; Sembène's use of, 109, 118, 119; Vautier's use of, 99, 107

Moore, Rachel, 21

Mortimer, Mildred, 76–77

Motion Picture Export Association of America (MPEAA), 38, 152

movie theaters, West African: categories of, 42–43; in Dakar, Senegal, 25–26, 30, 31, 162–63; film discussions in, 155, 180n78; increasing numbers of, 24, 26–27, 31, 95, 162; lewd behavior associated with, 34, 35–36, 39, 40, 43, 56, 169n61; monopoly control of, 30, 132, 141, 142–43, 146, 152–53; nationalization of, 152, 158, 159, 161; quota system, 37–38, 43, 154, 169n71; receipts from, 43–44, 88, 95, 134–35, 153, 161; regulation of, 39, 84; as sites of protest, 30–31; statistics on, 134–35, 178nn16–17. *See also* Laval decree of 1934

movies/moving pictures. *See* cinema; cinema, West African; films; films, West African

MPEAA, 38, 152

Mudimbe, V. Y., 76

Murphy, David, 15, 22, 27, 102, 126, 180n59

Muslims, 5, 49, 145; Islam, 35, 55, 169n55

narratives, 8, 76, 78, 123; cinematic, 13, 16, 18, 28, 32, 59, 64, 116–17. *See also* storytellers and storytelling

Nasser, Gamal Abdel, 34–35

nation-building, African, 10, 12, 72

nation-state, French imperial, 167n7; cinema as organ of, 32, 82, 95; development projects of, 45–46; film politics in context of, 22, 24, 101; regulation of cinema by, 22, 27, 80, 110. *See also* film politics, French imperial; France; imperialism

nationalism, 31, 68; Egyptian, 35, 173n73. *See also* consciousness, emerging nationalist; West Africa: independence for

négritude, philosophy of, 52, 62, 87, 108, 151

Negro-African civilization, concept of, 87, 175n48

neocolonialism: in cinema industrial complex, 99–100; French, 8, 91, 132, 138, 140, 150; global capitalism and, 159; in Latin America, 90–91, 93; legacies of, 157, 162–63; struggle against, 73, 129. *See also* colonialism, French; postcolonialism

neorealism, Italian, 15, 74, 90, 108, 122

New Wave cinema, 12, 139, 142–43

Ngangura, Mweze, 83

Niger: film industry in, 36, 111, 154, 178n15; Niamey film summit, 7, 150–52, 161. *See also* Dakar-Niger rail strike of 1947–48

Noire de, La . . . (film, Sembène, 1966), 101, 114–17, 147; African images in, 110, 111; comparisons to, 121, 124, 125; making of, 138, 139; seminal stature of, 7, 119, 177n39

North Africa, 46, 48–49

novels, West African, 76, 77–81, 84, 117. *See also* literature

open-air viewings, 90, 112, 122, 178n15

oppression, 115–16, 144–45; liberation from, 3–4, 61, 104, 164. *See also* hegemony; imperialism

orality, literacy and, 60, 76–77, 78, 81

orature, 79, 80, 86, 93

Organisation international de la Francophonie, 7. *See also* "Francophonie, la": origin of term

Ouédraogo, Idrissa, and establishment of FEPACI, 146–47
overseas territories, French. *See* West Africa

Pabst, Georg Wilhelm, *L'esclave blanche* (film), 54–55
Pan-African cultural festival, 7, 129, 147, 151
"Pan-African Cultural Manifesto," 148
Parti communiste français (PCF), 103
Partisans, Les (film, Soviet Union), banning of, 36–37
paternalism, 46, 86, 100, 132, 157. *See also* racism
patriarchy, 100, 144, 145
Paysans noirs, Les (film and novel, Delavignette), 78, 86, 101, 134; as colonialist film standard, 62, 64, 67, 69, 109; comparisons to, 108, 116; film adaptation, 55, 57–61, 107n87; modernity depicted in, 84, 103. *See also* Delavignette, Robert
PCF. *See* Parti communiste français (PCF)
Pelerinage Touba (film, Senegal), 37
Pétain, Henri Philippe, 31, 53
Pfaff, Françoise, 71, 83, 93, 94, 102, 121
Pinay, Antoine, 68
Poirier, Georges, 54
police films, 29, 52
politics, 82, 168n46; of representation, 15, 102; socialist, 47, 48. *See also* film politics, French imperial; film politics, West African
Pompidou, Georges, 134
pornographic films, 36
postcolonialism, 10, 63; authoritarian rule under, 100–101, 117–18, 124, 141, 145, 160, 161; cinema's role in, 17–18, 21, 44, 86, 88–89, 97–127, 132, 135, 140; film politics, 89–96; films made during, 49, 50–51; France's efforts to maintain control, 8, 124, 128–29, 162; poverty under, 112, 113, 124. *See also* hegemony; imperialism
power relations, 6, 48, 60, 97; in West African federation, 81, 83. *See also* hegemony; imperialism

Présence africaine (journal), 18, 70; intellectual circle around, 81, 82, 85, 87; *Les statues meurent aussi* coproduced by, 102, 108–10, 176n22; Pan-African film festival sponsored by, 7, 129, 147, 151; rise of African literary tradition in, 74–81; showing of *Afrique 50*, 105, 106, 108
production, 10, 16, 99; control over, 15, 65, 138, 142–43, 148; independent access to, 11, 18–19, 70, 130, 152, 156, 157; postproduction facilities, 9, 132, 136–37, 146, 159
projection, 42, 90, 141, 168n27, 172n33
propaganda: cinema as instrument of, 24, 28, 33–34, 52, 67, 88, 171n25; pro-U.S., 35; Soviet, 36–37; Vichy France, 53

Rabemananjara, Jacques, 105
racism, 49, 59, 86, 121, 123; stereotypes reflecting, 45–48, 127; tropes of, 14, 15, 69, 114, 129
Rassemblement démocratique africaine (RDA), 36, 55, 102, 103, 176n20
reality, 11, 62, 76, 78; cinematic likenesses of, 32, 51–52; regime of representation and, 55–62. *See also* Africa and Africans, representations of; social realism
regime of representation, West African, 45–69, 82, 154; challenging Western control of, 96, 119, 129; cinema industrial complex and, 45, 62–69; colonial, 51–55, 74, 101, 104, 108; filmmakers' interventions in, 145, 161; literary forms in, 75, 77; in the 1950s, 62–69; postcolonial, 97–127; reality and, 55–62
Régnier, Georges, adaptation of *Les paysans noirs*, 82, 103
representation, as dimension of cinema industrial complex, 39, 85, 101, 127, 160–61; breaking monopoly in, 156, 158; colonialism and, 60–61, 71, 131; struggle for control over, 138, 150, 151
representation, in film, 13–15, 19, 27, 33, 86; achieving African independence in,

22, 78, 96; colonial context, 50–51, 73–74, 82, 128–29, 148; construction of, 22, 31, 70; control of, 15, 17, 21, 37, 65; hegemonic, 25, 127; imperial discourse of, 23, 34, 46–47; politics of, 92–94, 102; postcolonial context, 18, 80. *See also* Africa and Africans, representations of

Resnais, Alain. *See Statues meurent aussi, Les* (film, Cloquet/Marker/Resnais): revolution, cinema's role in, 89–96, 119–23. *See also* liberation: cinema of; liberation, West African: cinema's role in; Third Cinema movement

RIF. *See* Studio Realizzazioni industriali fotocinematographiche (RIF), "Civilisation européenne en Afrique"

Roof, Maria, 148, 179n45

Rouch, Jean, 79–80, 87, 99

Sadji, Abdoulaye, *Nini, mulâtresse du Sénégal* (novel), 80

Said, Edward W., 4–5

Saidou, Conte, "Une culture africaine" (essay), 61–62, 172n58

Salembere, Alimata, 149

Sama, Emmanuel, 153

Sarr, Mamadou, 82. *See also Afrique-sur-Seine* (film, Vieyra and Sarr)

Schwartz, Vanessa R., 167n11

SECMA. *See* Société d'éxploitation cinématographique africaine (SECMA)

Second Cinema, 143

Second World Congress of Black Writers and Artists (1959), 87–88, 95, 106, 175n51

Second World War. *See* cinema industrial complex, West African: postwar; France: liberation from Nazis; France: postwar reconstruction; Vichy France

Semaine du cinéma africain (film festival), 149–50, 152, 153–54

Sembène, Ousmane, 3, 42, 71, 73–74, 82, 92, 110–19, 154; censorship of, 12, 100–101, 161; childhood of, 162; and establishment of FEPACI, 146–47; film politics, 120, 127, 144; filmmaking approach, 98, 99, 100, 102, 107, 123, 143, 180n47; image-Africa constructed by, 11, 14, 50, 160; on representation in film, 19, 97; on revolutionary filmmaking, 93, 94, 142, 149; Soviet film training, 15, 89, 110–11, 113, 122, 129, 136; as storyteller, 16, 101–102; struggle for independence in filmmaking, 30, 90–91, 129–32, 157, 159; themes of, 121, 124, 126, 127, 161; as writer, 76, 77, 96

Sembène, Ousmane, works of: *Black Docker*, 78; *Borom Sarret*, 101, 111–14, 115, 119, 123, 136, 139, 145, 158; *Camp de Thiaroye*, 159; *Ceddo*, 144–45, 159, 161; docu-fiction films, 93, 108, 144; early, 18; *Emitaï*, 144–45; *God's Bits of Wood*, 1, 78; *La Mandat*, 138–39; novels, 78, 79, 84, 117, 138–39; *Xala*, 144–45. *See also Mandabi* (*Money Order*, film, Sembène, 1968); *Noire de, La . . .* (film, Sembène, 1966)

Senegal, 88, 145, 161; film industry in, 7, 37, 111, 147, 154, 158. *See also* Dakar, Senegal

Senghor, Blaise, 111, 146

Senghor, Léopold Sédar, 2, 7, 80, 82; "la Francophonie" coined by, 151; *négritude* philosophy, 52, 62, 87, 108, 151; Wright's debate with, 175n48

Seven Wonders of Dakar, 1, 2

Shaka, Femi Okiremuete, 21, 50, 56, 62, 64, 98, 139

Sherzer, Dina, 21, 50

Sissako, Abderrahmane: *Bamako* (film), 163, 164; Soviet film training, 175n56

Slavin, Henry David, 14, 15, 21, 46, 49

social change, West African, 14–15, 71, 118

social development, West African, 62, 80, 128; cinema's role in, 10, 43–44, 91, 163. *See also* cultural development, cinema's role in West African; economic development, West African

social realism, 112, 113–14. *See also* reality

Socialist Party of Austria, conference on Third World cinema (1966), 146–47

Société des films exotiques et coloniaux, 29
Société d'études pour la propagande colonial par la film, 29
Société d'éxploitation cinématographique africaine (SECMA), 23, 30; breaking monopoly of, 95, 152–54, 155, 159; and movie theater regulations, 37–38, 43, 134, 141, 146, 169n71
Société national voltaïque de cinéma (SONAVOCI), 153–54
Solanas, Fernando, 119, 146; revolutionary vision of filmmaking, 12, 91–94, 142–44, 156; on Third Cinema, 118, 147
Soleil Ô (film, Hondo, 1967), 7, 101, 120–23, 177n56; African culture in, 127, 128–29; comparisons to, 124, 125; as revolutionary cinema, 142, 143, 144
SONAVOCI, 153–54
Sorkin, Marc, *L'esclave blanche* (film), 54–55
Soviet Union: banning of films from, 36–37, 54, 169n64; cinematography in, 16, 74, 89–90, 110–11; early West African filmmakers training in, 15, 90, 111, 122, 129, 136, 175n56; politics in, 47
Spence, Louise, 46–47, 49, 59, 86
Stam, Robert, 46–47, 49, 59, 86, 92
Statues meurent aussi, Les (film, Cloquet/Marker/Resnais), 18, 96, 102, 108–11, 115, 120–21, 139
stereotypes, racist, 45–48, 127. *See also* racism; tropes, African
Stibbe, Pierre, 105–106
Stoller, Paul, 58
storytellers and storytelling, 63–64, 80, 101–102, 111, 116–17. *See also* griots; narratives
Studio Realizzazioni industriali fotocinematographiche (RIF), "Civilisation européenne en Afrique," 64–65, 66

Taylor, Clyde, 119
technology, filmmaking, 51, 67, 72; access to, 86, 110, 134, 138, 152, 161, 163; advances in, 145–46, 162–63; transfer of, 6, 7, 9; Western domination of, 3–4, 137, 149, 162. *See also* dubbing; equipment; projection
television, 135, 163, 178n17
Tête brûlée (film, Soviet Union), banning of, 36, 169n64
texts, reading filmic, 25, 28–29, 32, 54, 90
Thackway, Melissa, 101, 114
theater, 16, 176n20
Thiong'o, Ngũgĩ wa, 5, 14, 79, 80
Third Cinema movement: African filmmakers' inspiration from, 11–12, 15, 74, 156, 157; cinema as class struggle, 24, 145, 149; core aspects of, 154–55, 180n59; manifesto of, 91–94, 142–44. *See also* films: witness-bearing
Third World cinema: Cuban support for, 146, 147, 151; filmmakers, 148–49, 151, 179n45; Socialist Party of Austria conference on, 146–47
Thompson, Kristin, 33
Tiffin, Helen, 78–79
Togo: film industry in, 27
Tomlinson, John, 6
Touffait, Adolphe, 38
Touré, Mamadou, *Mouramani*, 174n33
training, in filmmaking, 6, 83, 136, 148. *See also under* Soviet Union
Traoré, Mahama Johnson, 111
tropes, African: challenging, 58–59; hegemonic, 144, 158; of primitivism, 27, 45–48, 49, 64, 65, 160, 161; racist, 14, 15, 69, 114, 129
Truffaut, François, 139
truth-telling, 55–56, 91. *See also* films: witness-bearing
Tunisia: film festivals in, 147, 155

UDF. *See* Union pour la démocratie française (UDF)
Ukadike, Nwachuckwu Frank: on French colonial film policy, 22–23, 110, 118, 132; on origins of West African cinema, 21, 24, 72, 167n26; on pioneer West African filmmakers, 12–13, 14, 99, 122, 179n19; on *Soleil Ô*, 123; on U.S. film companies' influence, 153

Union pour la démocratie française (UDF), 105
United States, 35–36, 153. *See also* Hollywood film industry
Upper Volta: film festivals in, 7, 149–50, 154–55; nationalization of film industry in, 10, 152, 153–54, 155, 158, 159
urbanization, 76, 81–82, 83, 114, 123, 124

Vautier, René, 127, 178n13; *Afrique 50*, 18, 96, 102–10, 111, 116, 143, 176n20; conviction for violating Laval Decree, 102, 104–105
vernacular, 67, 77, 78, 81, 86, 94
Vertov, Dziga, 99, 112, 122
Vichy France, 30, 31, 53–55
Vieyra, Paulin Soumanou: on adapting literature to film, 116, 139; on African cinema, 3, 7, 9–10, 92, 140; docufiction films, 96, 144; essays, 85–87, 88; film politics, 73–74, 81–89, 94–95, 111, 114, 119, 127, 148, 155, 174n33; on French neocolonialism, 90, 91; as head of GAC, 132, 147; image-Africa constructed by, 98, 160; on independent filmmaking, 129–30; as Senegal's minister of information, 89, 132; Soviet film training, 103, 111, 178n13, 179n19; statistics collected by, 134–35, 153, 178nn16–17; on struggle for liberation, 18, 71, 72, 154; themes of, 126, 127; work on *Mandabi*, 118. *See also Afrique-sur-Seine* (film, Vieyra and Sarr); cinema, West African: in service to the people
violence, 30–31, 35, 93, 115, 120–21

Wade, Abdoulaye, 1
Wallerstein, Immanuel, 166n41
Wesseling, H. L., 173n74
West, the, 14, 100, 145, 149, 156. *See also* Europe; United States
West Africa: development of cinema in, 2–4, 7, 51–55; disorder in, 45, 47, 60; French films exported to, 135–36; independence for, 1–2, 21–22, 73, 75, 82, 85, 87–88, 94–96, 132; indigenous voting rights in, 168n46; relationship with France, 4–5, 46, 49–50, 59–60, 84, 106, 109, 128–29, 131, 162, 168n46. *See also* Benin; Côte d'Ivoire; Guinea; Mali; Mauritania; Niger; Senegal; Togo; Upper Volta
Westerns (films), 35–36, 39, 169n61
Wilder, Gary, 4, 52, 60, 167n7
Williams, Patrick, 15, 22, 27, 102, 126, 180n59
Woll, Josephine, 89, 114
Wollen, Peter, 160
World Bank, 164
Wright, Richard, Léopold Senghor's debate with, 175n48

youth: films' negative influences on, 34, 35–36, 39, 56, 169n61; in Paris, 83–84; protests by at movie theaters, 30–31

Zimbabwe: film industry in, 46, 58

JAMES E. GENOVA is Associate Professor of History at Ohio State University–Marion. He is author of *Colonial Ambivalence, Cultural Authenticity, and the Limitations of Mimicry in French-Ruled West Africa, 1914–1956* and several articles on colonialism, post-colonialism, identity formation, and West African cultural politics.